Pelican Books

Politics and Deviance

Ian Taylor was born in Sheffield in 1944 and
educated at the Universities of Durham and
Cambridge. He is now Lecturer in Criminology
at the University of Sheffield. He contributed an
article on soccer hooliganism to *Images of
Deviance* (also available in Pelicans) and is the
author (with Paul Walton and Jock Young)
of *The New Criminology* (1973).

Laurie Taylor graduated in psychology at the
University of London and is now Senior Lecturer
in Sociology at the University of York. He has
published many articles on theories of delinquency,
alienation, the relationship between psychology
and sociology, the social world of interaction and
the motivation of sexual offenders. His publications
include *Deviance and Society* (1971), *Deviance,
Crime and Socio-Legal Control: A Comparative
Approach* (1973) (written with Roland Robertson)
and (with Stanley Cohen) *Psychological Survival*
(1972) (available in Pelicans).

Politics and Deviance

Edited by
Ian Taylor and
Laurie Taylor

Penguin Books

Penguin Books Ltd, Harmondsworth,
Middlesex, England
Penguin Books Inc., 7110 Ambassador Road,
Baltimore, Maryland 21207, U.S.A.
Penguin Books Australia Ltd, Ringwood,
Victoria, Australia

Published in Pelican Books 1973
This collection copyright © Penguin Books Ltd, 1973

Made and printed in Great Britain by
Hazell Watson & Viney Ltd,
Aylesbury, Bucks
Set in Linotype Times

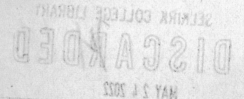

Introduction

This is the second volume of papers taken from the proceedings of the National Deviancy Conference. In his introduction to the first volume,* Stan Cohen described the development of what he called the 'sceptical' approach to the study of crime and deviance. This 'scepticism' – exemplified in the papers reproduced in *Images of Deviance* – inverted many of the positions traditionally taken by criminologists, and, in particular, involved a rejection of the simple idea that 'deviance' is the manifestation of some individual pathology. Deriving many of his arguments from contemporary deviancy theorists in America (in particular, the so-called 'labelling theorists'), Cohen argued that criminologists and sociologists of deviance should become increasingly concerned with the way in which the fact of social control itself (the demand for law and order) can give rise to, and shape, the facts of crime and deviance.

This book takes up the theme of social control more explicitly than did *Images of Deviance*. As the title indicates, the writers in this volume are all concerned with the political nature of social control – in the sense that they each want to describe the ways in which laws, regulations, customs, and control and repression can shape the form and content of what is called 'criminality' or 'deviance'. The argument that holds this book together is that the concept and the reality of crime is created through political action by those groups and institutions which possess the power to enforce their will. The writers in this volume are not content, with Howard Becker, to identify the question of rules and their enforceability as political, and then to leave the matter there. Rather they go on to examine –

* Stanley Cohen, ed., *Images of Deviance* (Penguin Books, 1971).

in various ways and in different areas – why particular kinds of politically-enforceable rules arise in particular periods, in particular cultures, and in respect of particular behaviours.

The book makes no claim to overall homogeneity. There are obvious differences of stress and style. But there are four questions which dominate and recur in each of the papers.

1. Most central of all is the question of *what is meant when people talk about 'crime', or 'deviance'*. Criminologists have tended in the past to take the term as referring to a distinctive kind of behaviour, however critical they may have been about its shifting or elusive nature. They have tended to 'take for granted' the fact of criminality, for example, as being *fundamentally* different from the fact of conformity. Recently, a more radically sociological approach has emerged, questioning – from a variety of positions – whether the term has any clear behavioural reference at all, especially when viewed across a broad social, cultural and/or historical canvas.

In his discussion of corporate crime in the United States in this volume, Frank Pearce argues that we should extend the meaning of crime to encompass the activities of companies which might not necessarily involve those companies in any conflict with the law, but which might be widely regarded as being socially injurious. For him, the disregard of these kinds of violation within traditional American criminological discussion is reason enough for the dismantling of that criminological orthodoxy.

Martin Loney, in showing how old crimes may be abolished and new ones created in a revolutionary society, further underlines the political and historical relativity of the general concept of crime.

2. Closely tied in with this line of argument in contemporary criminology is the view that *crime is created by specifically political initiatives*. In this volume, the attempt is made to illustrate this view by reference to crime as created politically at the national level (as in Martin Loney's analysis of Cuba), internationally (as in Frank Pearce's discussion) and also at a very local level. In *Images of Deviance*, Jock Young showed how the day-to-day activity of policemen, magistrates, journalists

and other agencies of control involved the essentially political selection of certain behaviours – in stereotypical fashion – as crime. In this collection, Gail Armstrong and Mary Wilson, in the course of a detailed discussion of the situation of working-class youth on the Easterhouse housing scheme in Glasgow, are able to show how local political initiatives (in the Corporation Council Chamber, and in local elections), along with subsequent police behaviour, gave rise to the definition and selection of Easterhouse youth as 'gangsters'. In so doing, they highlight not only the relatively arbitrary nature of the selection process (i.e. that *all* Easterhouse youth had the same characteristics); but also the very real consequences of such selection for those who do the defining (e.g. in terms of political popularity) and for those who get defined (e.g. in stigmatization of Easterhouse youth by employers).

Ron Bailey has experienced similar processes at work on a very personal basis; and he was invited therefore to contribute a paper to this volume in order that he could use his experience of the 'grass-roots' of British politics to underline the consequences of such labelling. Writing as a participant rather than as an observer, Bailey describes the definers actually at work in local authority housing departments. He records the history of the squatters' movement in Britain, and, in particular, the ways in which politicians and administrators attempted to deny the authenticity of the squatters' attempts to act on the housing crisis by describing them as 'vandals' and/or 'anarchists'.

In both instances – in Easterhouse and in the London boroughs – the 'criminals' and the 'deviants' were the creations of political interests, and of the power possessed by those interests to apply spurious labels and to make them stick.

3. It would be too simple, however, to believe that we can lay bare the political underpinnings of social control (and the creation of deviance) only by reference to the formal institutions of the state, or (for example) local authority agencies. The significance of the papers by Simon Maddison and Jerry Palmer in the context of this volume is that they show how the ideologies of two particular groups within society, which might popularly be thought to be 'non-political', are in practice of

profound social and political significance. The ideology under-lying the work of the thriller writer, and the diagnosis of the university psychiatrist, are both shown to have conservative implications, and to contribute to the hold exercised by the formal control agencies at large. *Social control and repression, that is, are shown to be a fact of our everyday experience at the hands of the apparently 'non-political'.*

4. The kind of argument advanced in this book is not, of course, confined to small groups of radical criminologists. There is increasing evidence to suggest that 'deviants' them-selves are coming to adopt, quite self-consciously, a similar perspective as a result of their experiences with agencies of social control and society at large. The Weathermen described by Paul Walton, and the hippies discussed by Jock Young, highlight in their own actions and beliefs the limitations of orthodox criminological explanation, not only in their self-conscious rejection of attempts to apply a pathological label but also in their articulate assertion that an alternative society, based on values currently considered deviant, is possible.

Whilst traditional criminologists may still refuse to bridge the gap between the explanation of social and criminal be-haviour (by refusing to analyse the state in a critical mood) some of their subjects are already 'doing it' in practice.

*

We would like to record that this book, like *Images of Deviance* before it, is very much a collective enterprise. The decision to go ahead with a second volume was prompted by the enthu-siasm of members of the National Deviancy Conference (which continues to grow in size) and by the general interest aroused, amongst sociologists and others, by *Images of De-viance*. This book is very much the result of collective editorial work, with ourselves as representatives only, to the best of our ability, of the *collective sentiments* of the National Deviancy Conference. We should like to thank all the committee for their work on this volume: Gail Armstrong, Roy Bailey, Stan Cohen, David Downes, Mike Hepworth, Mary McIntosh, Paul Rock, Mike Smith, Paul Walton and Jock Young; and also

express our thanks to Stuart Hall for general advice and Margaret Silcock and Glynis Spriggs for secretarial assistance.

Ian Taylor
Laurie Taylor
July 1972

Suggested Reading

In *Images of Deviance*, we suggested a few titles which may be of interest to readers. Most of these titles were American. In the last two years, several British sociologists have produced texts and readers in the 'sceptical' tradition, most of them with a more pronounced empirical reference to the British situation. These titles are listed below.

CARSON, W. G., and WILES, P., eds., *Crime and Delinquency in Britain: a Book of Readings* (Martin Robertson and Co., 1970).

COHEN, S., and TAYLOR, L., *Psychological Survival: the Experience of Long-term Imprisonment* (Penguin Books, 1972).

COHEN, S., *Folk Devils and Moral Panics* (Paladin Books, 1972).

PHILLIPSON, M., *Sociological Aspects of Crime and Delinquency* (Routledge & Kegan Paul: Students' Library of Sociology, 1971).

ROCK, P., *Deviant Behaviour* (Hutchinson, 1973).

ROCK, P., and MCINTOSH, M., eds., *Deviance and Social Control: Explorations in Sociology* (Tavistock, 1973).

TAYLOR, I., WALTON, P., and YOUNG, J., *The New Criminology: For a Social Theory of Deviance* (Routledge & Kegan Paul, 1973).

TAYLOR, L., *Deviance and Society* (Michael Joseph, 1971).

YOUNG, J., *The Drugtakers: the Social Meaning of Drug Use* (MacGibbon & Kee/Paladin, 1971).

Frank Pearce*   **Crime, Corporations and the American Social Order**

The 'crime problem' in America is an almost universal topic of discussion. American politicians and spokesmen are apparently frank about the extent and nature of the problem – even going out of their way to exploit it at election times. J. Edgar Hoover described the problem in a typically dramatic fashion:

Today the onslaught continues – with five offences being recorded every minute. There is a vicious crime of violence – a murder, forcible rape or assault to kill – every two and a half minutes; a robbery every five minutes; a burglary every twenty-eight seconds; and fifty-two automobiles are stolen every hour.[1]

This type of public exposure of national problems is not however so honest – or at least so comprehensive – as it might appear. For one result of this public stress upon such crimes as murder and burglary is that attention is shifted away from organized crime. Certainly burglary has involved an enormous amount of goods (estimated at $284 million by the F.B.I. in 1965); but this is almost trivial beside the $6 billion profit which organized crime was said to have made in 1967 on gambling. Neither is it only organized crime which is ignored by concentration on murders and muggings. The President's Commission which made the gambling estimate quoted above went on to note:

There is no knowing how much embezzlement, fraud, loan sharking, and other forms of thievery from individuals or com-

* This paper owes a great deal to the critical comments of Mike Hayes, Ian Taylor, Harold Wolpe and Tony Woodiwiss. Some of the arguments advanced here are to be expanded in greater detail in F. Pearce, Mike Hayes, Tony Woodiwiss, Harold Wolpe and Colin Prescod, *Crime, Law and the State* (forthcoming, Routledge and Kegan Paul).

mercial institutions there is, or how much price-rigging, tax evasion, bribery, graft, and other forms of thievery from the public at large there is. The Commission's studies indicate that the economic losses those crimes cause are far greater than those caused by the three index crimes against property.[2]

Senator Warren Magnuson recently claimed that deceptive selling is today's 'most serious form of theft, accounting for more dollars lost each year than robbery, larceny, auto thefts, and forgery combined'. An economist has argued that in 1957 in tax returns there was an illegal under-reporting of at least $27·7 billion, most of which was kept by the top 10 per cent by income of the population.[3] Probably, at least $11 billion of this was received by the wealthiest 1 per cent of the American population, which owns 80 per cent of the corporate wealth. This unreported income would be taxed at a rate of 90 cents to every dollar – on an income of $11 billion, some $9 billion plus would be owed the taxation department. This suggests that the richest 1 per cent of the American people defrauded the majority of more than $9 billion in one year alone. Violations of the anti-trust laws are however even more important. These laws are supposed to ensure that competition keeps prices at the lowest possible level, by outlawing monopolies and by stopping firms colluding to fix prices.

However, when calculated, the volume of *illegal* excess profits made by American industries who violate these laws is staggering. It was revealed in one famous case in 1961, 'The Heavy Electrical Equipment Case', that General Electric alone had made at least $50 million excess profits, in this one market. The $284 million cost of burglary begins to pale into insignificance beside the $7 billion made by organized crime. It looks trivial compared to the $9 billion year of which the wealthiest 1 per cent of the population defrauds the tax department and the millions of dollars which are made by corporations in *illegal* excess profits.

It appears then that the most economically significant crimes are the least publicized, investigated and punished. This discrepancy cannot be explained in terms of the ignorance of those responsible for dealing with crime, since the figures we

have quoted are derived in large part from government publications. These sources of information have been deliberately chosen in order to demonstrate that capitalist societies do not even abide by their own criteria of reasonableness. There is a contradiction between the way things are supposed to happen and what actually occurs.

The major aim of this paper is to explain why there is a discrepancy between the world (legitimate as well as criminal) portrayed by official agencies and the mass media, and that revealed by a more sophisticated radical analysis of capitalist societies. We focus here on American society, although a similar mode of analysis could be applied to other capitalist countries. In the remainder of this section I will make a schematic attempt to explain why the crimes of the poor, not the rich, are dramatized as the 'crime problem'. In the following section I examine the conventional account of the development of the major 'anti-business' legalization, the anti-trust laws. This account proves to be incapable of explaining big business's support for, and involvement in, the formulation and implementation of these laws. This can only be understood by relating the goals of corporate capitalists to the changing social, political, and economic environment from the latter half of the nineteenth century to date. I then focus on a famous antitrust prosecution in 1961 in order to try and determine the typicality of the behaviour of those involved in this case. This once again raises the question of the relationship between official portrayals of reality, in this case the economic system, and what seems to be actually taking place. In doing this I will have already moved beyond the confines of positive criminology,[4] and will continue to do so when examining criminal offences in the sphere of labour relations. However, it is in examining the international activities of corporations that I most radically break with these traditions. For it is only by understanding why certain actions are *not* prohibited by law, either international law or by those of certain 'underdeveloped' countries, that sense can be made of the social relationships inside the capitalistic world system. Thus the ultimate implication of this mode of analysis is the dissolution of criminology

as a separate discipline. In order to explain the distribution of criminal activity, and the nature of the social response to this it proves necessary to contrast the 'imaginary' social order in America, where it is portrayed as being a pluralist, democratic, free-enterprise society, with a more adequate (i.e. better theorized) description of its nature. Hopefully, having done this, certain hidden but significant social processes in capitalist societies will have been explained.

Edwin Sutherland pioneered the study of what he termed 'white-collar crime' in order to give an accurate picture of the distribution of criminal activity and also in an attempt to explain the misconceptions surrounding it. 'White collar' crimes were defined as being the kind 'committed by a person of respectability and high social status in the course of his occupation'. Sutherland claimed that because such groups were powerful, and because of the class bias of the courts, they were able to avoid prosecution and suffered little stigma if they were caught.[5] Their control over the mass media allowed them considerable power over the definition of the nature of the 'crime problem', and they were unlikely to dwell on their own illegal activities such as misrepresentation in advertising. 'Public opinion in regard to picking pockets would not be well organized if most of the information regarding this crime came to the public directly from the pickpockets themselves.'[6] Since their activities were little publicized, they were not watched much by the police, and detection was difficult anyway, because their transactions took place in private. These factors explained the relative immunity of the 'white collar criminals' and the absence of these factors explained the vulnerability of lower-class criminals. This explanation does not adequately account for the treatment of either group. I will deal with the lower-class case first and then with that of 'white-collar' criminals.

The concentration on lower-class criminals may be in a hidden sense rational. It is functional for maintaining a class system in America. Firstly, it strengthens the dominant individualistic ideology. If the criminals are also the social failures (those at the bottom of an open, competitive, hierarchical class system in which any man can succeed), then their

Contents

criminality is caused by their *inadequacies* (lack of determination, moral weakness, etc.) and the major social institutions are not exposed to critical assessment. Secondly, by defining them as non-citizens, with no *rights* to employment, education, etc., the system's failure to provide these for them (independently of their criminality) is obscured. Finally, by criminalizing them and treating them as asocial and amoral, the system can neutralize their potential for developing an adequate understanding of their situation; and by incarcerating them, it makes it difficult for them organizationally to realize any such ideas. The American class society would be threatened if an ideologically sophisticated 'lower-class' political movement were to develop.

Sutherland's category of white-collar crime implies that for purposes of analysis such crimes can be considered a 'natural category'. Embezzlement is similar to black marketing is similar to anti-trust violations. However, whilst it is true that little social stigma is attached to any of these crimes, it does not follow that they are all equally immune to prosecution. If, for example, embezzlement was left unprosecuted and there was a large increase in such activity, capitalism might well collapse. For financial transactions in this kind of economy cannot take place in a manner which gives foolproof protection from violations of trust.[7] Rather one must focus on the social effects of these crimes. Thus in the Second World War, it was imperative that the state should succeed in stopping those black market offences that undermined the American war effort, since American capitalism required military success in order to gain control of crucial Asian markets.[8] Immediate, easy profit, in this case, was opposed to long-term interests. But violations of the anti-trust laws (involving monopolistic control of certain markets) do not pose a threat to the social structure of American capitalism, as I will show below. They can, therefore, be tolerated. The crucial question, then, that must be asked of white-collar or any other offences is: what effects do these crimes, and public awareness of them, have on the social order? The answer to this question can only be given by examining the specific example of criminal activity in the particular sociohistorical context in which it occurs. This means that one must no longer focus primarily on the strategies by which prosecution is avoided, but rather on the effects of different kinds of crime, and thereby explain why the state wishes to prosecute certain offences and not others.

2

I want to illustrate these points by examining conventional accounts of the development of American capitalism and the related development of anti-trust legislation.[9] The inadequacies of such accounts call for a more sophisticated analysis, and one which entails a redefinition of the nature of American society, both in the past and at present.

According to such accounts, in the late nineteenth century America had a harsh *laissez faire* economy. Some of the businessmen, called 'Robber Barons', because of their treatment of customers, workers, and other businessmen, tried to make profits at all costs. They even sought to do so by violating the principles of the economy. They tried to gain monopoly control of industries by forming 'trusts'. (As used then, the term 'trust' was applied to an industry if it was effectively controlled by one firm or a working alliance of firms.) Because of general opposition to such monopolies, a number of laws were passed to stop them being formed. As Sutherland later expressed it:

The anti-trust laws are designed to protect competition; they are also designed to protect the institution of free competition as the regulator of the economic system and thereby to protect consumers against arbitrary prices, as well as being designed to protect the institution of democracy against the dangers of great concentration of wealth in the hands of monopolies.[10]

The first of these laws, the Sherman Act, was passed in 1890 at a time of general opposition to 'The Robber Barons'. The Act declared:

Every contract, combination in the form of trust or otherwise, or conspiracy, in restraint of trade or commerce among the several states, or with foreign nations, is hereby declared to be illegal.[11]

Although the Act seems explicit enough, a great deal still depended on judicial interpretation, and in fact, the legislation was rarely invoked during the McKinley and Roosevelt presidencies. In 1906 three more acts were passed regulating the meat industry (Meat Inspection Act), foodstuffs (Pure Food and Drug Act), and the railroads (Hepburn Act). Later, during the administration of Woodrow Wilson, to strengthen the anti-trust legislation, the Clayton Act and the Federal Trade Commission Act were passed, in 1914. The latter act provided for the setting up of the Federal Trade Commission. In a period of twenty-five years a whole new set of laws had been created to regulate the economy and a recent chairman of the Federal Trade Commission claimed that it resulted in the growth of economic individualism and the fostering of free and fair competition.[12] Monopoly, in whatever form, was condemned, at least in principle. As a result of popular pressure the free enterprise system was now protected by law.

Present-day society is seen as no longer completely dominated by the excesses of a *laissez faire* economy. Public relations men, the mass media, and school and college text-books picture it rather as a humane mixed economy where competition is regulated, stability is achieved and full employment is maintained by governmental intervention.[13] But the economy is still fundamentally based on the private ownership of wealth; U.S. Steel characterized it as a 'competitive system ... an acknowledged profit and loss system, the hope of profit being the incentive, and the fear of loss being the spur.'[14]

While there are large corporations, any advantage which they gain from their size is used either to reduce prices and/or to act in a community-conscious way. Overall, 'One needs only to look at the great achievements and standards of living of the American people to see the advantages of our economic system.'[15]

This persuasive picture of the nature and development of American capitalism cannot explain significant features of American society either now or at the beginning of this century. In 1918, the Export Trade Act allowed for the monopolization by certain firms of key foreign markets although this had been explicitly forbidden by the Sherman Act. Moreover, these anti-big-business acts had in many cases been supported by the businesses they were supposed to regulate. Thus, the railroads supported the Railroads Regulation Act of 1906 and the Chicago slaughter-house owners supported the Meat Inspection Act of the same year. These inconsistencies with the earlier picture can only be explained by re-examining the development of the American social, political, and economic structure during this period, and by conceptualizing more adequately the relationship between big business and the major institutions and social groups in American society. I suggest as a model the following:

1. The capitalist is committed to profit and growth, which are realized in an exchange economy,[16] and not necessarily a *laissez faire* economy. It could be that a monopoly, and indeed, a disguised monopoly, is the ideal.

2. In order to achieve this goal he requires an environment which is predictable, and as much as possible under his control; this is best achieved when,

(i) he has stability – when he can control competition, and prices – particularly of raw materials;

(ii) he can predict the actions of others – he can control consumers, dominate labour, and effectively influence the government;

(iii) he has security – from any kind of movement to limit his power, particularly those that may affect him through the formal democratic institutions.

3. The action of the large capitalists towards different institutions and groups is essentially calculative and will depend upon such factors as their consciousness of what is occurring, (e.g. consumers), on their degree of organization and strength (e.g. labour), the amount of interference that can be expected (e.g. government). The capitalist's loyalty to democracy is only provisional.[17]

4. Although the form of capitalist organization may change – particularly the present move to large corporate structures – and although the relationship of American capitalism to such things as the world market altered significantly during the

period being discussed in the body of this article, it is still comprehensible in terms of this paradigm.

3

The attitude of the large corporations to the anti-trust laws developed from hostility in the late nineteenth century to an active involvement in their administration by 1914.[18] Gordon's comments on anti-business legislation go a long way towards explaining why. He writes:

The State may be pressured either nominally or effectively to prosecute the wealthy if their criminal practices become so egregiously offensive that their victims may move to overthrow the system itself. In those cases, the State may punish individual members of the class in order to protect the interests of the entire class. Latent opposition to the practices of the corporations may be forestalled, to pick several examples, by token public efforts to enact and enforce anti-trust, truth-in-lending, anti-pollution, industrial safety and auto safety legislation. As James Ridgeway has most clearly shown in the case of pollution, however, the gap between the enactment of the statutes and their effective enforcement seems quite cavernous.[19]

The attempt by big business in the latter half of the nineteenth century to gain control of an entire industry must be seen as a strategy used to achieve their major goals of profit and growth. Thus their trusts (whisky, sugar, lead, oil, etc.), brought all aspects of the manufacture and distribution of goods under monolithic control. These trusts used any method, legal or illegal, in order to gain, consolidate and maintain their monopolies. By their control of raw materials, firms such as Standard Oil bankrupted competitors.[20] Where these methods were not possible, this firm used violence against rivals; for example, in 1887 Standard Oil paid another company's employee to blow up his employer's oil refinery. Violence was also frequently used against organized labour. In one incident gangsters were sent from New York to break a strike of Erie brakemen. Government intervention, if it occurred, invariably aided the employers.

The 'Robber Barons' were indifferent to the law. This was

made clear by Daniel Drew, who said: 'Law is like a cobweb; it's made for flies and smaller kinds of insects, so to speak, but lets the big bumblebees break through. When technicalities of the law stood in my way, I have always been able to brush them aside easy as anything.'[21] They seem to have changed their attitude to the law in the subsequent twenty years. Or perhaps, more accurately, they broke the law less flagrantly.

One reason for their change in behaviour was their fear of radical agitation. There was widespread popular opposition to them and their methods. Political pressure from other businessmen, farmers, workers and consumers made them liable to unpredictable court interference, particularly at the local state level. There was a very general recognition of the dangers of this resentment developing into some kind of socialistic movement that would fundamentally transform the social order. Sherman placed strong emphasis on this when he argued for his anti-trust act.[22]

The Sherman Act, however, did not suffice to quieten popular sentiment, and this sentiment was particularly strong at the local state level. Local prosecutions under state laws against monopolies were frequent. This led companies, and their papers, such as the *Railroad Gazette*, to agitate for the transfer of these powers to the federal level where they would be able to effectively control the federal regulation of their activity.

However, it was not the fear of radicalism that led big business to view legislation favourably. Despite the general view that the merger movement was widespread in America in the late nineteenth century, and that it was due to the superior efficiency of large scale business, 'in effect the merger movement was largely restricted to a minority of the dominant American industries and that for only a few years.'[23] Despite their ruthlessness, despite their size and the supposed advantages derived from economies of scale, the merger movement had more or less fizzled out by the end of the nineteenth century.

Year	No. of Firms Merging	Capital in Millions
1895–1906	301 average	$691 m average
1905–1914	100 average	$221 m average [24]

The merger movement had been given strong stimulus by promoters who benefited from the return of economic prosperity in 1897. It was not inspired by a desire for efficiency; U.S. Steel was capitalized at $1,403 million when around that time maximum efficiency was achieved for plants costing $25 million. The movement was an attempt to achieve effective control of the key industries in America, but due to the expansion of markets and the availability of alternative capital, they failed to achieve this control.[25]

With the failure of illegal and merger techniques, the larger trusts turned to two other methods of achieving domination. In certain key industries acts were passed allowing for governmental regulation of rates and prices, outlawing unfair methods of competition (which usually meant outlawing dangerous small rivals), and sometimes introducing production standards that only the largest firms could afford. The 1906 Meat Inspection Act may have gained much popular support because of the muck-raking activities of Upton Sinclair, but in fact, it also delighted the large meat packers. It helped them export successfully by fulfilling the high safety standards demanded by the European countries who imported the meat, but it crippled smaller companies. Americans were left with poor-quality meat, and the working conditions and wages of the workers were left unaffected. Governmental regulation provided a means by which monopoly could be achieved against dangerous competitors and without the dangers of popular reactions.

The large corporations also attempted to influence the government. They succeeded with President Roosevelt. Despite his reputation as a reformer, the few anti-trust prosecutions he initiated had little bite. He preferred the weapon of 'publicity' and formed the Bureau of Corporations with this in mind. He was, in fact, confused as to the nature, merits, and dangers of big business. He saw it as efficient and inevitable, yet he was concerned about the political and economic power it might yield. The dangers could be avoided if there were 'good' men in control and if the 'bad' men and 'bad' trusts were punished. Thus, those like U.S. Steel's Judge Gary, who gained his confidence, avoided prosecution. In 1907, Roosevelt approved of

U.S. Steel's takeover of Tennessee Coal and Iron for $45 million, although a little investigation would have shown that it was worth $180 million and unfair coercion was used in the sale. Others, like Standard Oil, made a poor impression and became the epitome of the 'bad' trust.

Although Roosevelt initiated the investigation of Standard Oil, it was in 1909, during President Taft's term of office, that the corporation was eventually prosecuted. In 1911 the American Tobacco Company was broken up and sixty-three other prosecutions were initiated during Taft's presidency (compared to forty-four during the eight years of Roosevelt's). For various situational reasons the system of informal detentes had broken down. The corporations became aware of their precarious position and at the same time were recognizing their vulnerability to prosecution by socialist-controlled state legislatures. President Wilson shared their concern, and during his Presidency the legal situation was radically modified. Legislation was passed making regulation a federal responsibility, and creating agencies responsive to the interests of big business.

The most important of these was the Federal Trades Commission Act of 1914. The provisions of the Bill were formulated by Davies, Head of the Bureau of Corporations, who himself was strongly influenced by prominent corporation lawyers. A presidentially appointed five-man commission was set up with jurisdiction over areas already dealt with by the Justice Department.

'Unfair methods of competition' were declared 'unlawful', and the commission was authorised to prevent them from being used. Upon calling a hearing, the commission could issue 'cease and desist' orders which could be enforced by Circuit Courts. The commission might also compel the production of information and utilize the power of subpoena, with penalties for refusal to co-operate. The commission could gather and issue information of a more general sort, and advise the Attorney General on correcting illegal corporate actions.[26]

The precise meaning for this Act was unclear; there was little direct specification of appropriate penalty and there was little guidance on what constituted an offence. Both of these would, in practice, be defined by those who administered the Federal Trade Commission, the Inter-state Commerce Commission and the Anti-trust Division of the Justice Department. Of these three, the most significant was the Federal Trade Commission. The first chairman, Hurley, made it abundantly clear in 1916 how he conceived his role: 'When I was offered the place, I told the President that all I knew was business, that I knew nothing about the new laws, nor the old ones and that I would apply the force that I might have in the interest of business.' [27] The previous year he had made concrete his intentions. 'We are making an enquiry into the coal industry today with the hope that we can recommend to Congress some legislation that would allow them to combine and fix prices.' [28]

The large banks were similarly aided by the Federal Reserve Act of 1913, and even seemingly progressive acts such as the Underwood Act of 1913 attacked small businesses by reducing tariffs where they predominated. Thus, an analysis of the force and meaning of this legislation (and any legislation) must be clear about what is being prohibited, *who* is prohibiting whom, and what sanctions are being applied.

By 1914 the major foundations for the new social order were well established; big business was consolidating its control over the major political parties, much of the wind had been taken out of radical movements because 'something' had been done, and the legal structure was one that would help rather than hinder the actions of these powerful men. However, their commitment to this legal system was and is pragmatic, their attitude being determined by whether it helps them to realize their goals and the consequences of ignoring it.

4

In the previous section I presented an account of the development of the anti-trust laws which suggests that their content and the mode of their implementation have been very different from what one would expect from the accounts of Sutherland, Kintner, etc. In order to understand their importance in American society I shall now turn to the number of prosecutions under these laws; analyse who was prosecuted and under what conditions; and relate these to the frequency of actionable practices by corporations. These prosecutions serve to dramatize an imaginary social order and hence legitimate the economic structure in terms of a misleading portrayal of its nature. They also vindicate the claim that the state is neutral, in that it seems that every group, no matter how powerful, is subject to the will of the majority. However, these 'ideological' interpretations of social reality turn out to be inadequate in explaining the 'real' course of events.

The frequency of prosecutions under the anti-trust laws has been calculated by Hofstadter. He points out that after the demise of the anti-trust movement, surprisingly, the number of prosecutions increased.

During all the years from 1891 to 1938, the government instituted an average of nine cases a year.... In 1940, with the Roosevelt-Arnold revitalizations well on its way, the number of cases jumped to 85 – only two less than the number instituted during the entire first two decades of the Sherman Act. Thereafter, the number of cases, though still fluctuating, stayed at a level considerably higher than that maintained before 1938. In 1962, the Anti-Trust division employed 300 lawyers and working with a budget of $6,600,000 instituted 92 cases.[29]

Interesting as these figures are, they do not justify Hofstadter's view that the anti-trust laws are significant regulators of business activity. Ninety-two prosecutions hardly constitute an avalanche, since business activity more than doubled in the same period. The significance of this number of prosecutions can only be understood in relation to some estimate of the amount of forbidden activity taking place, with some attempt to generalize to enforcement levels.

Enforcement is undertaken by both the Justice Department and by the Federal Trade Commission. The Commission, which has an annual budget of $14 million and 1,200 staff members, has powers to issue cease and desist orders, demand information from firms, and publish what it feels should be made general knowledge, initiate binding actions on companies for contempt, and also alert the Justice Department to infractions which might well lead to prosecution. The Justice Department itself is less actively involved in the regulation than is the Commission, but some of the more important prosecutions have been initiated by it, for example, the prosecutions of the large electrical companies in 1960 after the Tennessee Valley Authority had complained of price fixing. An examination of this case is revealing, because it shows the conditions under which prosecutions are likely, and it also provides information which can be used to help determine the 'normal' practices in American industry. The T.V.A. announced in 1959 that it had once again received identical secret bids for three contract awards it had advertised to the electrical industry. Further investigation took place, and 'a sampling of T.V.A. records turned up 24 instances of matched or identical bids in just over three years. Some of these bids figured down to a hundredth of a cent.'[30] Pressure was then brought to bear on the Justice Department to prosecute. Only then did it do so, although it had already been investigating this industry for ten years. The companies entered a plea of *nolo contendere*, thereby admitting their guilt but limiting the details of their offences that would be made public. When judgement was given, twenty-nine corporations and forty-five individuals were punished. The twenty-nine corporations payed fines *totalling* only \$1,787,000, with General Electric paying \$437,000 and Westinghouse \$373,000. The forty-five executives were fined a total of \$137,000 and seven served thirty-day jail sentences.

It is difficult to know how many illegal, excess profits were made by these companies in this particular market. However, some indication of its scale is provided by the amount of money that General Electric paid out in treble damage suits to companies and governmental agencies who claimed compensation. By 1964, General Electric had paid out \$160 million; this meant (because of the treble damage clause) that it had made at least \$53 million excess profits in that market area. But was this an atypical way of doing business, and therefore not a generalizeable case? The President of General Electric said that it was atypical. He claimed that as early as 1946, employees had been warned against collusion, and that he himself in 1954, and again in 1958 and 1959, had sent out Directive Policy

20.5, which reaffirmed this. The prosecuted employees thought otherwise. The ex-Vice-President claimed that he had been told early in his company career that if he wished to be successful, he should involve himself in such activity. Another employee agreed with Senator Carroll that he had been: 'thrown to the wolves to ease the public relations situation ... that had developed since these indictments.' [31] There is indeed additional information which suggests that these directives were pragmatic, *ad hoc* in inspiration – and not to be seen as interfering with normal business practice.

When Directive Policy 20.5 was reissued in 1958, the price-fixing agreements in the switchgear and transformer markets had just broken down, thereby allowing for righteous competition. The 1959 Directive was issued at the time when Philadelphia juries were deciding whether there was a *prima facie* case for prosecution or not. De Munh provides evidence that in the months immediately following the plea of *nolo contendere*, identical bids were still being made by these companies for T.V.A. contracts. On 14 December 1960, General Electric and Westinghouse put up identical estimates of $1,680·12 for lightning arresters; on 12 January 1961, both General Electric and Westinghouse made bids of $604·8 for current transformers; and on 30 January 1961, six firms, including General Electric, bid $4,274·50 for bus-type insulators. It does not seem possible to explain this systematic continuous behaviour in terms of the 'greed' of a few individuals. Price fixing was part of the standard *modus operandi* of the large firm.[32]

More recently, in 1963, the Federal Trade Commission itself estimated that, when robbery netted $55 million, *detectable* business fraud netted in excess of one billion dollars, and also that large corporations are knowingly involved in frauds, such as those concerning home improvement where Alcoa and Reynolds play an important role.[33] Yet there have been few prosecutions initiated by this body, and its Chairman, Paul Reid Dixon, recently said that contrary to the Nader Group he believed the American businessman to be basically honest. The primacy of big business interests is demonstrated by the interchange of personnel between them and the F.T.C. and the pattern of enforcement. This underlines the importance of asking of laws not only what they forbid, but who administers them.

The particular 'imaginary social order' subscribed to by men like Reid Dixon is that communicated by public relations men, school texts etc. The full picture seems to have these elements:

1. Economy is based on private property; there are many shareholders (Magruder quotes 25 million).

2. Mixed economy still has as an essential feature, the pursuit of profit in a competitive market.

3. Large corporations grew naturally because of their efficiency compared to other firms.

4. They maintain their importance because they benefit from economies of scale, and invest most money in research and development.

5. Nevertheless, if they were not efficient, the market would ruthlessly remove them; the market breeds efficiency; competition is central to the system.

6. Ownership and control are separated, allowing for a community-conscious managerial group.

This view is naive and misleading. Although there are many shareholders in America, most of the corporate wealth, more than 75 per cent of the marketable stock, is owned by the top 1 per cent of the spending units.[34] Many of the top managers are themselves substantial shareholders,[35] and above all else pursue high profits with efficiency and dedication.[36] The wealthiest shareholders have most of their money invested in the '500 corporations that control two-thirds of the non-farm economy'.[37] The continuing success of these large corporations cannot be explained by them having a competitive superiority through the relative cheapness of their products. They are usually many times larger than that required for economies of scale,[38] and even if there are savings, they are not necessarily passed on to the consumer.

The Senate Small Business Committee announced that for one contract in 1959, General Electric had charged the navy $82 per unit of carbide blacking, while a smaller company in Hackensworth, New Jersey, had charged $15, representing an over-charge of 446 per cent.[39]

Despite their size, they are not even responsible for most of the innovations which have been so crucial for technological development.[40] Their continuing success is due to their economic power, by means of which they either take over or intimidate competitors. From the available evidence, it is clear that they control the economy in an essentially monopolistic way. Firms either collude illegally to fix prices, or the large firms, such as U.S. Steel, dictate prices via price leadership.[41]

On closer analysis then, the common-sensical picture of the nature of the American economy and of the relationship between large corporations and the government, proves to be illusory and misleading. For example, although price leadership is not itself illegal, it is unlikely that it could even take place if there were not an 'unreasonable' concentration of market power. This is recognized even by the Federal Trade Commission itself:

The Federal Trade Commission has estimated that if highly concentrated industries were broken up by the anti-trust laws into more competitive companies so that the four largest firms in any industry would not control more than 40 per cent of that industry, prices would fall by 25 per cent or more.[42]

5

The analysis of the nature and extent of anti-trust violations required an appreciation of the way in which the capitalists' commitment to profit and growth, and their calculative attitude to their economic, political and social relationships, made them willing to act illegally if it was in their best interest to do so. A similar framework enables one to make sense of the patterns of Labour Law violations. Capitalists view labour as a factor of production, and one which in its role as *consumer* benefits from the capitalistic order. Hence workers are viewed in a two-dimensional manner, and aspects of their potential such as creativity and control over their life space, are viewed as epiphenomenal. They are taken account of not because of their intrinsic worth, but only because of their contribution to the development of man as producer and/or consumer. Historically, laws concerning 'fair labour practices' were supported in so far as they helped achieve capitalist goals; when they did not do so, they were ignored.

Offences against the Labour Laws in the U.S.A. have often been committed by business. Sutherland found that, in the period 1890–1949, 444 out of 700 large corporations had been prosecuted for unfair labour practices.

According to the 'capitalistic' world view, labour, as a factor of production, should be calculable and controllable. But since labour may not accept such an interpretation of itself, certain problems may arise which will then be solved pragmatically. Whatever solutions are chosen, however, there is an ongoing belief that the interests of labour are essentially the same as those of capital. *Corporatist pre-suppositions are fundamental to their view of these relationships.*

In 1901, for example, the 'Banker's Magazine' wrote:

The growth of corporations and of combinations tends to strengthen the forces which seek to control the machinery of the government and the laws on behalf of special interests.... That they are not entirely controlled by these interests, is due to the fact that business organization has not reached full perfection.... Every professional man, as well as all who pursue every other mode of livelihood, will be affiliated by the strongest ties to one or other of the consolidated industries. Every legislator and every executive officer will belong to the same head. Forms of government may not be changed, but they will be employed under the direction of the real rulers ... The direction of the industrial and producing forces would enlarge independence in some direction while it might restrict it in others. Wisely conducted, every citizen might, according to his merit and ability, attain higher prizes in life than is possible at the present time.[43]

In the 1950s, this view was still retained in its essentials, but modified to the extent that unions, rather than individuals, would be co-opted. In the new order, self-governing but *non-democratic* corporations would be the basic units. These would include everybody, and labour unions could play a consultative role, provided that they abandoned the right to strike. In this neo-corporate feudal order, the central government would be little more than *primus inter pares*, because: 'You don't hand such a function (coping with economic, political and military problems) over to the government. You hand over this function to a new kind of corporation.'[44]

Adolf Berle, who had been Chairman of President Kennedy's Task Force on Latin American Policy and Special Assistant to the Secretary of State, made clear the basis of legitimacy of such a system. It was pointless using normal democratic procedures and consulting the people as a whole, because one only received superficial public opinion. Rather, the system was legitimate if it was acceptable to the public consensus. That is:

The conclusions of careful university professors, the reasoned opinion of specialists, the statements of responsible journalists, and at times the solid pronouncements of respected politicians. (These constitute) the real tribunal to which the American system is finally accountable.[45]

This corporatism expressed itself in the efforts of business to involve the unions in organizations such as the National Civic Federation, which was founded in 1900. This was supported by business and liberal political leaders and publicly advocated the right to unionization. It attracted conservative trade unionists, and supported them against those radicals who claimed that there was an irreconcilable conflict of interest between labour and capital. These views were significant because unionism was strong at this time. The NCF continued to be important into the 1930s. It succeeded in attracting Samual Gompers and many of his followers in the movement. Under Franklin Roosevelt and the New Deal, the proclaimed unity of interest of state, labour and capital was given an institutional expression in the National Recovery Administration.

Although fair labour laws had been passed (paralleled by the corporations' exemption from prosecution under the anti-trust laws), by 1934 many of the conservative trade-unionists were disillusioned with this cooperative arrangement. They argued that the unions were losing many rights and gaining little real say in the important decisions being made. There was strong rank-and-file discontent because of the contradiction between the publicly declared policy of the corporations on unionization (they supported fair labour laws), and their actions in their own industries. As early as 1919, the Inter-Church World Movement had condemned the hypocrisy of U.S. Steel for preaching welfare capitalism at NCF meetings, but practising the worst tyranny against their workers, using intimidation, blacklists and discharge of union men. Although some of these inconsistencies were particularly blatant, in fact the pragmatic nature of the commitment to conservative labour unionism as a way of incorporating labour, was being made clear. When the situation changed, the goals of profit and control could be achieved without the mediation of unions – in a sense, they disappeared as 'real' factors in the situation.

The large corporations violated N.L.R.B. regulations based on laws which were passed at times when it was necessary to recognize, institutionalize and incorporate trade unions via their conservative leadership.

At other times, when the unions seem weak, attempts are made to establish the primacy of the individual contractual relationship between the corporation and the employee. Thus, the laws lose their binding power, because they no longer are based on realities of power. When they are enforced in such periods, penalties are relatively light and do not worry the corporations. Thus, corporations are willing to break the laws they themselves have advocated.

6

I have attempted to locate the contradiction between the actual workings of the social order (actual corporation behaviour) and the ideological picture of the nature of capitalist society (enshrined in part in the law) in the workings of the capitalist economy. I have shown that the knowledge of the laws is a poor guide to how the corporations will act and a poor guide to how the state will react. Thus, I had to go beyond the commonsensical (and legal) understanding of the legal institutions.

But it is not enough to ask why laws have been passed (and whether they are implemented). We must also query why they have not been passed. This question is particularly relevant when the organization of institutions seems to violate their declared purpose. Thus the oligopolistic organization of the press in England seems to be at variance with the notion of an open market of information and opinions. However, there is a voluntary body that is meant to oversee the situation, the Press Council. On closer analysis this proves to be under the control of the major newspaper publishers (even the lay members of the council are chosen by the professionals), and was probably constituted to pre-empt the formation of a body under public control. The foreign relations of America are justified to her people in terms of her commitment to the 'Free World' – a world of democracy and free enterprise. The compatibility between this picture and the nature of the relationship to other countries rarely becomes fully manifest because few laws concerning the regulation of international commerce and intercourse exist that can highlight these relationships. Moreover, although capitalism is itself an international system, dominated for the last twenty years by America, people still think in national terms. (This includes criminologists, who, even when they talk about social control, are bound by commonsensical nation-state units of analysis.)[46]

This section attempts to examine corporate crimes committed in an international context and show that they are only a minor part of the behaviour in which sociologists should take an interest. In so doing it is intended to integrate the study of crime into the study of social life, and to drop the commonsensical categories that have inhibited the full development of an adequate criminology. The large corporations have not confined their activities to America itself. Since the First World War, they have been involved in the administration and direction of American foreign policy. Their confidence in the competitive advantage held by American business, their need of new markets, and the importance of raw materials that were either naturally available abroad, or could be more cheaply produced in 'underdeveloped' countries, explain this involvement. Since the Second World War, the importance of military expenditure to the revenues of the largest corporations has strengthened their interest even more. The government (mainly defence) and foreign buyers now account for 20 per cent to 40 per cent of the total demand for the products of all the major industries, with the exception of agriculture.[47] The corporate rich are involved in foreign policy decisions of the American government, in order to protect and develop their overseas interests, and also in their capacity as a virtually co-equal partner to the military. That their interests have been by far the most important in shaping American foreign policy, is now extremely well documented. The change of attitude towards Russia after the Second World War can no longer be explained in terms of Russia's aggression,[48] but must rather be understood as due, in part, to the economic consequences of the spread of communism. As America's former Ambassador to Russia expressed it, 'Every time Russia extends its power over another area or state, the United States and Great Britain lose another market.'[49]

International business activity is supposedly governed by certain conventions and laws, and is, in fact, legitimated to the peoples of the world in those terms. But there has been little development of either international or national laws to cope with the emergence of the large American-based monopolies. These companies attempt to control their foreign markets, and also to control their sources of raw materials. They achieve this by methods that continually violate international norms and national laws. However, information about this is systematically denied to the American people by governmental and corporate misrepresentation.

In the 'underdeveloped' countries, similar attempts are made to mislead the indigenous peoples who are said to have an irrational distrust of American business. One writer[50] suggested that the 'image problems of American corporations abroad' would be solved by the general adoption of an advertising programme which had been designed for such an organization. Nine features of a desired image were outlined, four of which were:

35

1. The company is an important tax contributor to the national government.

2. The company puts the broad national welfare above immediate profits.

3. The company does not interfere in any way with national political decisions.

4. The company takes a sincere interest in community problems.[51]

It is interesting to apply this model to Guatemala. In 1950, Jacob Arbenz, having received 267,000 of the 350,000 votes cast, became President of his country. He continued and developed social reforms started by his predecessor, Juan Jose Arrevalo. One such reform involved distributing idle land to poor peasants. The American-owned United Fruit Company was informed that it would have to surrender some of its land. It was offered compensation based on the value set on the property in 1952 for tax purposes 'by the owner himself'. Although United Fruit objected, the expropiation took place. In 1954 a group of Guatemalan exiles, led by Colonel Carlos Castillo Armas, invaded Guatemala from Honduras, and Arbenz fled into exile.

America still claims that Arbenz's government had been taken over by communists (despite all the evidence to the contrary), and does not mention its own connection with Armas.[52] He was trained at the U.S. Command and General Staff School at Fort Leavenworth, Texas; and the whole operation was financed, armed and organized by the C.I.A. The Secretary of State at the time, John Foster Dulles, was a major stockholder and long-time corporation counsel for the United Fruit Company.[53]

This not atypical example is revealing for a number of reasons. Clearly, both the United States Government and the United Fruit Company colluded in *illegally* undermining a legitimate government. The willingness to sacrifice democracy when it interfered with corporate action underlines the tenuous and provisional nature of their commitment to democratic institutions. If those who espouse socialistic ideas are elected, they can be removed relatively easily because of the vast military might of America compared to that of poorly organized local people. The need to take such action is often avoided by actively funding undemocratic regimes which would otherwise be replaced by the inhabitants of these countries.

One quarter of outright U.S. grants in the period 1946–61 went to five countries – Turkey, Greece, South Korea, South Vietnam and Formosa – all right-wing dictatorships opposed to social change, and with the exception of Formosa, all hopelessly backward economically[54]

There can be no theoretical justification for confining one's analysis to those occasions when regimes are illegally undermined. Rather, that must be understood as only one strategy developed to control and guarantee the supply of raw materials.

7

I have attempted to show that to understand the 'crime' problem in America one must relate four things:

1. The publicly declared 'crime' problem.

2. The 'ideological' portrayal of American society as being a *democratic*, free-enterprise system, wherein the majority rationally control the legislature and the government. This is the *'imaginary social order'*.

3. A more accurate picture of the distribution of criminal activity in the American social structure – using as criteria of significance those adopted in 1 above.

4. A picture of American society based on a radical, more sophisticated analysis of the relationship between the capitalist class and the state, the nature of the economic order and the problems posed by insulating this against democratic attack. I focus here on the 'real social order'.[55]

When examining specific kinds of criminal acts and the actual societal response to them, I have shown that the major determinant of police action is the relationship between the criminal activity and the 'real social order'. Actions that pose a real threat to this must be controlled, e.g. embezzlement or lower-class attacks on private property. I have also suggested that police action by the state stabilizes the system by mystifying the people. The very existence and occasional implementation of laws that sanction the rich seemingly gives content to the claim that the state is neutral and controlled by the people. Furthermore, in focusing on and incarcerating lower-class criminals, the centrality of an individualistic ideology is upheld and the potential for developing lower-class-based radical political movements is partially neutralized.

Although I initially started the analysis of corporate crimes within a very legalistic framework, I progressively moved further and further away from the confines of positive criminology. Once criminal activity is viewed merely as one amongst other strategies used by corporations, then the overall social structure within which they act must be analysed. This not only leads to posing the questions why are laws implemented in this way, and why are laws not passed, but also to recognizing that the international nature of the capitalist system is not reflected in either the system of regulation *or* in most theorizing about it.

References

1. EDGAR J. HOOVER, 'The Faith of Free Men', in *Criminological Controversies*, ed. R. D. KNUDTEN (New York: Appleton-Century Crofts, 1969), p. 10.

2. THE PRESIDENT'S COMMISSION ON LAW ENFORCEMENT AND ADMINISTRATION OF JUSTICE, 'Crime and Victims in a Free Society' (1967), in *Crime and Delinquency*, ed. C. A. BERSANI (Macmillan, 1970), p. 8.

3. G. KOLKO, *Wealth and Power in America* (New York: Praeger, 1962), pp. 20–22. For figures in income distribution see R. J. LAMPMAN, 'The Share of Top Wealth Holders in National Wealth 1922–1956' in *American Society Inc.*, ed. M. ZEITLIN (Markham, 1970).

4. See the general discussion of the confines of traditional criminological thought in 'Defenders of Order or Guardians of Human Rights?', JULIA and HERMAN SCHWENDINGER, *Issues in Criminology*, Vol. 5, No. 2 (summer 1970).

5. E. SUTHERLAND, 'Crime of Corporations' in *White Collar Criminal*, ed. G. GEIS (New York: Atherton Press, 1968), p. 58.

6. E. SUTHERLAND, ibid., p. 47.

7. Sutherland quotes WENDELL BURGE, Assistant at the head of the Anti-Trust Division of the Department of Justice, who said, 'Most of the defendants in anti-trust cases are not criminals in the usual sense.

Crime, Corporations and the American Social Order

There is no inherent reason why anti-trust enforcement requires branding them as such.' G. GEIS, 'The Heavy Electrical Equipment Anti-trust Cases of 1961', in *White Collar Criminal*, ed. G. GEIS (New York: Atherton Press, 1968), p. 359.

8. See the discussions of the Second World War by J. BAGGUELEY, 'The Cold War and the Second World War', in *Containment and Revolution*, ed. D. HOROWITZ (A. Blond, 1967).

9. See the accounts presented by Sutherland in the various works quoted; E. W. KINTNER, *An Anti-Trust Primer* (New York: Macmillan, 1964).

10. E. SUTHERLAND, op. cit., p. 354.

11. E. W. KINTNER, op. cit., p. 226.

12. ibid., p. 15.

13. The following picture is a composite, relatively consistent one, communicated by these diverse sources. The school texts I consulted are used in Californian high schools as standard texts: economics courses use J. M. DODD, *Applied Economics* (Cincinatti: South-Western Publishing Co., 1945); compulsory civics courses use W. A. CLENAGHEN, *Magruder's American Government*, 52nd edition (Boston: Allyn & Bacon, 1969).

14. From the corporation Report of U.S. Steel in 1958, quoted in J. K. GALBRAITH, 'The Corporation', in *Crisis in American Institutions*, ed. J. K. SKOLNICK (Boston: Little, Brown & Co., 1970).

15. W. A. CLENAGHEN, op. cit., p. 16.

16. A more accurate characterization of a capitalist economy requires a discussion of the 'capitalist mode of production'; see K. MARX, *Capital*, Vol. 1 (Moscow: Progress Publishers, 1965).

17. This really is the logical conclusion of Weber's analysis of capitalist rationality. In other words, I am sceptical of the utility, for understanding this rationality, of his distinction between *zweckrational* and *wertrational*. Furthermore, I would argue that the capitalists' provisional attitude to democracy explains their ability to work in collaboration with undemocratic societies. Thus militarist Japan and Nazi Germany were both explicitly committed to a capitalist mode of ownership and production. On these points see H. MARCUSE, *Negations* (Allen Lane the Penguin Press, 1968), p. 10; C. B. MACPHERSON, *The Real World of Democracy* (Oxford University Press, 1969), pp. 201–22; and B. L. INGRAHAM and K. TOKORO, 'Political Crime in the United States and Japan: A Comparative Study', *Issues in Criminology*, Vol. 4, No. 2; and also Section VII below.

18. For this analysis I have relied mainly on the following works: G. KOLKO, 'Railroads and Regulations 1877–1916;
G. KOLKO, 'The Triumph of Conservatism;
M. J. SKLAR, 'Woodrow Wilson and the Political Economy of Modern United States Liberalism';
J. WEINSTEIN, 'Gompers and the New Liberalism 1900–1909;

39

R. RADOSH, 'The Corporate Ideology of American Labour Leaders from Gompers to Hillman'. All are in J. WEINSTEIN and D. W. EAKINS, eds., *For a New America* (New York: Random House, 1970). R. HOFSTADTER, 'What happened to the Anti-trust Movement?' in *The Paranoid Style in American Politics* (New York: Vintage Books, 1967). M. JOSEPHSON, *The Robber Barons* (Eyre and Spottiswoode, 1962).

19. D. M. GORDON, 'Class and the Economics of Crime', *Review of Radical Political Economics*, Vol. 3, No. 3 (summer 1971), p. 62.

20. M. JOSEPHSON, op. cit., pp. 109–20, 269, 364, 372, 379–80.

21. G. GEIS, op. cit., p. 48.

22. R. HOFSTADTER, op. cit., 1967, p. 197.

23. G. KOLKO, 'The Triumph of Conservatism', p. 19.

24. ibid., pp. 10–19.

25. In the telephone industry, for example, the competition from the independents broke the American Telephone and Telegraph Company's monopolistic position, which it had held from 1885 to 1894. By 1910 the telephone rates had been forced down by this competition, and the dividends paid out by A.T. & T. had sharply declined. Whereas, those paid out by many of the smaller companies were still healthy. ibid., pp. 47–50.

26. ibid., p. 267.

27. ibid., p. 275.

28. ibid., p. 270.

29. R. HOFSTADTER, op. cit., p. 194.

30. J. HERLING, *The Great Price Conspiracy* (Washington: R. B. Luce, 1962).

31. G. GEIS, op. cit., p. 111.

32. *Illegal* excess of the American Telephone and Telegraph Company's current revenues over the maximum supposedly in force (the rate of return is set by the Federal Communications Commission) is approximately $169 million per annum. See P. LASSELL and L. ROSS, 'Nixon's Economic Melodrama', *The New York Review of Books* (23 September 1971).

33. E. F. COX, R. C. FELLMETH *and* J. E. SCHULTZ, *Nader's Raider Report on the Federal Trade Commission* (New York: Grove Press, 1970), p. 56.

34. R. J. LAMPMAN, op. cit., p. 103.

35. G. KOLKO and W. DOMHOFF, *Who Rules America* (Englewood Cliffs: Prentice-Hall, 1967).

36. P. A. BARAN and P. N. SWEEZY, *Monopoly Capital* (Penguin Books, 1966).

37. A. BERLE, 'Economic Power and the Free Society', quoted in J. SKOLNICK, op. cit., p. 123.

38. W. ADAMS, 'Competition, Monopoly and Planning', in M. ZEITLIN, op. cit.

39. J. DE MUNT, 'G.E.: Profile of a Corporation', *Dissent* (July–August 1967), p. 593.

40. P. A. BARAN and P. N. SWEEZY, op. cit., p. 9.

41. ibid., Ch. 3.

42. R. NADER, 'A Citizen's Guide to the American Economy', *New York Review of Books* (2 September 1971), p. 15.

43. G. KOLKO, op. cit. (1963), p. 162.

44. Quoted in HAL DRAPER, 'New Corporations and New Reformers', *New Politics*, Vol. 1, No. 1 (1960).

45. ibid., p. 96.

46. JULIE and HERMAN SCHWENDINGER, op cit., p. 149.

47. H. MAGDOFF, *Economic Aspects of U.S. Imperialism* (New York, Monthly Review Press, 1966), p. 16.

48. Whatever Russia's intentions, she was in no position to engage in aggression, since during the Second World War she had lost 20 million dead, one third of her territory had been devastated, and she lost two thirds of her industrial base. D. HOROWITZ, *Empire and Revolution* (New York: Vintage Books, 1969).

49. ibid., p. 71.

50. HELEN DINERMAN, 'Image Problems of American Corporations Abroad', in *The Corporation and its Publics*, ed. J. W. RILEY (New York: Wiley, 1963).

51. ibid., p. 157.

52. See for example the account of these events in *The U.S. Department of State Fact Book for the Countries of the World* (New York: Crown Publishers, 1970), p. 270.

53. D. HOROWITZ, *The Free World Colossus* (New York: Hill and Wang, 1965).

54. ibid., p. 195.

55. By contrasting 'ideological' and 'real', I am not implying that we can interpret social reality other than theorizing about it, merely that I have proposed an analysis that not only provides a better explanation of what is going on than does the 'ideological' one but also explains the functions of this inaccurate portrayal. Cf. K. MARX, *The German Ideology* (New York: International Publishers, 1947).

Martin Loney*   Social Control in Cuba

Discussions of 'social control', whether in sociology at large, or in criminology and the sociology of deviance in particular, have been mainly confined to the forms of control in capitalist societies. This paper is an attempt to rectify that omission. If there are any intrinsically theoretical concerns in this paper, they are, firstly, to illuminate the ways in which social control in a revolutionary society is a product of *conflicts* of interest within the revolution itself, as well as being a product in part of the wider cultural context within which the revolution occurred, and, secondly, to indicate, in a very preliminary fashion, that the functions and content of 'social control' in a society intent on *liberating* men's potential are rather different from the functions and content of control in a society which is avowedly concerned to *repress* the 'passions' (or the allegedly baser instincts) of men.

In this paper I am interested in an empirical description of three broad areas of social control in Cuba: the regulation of absenteeism in Cuban industrial and agrarian life; the control of political expression and activity; and the Cubans' attempt to come to terms with 'classical' social problems. None of these can be understood, however, without a basic understanding of the Cuban Revolution itself.

The Revolution

The distinctive features of the Cuban revolution are often ignored in popular political discussion. The origins of the 1958

* The author would like to thank Mary McIntosh, Ian Taylor and Paul Walton for comments on an earlier draft of this paper.

revolution have, in fact, to be traced to the struggle waged against Spanish colonialism in the last century. This struggle remains an important theme in post-revolutionary culture in Cuba.

In 1868, Cuban coffee planters engaged the Spanish in the Ten Years' War, an uneasy peace settlement in 1878 being disturbed only eighteen years later by the revolt under the leadership of the legendary José Marti. On this occasion, the revolt was successful in expelling the Spanish – but only at the cost of American intervention, and the imposition of American military rule until 1902.

The Americans had good reason to intervene. In the latter half of the century, American investments in Cuba had increased by leaps and bounds, until, in 1895, they were estimated at $50 million; and Cuba purchased about one fifteenth of American exports. The Platt Amendment – giving America the right to intervene to maintain a government 'adequate for the protection of life, property and individual liberty' – convinced Cuban nationalists of the need to resume the struggle for national independence. In 1933, the revolutionary nationalist government of Grau San Martin was denied recognition by the United States, and the repressive tyranny of Batista was installed in its place.

Fidel Castro explicitly saw himself as an heir to the traditions of the struggles of the nineteenth century: the leading column of the 26th July Movement, indeed, was called the 'José Marti Column Number One'. Thus, the triumph of the Cuban revolutionaries in 1958 was the final act of a dramatic struggle instigated some ninety years earlier: a national mission cutting across the lines of class (although in time the support for the revolution assumed distinctive contours of class and status) and accomplished (unlike in Russia) without a significant internal counter-revolution claiming the mantle of national interests.[1] Even today, some thirteen years into the revolution, *Granma,* the official newspaper of the Castro government, carries numerous articles on leaders of the various revolutionary struggles in the nineteenth and twentieth centuries.[2] Side by side with the commemoration of Cuban martyrs, articles recall the squalor and poverty of life for many people in a society where unemployment was often as high as 25 per cent.

Continued American aggression – whether political, military or economic in form – acts as a constant reminder of Cuba's ongoing battle against external domination. Thus, the Cuban leadership frequently describes the revolutionary process largely in terms of the *national* struggle against the United States. On 3 September 1970, Fidel said:

> ... the fact that our country has come this far, that our country has successfully put up resistance for eleven years, against the world's most powerful imperialist country – the one which could do most damage to us economically, militarily and ideologically; a country which had us completely indoctrinated, which had inculcated us with its capitalist, egotistical, thoroughly reactionary policy and vices, with everything – the fact that our country was capable of holding up against all this demonstrates the strength of the revolution, the power of the revolution.[3]

The nationalistic features of the revolution are accompanied – and sustained – by the populism of the revolutionary leadership, a populism which also derives from the traditions of the nineteenth-century struggle. Although Castro is now leader of an organized Communist Party, he is also a popular figure intent on keeping in contact with the Cuban people at large. Castro maintains his personal authority in frequent trips to the country, and in his lengthy speeches, in which he will deal in great detail with, for example, technical problems of milk production. The leadership – avowedly interested in the creation of a new 'Socialist Man' – is seen as legitimate, not so much by virtue of a monopoly over the possession of force nor by virtue of bureaucratic rationality, but primarily by virtue of its role in the defeat of Batista and the final achievement of Cuban independence. This legitimacy is strengthened through the leadership involvement in *popular* discussion and its concern to open the channels of communication and mutual education. In the 26 July speech for 1971, Castro said:

> I believe, that we, the leaders of this revolution, have cost the people too much in our process of learning ... when we spoke of

illiterates we didn't include ourselves ... we could best be classified as ignorant.

The Cuban revolution has to be understood, then, not just in terms of the undeniable improvements in material living standards it has brought to the Cuban people, but also in terms of its popular, nationalist base: powerful sentiments which have wrested a nation from 450 years of foreign control, and powerful sentiments which gave rise to a system of social control and social order quite unlike those in existence elsewhere.

Problems of Social Control: 'Loafing'

Successful revolutions do not result in the complete abolition of pre-revolutionary 'crime' and 'social problems'. These live on, perhaps taking a different form, certainly being influenced by new factors. Some kinds of behaviour previously classified as a 'problem' or a 'crime' will now be acceptable while kinds of behaviour previously approved will now be labelled antisocial. The major problem facing the national revolution in Cuba in 1959, and the major problem facing any national revolution of this kind, was to guarantee minimum living standards. The Cuban attempt to achieve this, however, was to be made without the aid of economic incentives to productivity – since one of the distinctive features of the attempt to create 'Socialist Man' in Cuba was the attempt to eliminate capitalist wage incentives. In his 1971 speech, Castro noted that the attempt to replace 'motivation by hunger and death' with 'motivation by honour' in the economy had meant that the sixteen- to seventeen-hour working day imposed on peasants in the sugar harvest in pre-revolutionary periods could no longer be expected. Moreover, the equalization of salaries and the small capital base in the post-revolutionary economy had resulted in a serious shortage of consumer goods, the majority of which could still only be obtained on ration cards. This in turn resulted in an anomalous situation in which many workers could earn in two days all that they were able to buy in seven, and in which other workers were content merely to live on

friends or on the welfare system. The goods were not there to
be bought.

The surprising fact is that most workers continued to work
a full week, apparently vindicating the exponents of the 'moral
incentives' school in Cuba. But large numbers of workers did
not. The average number of hours worked per day did decline,[4]
and the problem of absenteeism, or 'loafing' (as the Cubans
call it), did increase. Such a situation obviously threatened the
ability of the revolution to achieve one of its central aims,
that is, to guarantee the minimum standards of life which had
been denied before.

The Cuban leadership had constantly referred to the problem in speeches and conventions, but it was clear by the
autumn of 1970 that political appeals and moral suasion were
insufficient. The leadership began to canvass proposals for the
regulation of 'loafing' and absenteeism. In September 1970,
the meeting of the Central Organization of Cuban Trade
Unions devoted a large part of its time to the discussion of the
problem, and Jorge Risquet, the Labour Minister, announced
that a draft law had, in fact, been drawn up a year earlier, and
that, now that information and personal records were available from the earlier national census, it would be feasible to
implement the law. Risquet also announced that the draft law
would be submitted for discussion and amendment to the
Trade Unions, the neighbourhood Committees for the Defence
of the Revolution, the Federation of Cuban Women, the
National Associations of small farmers, students, and the
armed forces.

Subsequently, the press paid great attention to these debates;
and, throughout, the law was presented as having been a
response to pressure from the workers. Presenting the law to
the Central Organization of Cuban Trade Unions, Risquet
asserted that: 'The working masses have for years demanded
that the revolutionary government adopt rigorous laws against
laggards and absentees.' *Granma* stated that 3·75 million people
had participated in discussions of the draft law in 115,000
assemblies. Furthermore, among the Trade Unions and the
Committees for the Defence of the Revolution, 76 per cent of

participants approved of the law unanimously, 24 per cent proposed changes and 1 per cent voted to make the law more lenient.[5]

The widespread mobilization around the issue, coupled with the advent of the law itself, served to put moral pressure on those defined as 'loafers'. Some 90,000 people signed up for work. In an editorial following the passage of the law, *Granma* urged Cubans to continue this re-educational process 'making them feel, think and act as members of the working class'.[6]

For those 'loafers' who were unresponsive to re-educational attempts, the law imposed sentences ranging up to one year's work in a rehabilitation centre. The sentence, however, would initially take the form of a recommendation from an individual factory Labour Council (a popularly elected factory-level committee), which would then have to have this recommendation ratified by the General Assembly (the factory as a whole). Even in a situation where the interests of the revolution demanded the identification and regulation of individual 'deviants', therefore, the popular and democratic nature of legal process was maintained and in fact seen as an essential element of the process.

Two tactics, then, were used in the attempt to assert social control in the name of the Revolution. The first tactic (consistent with the espoused Cuban policy of building 'Socialist Man') was the process of social mobilization and education. The second (necessitated by the partial failure of the first) was the direct coercion of those who 'intended to lead a parasitic life'.[7]

Significantly, however, even when coercion was introduced, the goal of 're-education' remained paramount, and Labour Minister Risquet expressed concern that those who did not like to work should not be placed in institutions for the 'lumpen elements, thieves or homosexuals' but rather in 'schools to combat loafing'.[8]

The continuing emphasis on 're-education' (and the relatively gentle sentences imposed on 'loafers', compared, for example, to those imposed on 'counter-revolutionary' elements in post-revolutionary Russia) can be understood in terms of

the popular nature of the Revolution itself, and the institution-
alization of a level of popular democracy in Cuba after the
Revolution. Debate is real; at the 1970 Trade Union Congress,
for example, many of the delegates attempted to explain
absenteeism and 'general dissatisfaction' as a response to the
inefficiency of many local administrations. One dockworker,
whilst calling for stronger measures against absentees, nevertheless denounced the absence of drinking water on the dock-
fronts, and the lack of washing facilities for workers who were
called upon to handle dirty cargoes. A telephone worker denounced faulty management methods and the indifference of
some political leaders to problems of detail, and argued that
these failings could be significantly related to the absentee
problem. Not only was the criticism of government open and
unrestrained, compared, for example, to that in Soviet Russia
in its early period of revolutionary consolidation; it was also
criticism which provoked a positive response from the leadership itself. In his closing speech to the Congress, Castro discussed the issue of privileges and concluded:

... the administrative official – or, even worse, the political leader
– who gets preferential treatment in obtaining a house that becomes available, right before the eyes of thousands of people who
don't have a single room ... does a tremendous amount of damage
to the authority and prestige of the Revolution.... If a cadre or
Party member has gone sour he must be replaced.

The Cuban Revolution is still an isolated political force in
the Americas, although it is conceivable that the Allende regime
in Chile may alleviate some of the problems that stem from
Cuba's economic and political isolation. But any examination
of Cuban revolutionary culture, and in particular of the system
of social control, must take account of that isolation. Although
the Revolution may be seen as democratic and popular – in
form – in that the membership level of the various Cuban
organizations is high and in that criticism within those organizations is relatively open and unrestrained – it is still very
much the case that the *content* of that democracy, and thus the
imperatives of social control – are dictated by the need – in

more or less siege conditions – to build a productive economy. The Federation of Cuban Women, for example, is an organization that is largely devoted to the task of bringing women into the labour force. Cuban Trade Unions constantly commit themselves to increasing their productivity. The Federation of University Students mobilizes its members for voluntary work. In this atmosphere, little time is left for thoroughgoing debate, and questions that are not directly related to production targets almost inevitably come to be defined as 'disruptive', and certainly unpatriotic. The legislation on absenteeism and loafing – accompanied by a degree of discussion on the nature and causes of the problem in question – was nevertheless dictated by the economic context of the revolution itself. In his May Day speech for 1971, Castro confirmed, once again, that 'work productivity must from now on be the number one objective of the labour movement'.

Political Deviance in Cuba

During its prolonged period of isolation as the only revolutionary society within the American 'sphere of influence', Cuba has had to rely on the U.S.S.R. for aid and for economic trade agreements in general. In return, the Cuban leadership has been compelled to maintain reasonable relations with the Soviet bloc at large. The relationship has fluctuated, but, more recently (and particularly after Castro's ambiguous statement on the Russian invasion of Czechoslovakia), observers have detected the increasing influence of the Soviet Union on the politics of the Revolution.[9]

Earlier however, there were a number of crucial issues on which the Cubans were divided from the U.S.S.R. (notably, the Cuban stress on 'moral incentives' and the validity of the armed struggle against imperialism as opposed to Russia's own reliance on the monetary economy and the road to socialism via 'peaceful co-existence'). Many internal developments in Cuba, and notably the ways in which attempts have been made, in the courts, to define the appropriate forms of revolutionary political behaviour, in part reflect the uneasy nature of the

Cuban-Soviet relationship. Two of the outstanding 'political trials' in Cuba can be seen to reflect a change in the definition of correct revolutionary politics in two different periods in the Revolution's development.

In the so-called 'micro-factional' trial of February 1968, thirty-seven people were given prison sentences. Eight of these defendants were members of the Cuban Communist Party, amongst them Annibal Escalante, a major leader of the Party in the pre-revolutionary period. The charges against the thirty-seven were vague but extensive. The defendants were variously alleged to have opposed the elimination of bus conductors, to have worked for the restoration of material incentives and to have passed information to Soviet or eastern European officials. The general tenor of the charges was that the defendants had exhibited 'pseudo-revolutionary' (i.e. pro-Soviet) attitudes and that they had built a faction within the Cuban Communist Party to propagate these views. This in itself was not illegal, although it may have been a breach of the rules of the Party. The evidence presented at the trial consisted of a series of documents from police files, records of telephone conversations, denunciations, 'confessions' and photographs of the defendants talking. At no time did the accused address the court; and the trial was preceded by a meeting of the Party's Central Committee in January, in which both Raul and Fidel Castro made extensive speeches, setting the tone for the trial: a tone of accusation and stigmatization taken up in full by *Granma*, the official paper of the Revolution.

There had, of course, been other political trials in post-revolutionary Cuba. Many of these involved individuals or groups who were working for Batista; and some of them involved individuals whose political affiliation was unclear and never explicitly revealed; one notable exception was the trial of one of the first Communist Party members to join Castro in the Sierra Maestre immediately before the Revolution, who was imprisoned for attempting to organize a Black Power group – not an unreasonable aspiration in a society where some 30 per cent of the population is black and where racism has certainly not been altogether eliminated. But the Escalante trial was outstanding for the scale on which it was mounted; for the *ad hominem* nature of the charges and accusations; for the directness of the intervention by the Cuban leadership; and for the extent to which widespread publicity was accorded the trial. It was indeed a 'show trial' intended to alert the population at large to the existence of 'pseudo-revolutionary' activity, and to cement in the popular mind the only legitimate (Cuban) alternative.

Some three years later – on 20 March 1971 – the prize-winning Cuban poet, Heberto Padilla, was arrested and arraigned for trial – on the direct orders of Castro himself. The charges against him were even more ambiguous and vague than those placed against Escalante and his friends; and were concerned only with the nature of Padilla's *ideas*.

In contrast to the micro-factional trial, little publicity was given to the Padilla hearings; and most of the references were oblique and concerned largely with the role of foreign intellectuals who had interceded on Padilla's behalf. On 5 April, Padilla signed a statement in which he castigated himself for his egoism and his desire for fame abroad.[10] He admitted giving erroneous analyses of Cuban life to K. S. Karol, René Dumont (whom, it is now said, he has never met) and Hans Magnus Enzensberger. He called on other writers to overcome weaknesses which 'could lead to political and moral degradation'. And in a speech to Havana University students, Castro is reported to have warned other intellectuals engaged 'in this type of activity' that they could expect to meet the same fate as Padilla.[11] In the meantime, intellectuals who know Padilla have been saying that the 'confession' he is alleged to have signed is totally out of character. The structure of social and political control appears, to put it no more strongly, to be assuming the forms of the Soviet model, where once it was concerned to identify this alternative to be 'pseudo-revolutionary' and politically deviant.

Some clues to this change in policy can be found in statements made by the leadership on the questions of revolutionary culture and intellectual life.

In 1961, Castro's 'Address to the Intellectuals', had allowed 'everything within the revolution, nothing against the revolution'. In *Socialism and Man*, Guevara, whilst a member of the revolutionary leadership, had referred to 'socialist realist' painting as the 'corpse of nineteenth-century bourgeois painting'.[12] And in 1965, Castro told the American journalist, Lee Lockwood, that: 'I especially am a partisan of the widest possible discussion in the intellectual realm ... ideas must be able to defend themselves. I am opposed to the blacklist of books, prohibited films and all such things.' Finally, in 1968, in his speech to the Cultural Congress in Havana, Castro warmly praised the intellectuals present who had stood by Cuba during the missile crisis 'who were the ones who mobilized the people, painted signs and organized meetings in Europe ... precisely (among) the intellectual workers. It was not organizations, it was not parties! It was honest, sensitive men and women, who were able to assimilate, understand and to do justice.'

By 1971, the situation had clearly changed. In April, Castro proclaimed to applause at the First National Congress on Education and Culture that: 'As a matter of principle there are certain books of which not a single copy, chapter or page should be published, not even a letter.'

At the same conference, in an oblique reference to the signatories of a letter urging Padilla's release, Castro referred to those '... bourgeois liberal gentlemen ... two-bit agents of colonialism ... bourgeois intellectuals and bourgeois libellants, agents of the C.I.A. and intelligence services of imperialism ... you will not be allowed to come to Cuba.'

And in the Congress declaration it was stated that: 'We reject the claims of the Mafia, of pseudo-leftist bourgeois intellectuals to become the critical conscience of society.'

Many of the intellectuals being rejected were the same men who had been feted in 1968, and, whether or not the Congress was aware of the fact, included people like Jean Paul Sartre, Simone de Beauvoir and Carlos Fuentes. Sartre's position on the role of the intellectual is clearly on record, and Castro's caricature of his politics, and those of his co-signatories, does the new Cuban position on culture no credit at all.[13]

The process has not been confined to definitary statements

at congresses. In his recantation, Padilla explicitly referred to K. S. Karol and to René Dumont (authors of sympathetic socialist analyses of the Revolution) as C.I.A. agents (although, significantly, this particular passage was omitted from the version released by the Cubans in New York). Within Cuba itself, the press pursued the matter – alleging that Dumont had received information from a Cuban agronomist who later was shown to be an agent of the C.I.A.[14]

The changes in Cuban cultural, political and social policies can only be seen to reflect changes in the power possessed by different political tendencies within Cuban society; and, in particular, the increasing power of traditional Communists within the Revolution. The struggles of these groups for 'socialist orthodoxy' considerably predate the Escalante trial. In 1961, hard-line Stalinists claimed responsibility for the suppression of the widely-read cultural journal *Lunes de la Revolucion* and the film *P.M.* In 1966, another offensive was mounted, culminating in the establishment of the 'Military Units for Aid to Production' (U.M.A.P.) – which were supposed to be productive alternative employment for young men of draft age whose 'moral outlook' make them unsuitable for regular military duty. In effect, however, the U.M.A.P. were prison camps for homosexuals and other 'undesirables'; and they were used as a base from which to attack libertarian tendencies, particularly among intellectuals. In 1966, five prominent artists were called to report to U.M.A.P. The Cuban Writers' Union demanded that the order be rescinded and Castro eventually intervened and promised to close U.M.A.P.[15]

In 1968, however, the hard-liners were a little more successful. Padilla having been awarded the U.N.E.A.C. poetry prize by an international jury (of their nomination), but against their opposition, the Stalinists produced a denunciatory introduction to the published works themselves. In particular, they expressed their outrage at Padilla's poetic criticism of the Soviet Fatherland; and, in the armed forces newspaper, *Verde Olivo*, they published an accusation to the effect that Padilla had once been dismissed from the Cuban foreign trade agency for corruption.[16]

The trial and 'denunciation' of self by Padilla completed their victory over a man who, in the same year, had attacked his former friend, Cabrera Infante, for leaving Cuba, with the words: 'I am here and will continue here ... for a revolutionary writer there is no alternative: the revolution or nothing.'[17]

At the time of writing, little further information is available on the Padilla trial; and *Granma* is taken up with reports of Castro's visit to Chile. Some tentative remarks can be made, however, in the light of the discussion of these two trials, about the content and direction of social control, as applied to the conduct of politics, in post-revolutionary Cuba.

In the first place, although the Escalante trial was in many senses a 'show trial' in which a powerful political leadership decided to bring a certain kind of politics within the jurisdiction of the law, and thus to end the dialogue, it was also an indication of the Cuban leadership's determination to open up the Revolution – in particular, to revolutionaries of non-Stalinist complexions, intent on building a new Socialist Man in Cuba on the basis of continuing, democratic and militant struggle. This objective needed clearly to be distinguished from the 'pseudo-revolutionary' concerns of men like Escalante and the pre-revolutionary Cuban Communists. Thus the Escalante trial served the function of marking the 'moral contours' of Cuban socialism, in rather the same way that some of the trials in early Puritan settlements in America served to define the contours of a religious and frontier society.[18]

Like those earlier trials, the Escalante trial was made the subject of considerable publicity; and similarly the attempt was made to mobilize opinion on the basis of mass involvement. In place of the market-place accusation, however, the Cubans made use of (for example) the neighbourhood Committees for the Defence of the Revolution. There they held popular discussions on the interpretation of the charges and the findings; and in this way what was formally a criminal trial of some thirty-seven individuals took on an alternative importance as the public affirmation of proper and appropriate revolutionary behaviour.

The Padilla trial could be seen as a necessary development,

then, following on from the leadership's failure to democratize and consolidate the revolution as much as was hoped. Crises in the Revolution, notably the failure to achieve the 10-million-tons target in the 1969 sugar cane harvest, and also the failure of the Revolution to spread, in the rest of Latin America, provided the opportunity for a Stalinist resurgence: a resurgence, of course, that carried with it the promise of increased Soviet aid. Padilla, in this sense, was a pawn in the political struggle for the control of the Revolution. As a popular poet for the new socialism, and thus as a sworn opponent of Stalinist orthodoxy, he was the natural symbol around which to renegotiate the 'moral contours' of Cuban socialism.

Social control in Cuba, therefore, in the political and in the economic spheres, can be seen to have a changing *content* – a content which, in large measure, can be traced back to the fact of the Revolution's isolation and dependency on a changing international economy and political situation. In a revolutionary society (as much as in the capitalist societies of East and West) the actual nature of social control is in large part the result of the clash of interests within (and outside) the society, as much as it is a response to apparently disruptive or problematic characteristics of *individual* members of that society.

'Social Problems' in Cuba

The clash between different political and ideological interests in Cuba, however, does not occur in a cultural vacuum. There are features of social control in Cuba that seem to owe more to broad cultural traditions, and which have not been specifically questioned by the revolutionary leadership in Cuba itself.

Earlier, mention was made of the Stalinists' attempt to mount a campaign against sections of the intelligentsia, in the course of which some of the intellectuals were stigmatized as homosexuals. The Cuban – indeed the Latin American – attitude to homosexuality is extremely simple: it is regarded as a form of human degeneration. The favoured cultural trait in Cuba is still 'machismo', the one difference from the pre-revolutionary period being the implication that the only really good, strong males are fully conforming revolutionaries. The adulation of Che Guevara is the obvious but not unexceptional example. Far from confronting the arguments of revolutionaries in the West who argue for a liberatory sexuality and a breakdown of restrictive sexual roles as a prelude to human liberation, the Cubans have systematically equated homosexuality with the possession of counter-revolutionary sentiment. Moreover, insofar as the Cubans have referred explicitly to sexuality as a 'problem' at all, they have tended to argue that homosexuality is an unnatural 'survival' from pre-revolutionary society. This is, of course, the kind of explanation that Soviet criminologists have, until recently, tended to advance for the continuation of various 'capitalist' social problems in post-revolutionary Russia,[19] and it is an explanation which is superficially more satisfactory some twelve years after a revolution, as in Cuba, as compared to the fifty-four years which have elapsed since the Bolsheviks' success. The Cubans' position is clear in the declaration made at the First National Congress on Education and Culture, in 1971, that:

... the structural transformation and development of our society ... has brought about new contradictions which demand a constant effort at creative renovation in behaviour, social habits and ideas.[20]

This same congress resolved also to 'struggle against all forms of deviation among our young'. The specific reference was to groups of youth who adopted extravagant dress and life-styles; behaviour, which in the view of the Congress, was very much the result of 'contamination' of Cuban youth by Western influences.[21] The Congress determined to take action against such contamination by calling for the establishment of state agencies whose responsibility it would be to develop 'fashion guide-lines' for the young.

There may be very good reasons why a revolutionary society which is trying to consolidate and industrialize should want to take a firm, and indeed (to Western eyes) repressive, line on matters of life style and associated 'symbolic' behaviour. Whilst affluent capitalist societies appear to have an almost infinite capacity for the (profitable) absorption of 'counter-cultural' symbols, a revolutionary society with a severely restricted economic base does not. The Revolution, in order to survive, has not only to draw the accepted lines of behaviour very clearly in 'show trials': it is also important to maintain a monopoly on cultural symbolism. Fidel still wears the uniform in which he came down from the hills. He offers a hundred prisoners selected by the C.I.A. in exchange for the return of Che's dead body, as clear expression of the Cuban view that Che dead is worth any hundred counter-revolutionaries alive. The symbolic (functional) alternative in Cuba to the possession of goods is the struggle for socialist consciousness; and the adulation of Che replaces the worship of media heroes in capitalist societies. In this situation, it may be that the development of counter-cultural symbols, whether or not they are really dissident in a political sense, may indeed serve to undermine revolutionary legitimacy, associated as it is with a certain set of cultural symbols.

Cuban discussions of juvenile delinquency, narrowly defined, and its causes, are carried out almost entirely in terms of a straightforward positivistic frame of reference. The contributing 'factors' are identical to those used by Western criminologists in 'explaining' delinquency under capitalism: broken homes, poverty, unemployment, lack of schooling, 'under-socialization', etc. The discussion of treatment alternatives has not been markedly different from contemporary Western dialogues either, the dominant emphasis being on 'education' and 'remedial action' and similar ideas. One short-lived exception was the proposal in 1969 by the Minister of the Interior that the death sentence be introduced for a wide range of crimes. This proposal, reminiscent of the solutions proposed in Russia during the Stalinist period to deal with those who failed to appreciate socialism, has happily not been repeated. However, for so long as the Cuban experts continue to use arguments developed by Western sociologists in the search for order within capitalist social structures, refusing to contemplate the qualitatively different problems posed by the struggle for human liberation, then the return to a crude, neo-Stalinist 'penology' – death penalty, exiles and all – must be a possibility in Cuba.

Conclusion

My purpose has been to clarify some aspects of social control in Cuba, and, in so doing, to provide some kind of addition to the literature on social control, which has necessarily had to concentrate on the structures of control and repression under capitalism. I have tried to show that the nature of social control in Cuba (and, by implication, in societies which are much more markedly divided into different interests – and particularly different classes) is not the product of some objectively given set of individual pathologies in the population at large, nor even the product of *individual* 'moral entrepreneurial' activity by powerful reformers or reactionaries. Rather, I have argued, the structure and content of social control is very much bound up with the political economy of the Cuban situation. I think it follows that those who would take moral stances on Cuba and the system of control in operation there must also be prepared, therefore, to consider the *real* (as distinct from the hypothetical) possibilities. It also follows, of course, that anyone who would believe that the fact of revolution is sufficient in itself to hasten in a problem-free utopia, whether in Latin America or the more developed societies, would do well to consider the ways in which 'progressive' and 'reactionary' tendencies appear to continue, and uneasily to co-exist, in the systems of social control in post-revolutionary Cuba.

The method I have followed has been to portray, as accurately as the scanty data will allow, the recent developments in the system of social control in three different areas. An accurate picture of Cuba can be attempted in other ways. Jose Yglesias and Barry Rekord have provided narrative accounts of Cuban life which frequently highlight the 'dialectics' of the situation rather more naturalistically – whether it be a dialogue with an absentee who is arguing that he prefers hedonism to production, or whether it is an account of a factory meeting in which the Manager uses the necessity of meeting production targets, and the need to use time 'productively', as an excuse for closing potentially critical meetings.[22] My method here has necessarily been more assertive and less detailed, constrained by the difficulties of data collection and the paucity of existing secondary sources, but the attempt has been made to stress the changing inter-relationship of social control initiatives.

The Cuban experience is important in that it represents, however imperfectly, an attempt to operationalize the humanistic goals of Marxism. We do not know what 'social control' would look like in a liberated society, but this examination of the experience of a *revolutionary* society raises questions, perhaps, in a way that contemporary deviancy theory, working under and on capitalist social structures, does not. A *political* sociology of deviance unconcerned with these questions would indeed be an academic exercise. In the meantime, the last words must rest with C. Wright Mills, writing of Cuba. He simply said: 'I do not worry about it. I worry for it, and with it.'

References

1. Whilst there is considerable evidence to show that the support for the revolution in Cuba was mainly from workers and peasants, it is also clear that the support was highest among Cubans of Castro's own generation and also Cubans who had participated in, or witnessed, the abortive revolution of 1933. The continuous nature of the Cuban *national* struggle is emphasized. Cf. MAURICE ZEITLIN, 'Political Generations in the Cuban Working Class' in M. ZEITLIN and J. PETRAS, eds., *Latin America: Reform or Revolution?* (New York: Fawcett, 1968).

2. For example, a member of the central committee of the Cuban Communist Party, Armando Hart, in a speech commemorating the death of Antonio Maseo, a leader in the Ten Years' War, argued that: 'the greatness and profundity of our revolutionary movement today derives from a series of historical situations which are to be found in great part in the struggles for independence and the process of national formation in our country'. ARMANDO HART, 'La Instransigencia del Movimiento Liberador Cubano', *Pensamiento Crítico* (Havana, September 1967), No. 8.

3. *Granma* (Havana, 6 September 1970). Quotations from Cuban speeches in this article – unless otherwise stated – are taken from *Granma*.

4. One estimate is that the national average of productive hours worked per day between 1966–8 was four. K. S. KAROL, *Guerillas in Power* (New York: Wang & Hill, 1970), p. 426.

Politics and Deviance

5. *Granma* (14 March 1971, 28 March 1971).

6. *Granma* (11 April 1971).

7. JORGE RISQUET, Speech to the Central Organization of Cuban Trade Unions, *Granma* (3 September 1971).

8. ibid.

9. Cf. for example: RENÉ DUMONT, *Cuba: Est-il Socialiste?* (Paris: Seuil, 1970); K. S. KAROL, op. cit.; P. BARAN and P. SWEEZY, *Socialism in Cuba* (New York: Monthly Review Press, 1969).

10. H. PADILLA, *Intervencion en la Union de Escritores y Artistas de Cuba, Casa de las Americas*, Nos. 65–9 (Havana, 1971).

11. Fidel Castro, reported in *Indice* (Madrid, June 1971).

12. E. Guevara, quoted in HUGH THOMAS, *Cuba* (Eyre & Spottiswoode, 1971), p. 1,465.

13. In interview, Sartre has argued that 'the intellectual who does not put his body as well as his mind on the line against the system is fundamentally supporting the system, and should be judged accordingly'. Interview with John Gerassi, *The Guardian* (4 September 1971). His recent defence of the illegal French 'groupuscule', *La Gauche Proletarienne* (in which Sarte sold the group's illegal paper), is further evidence of Sartre's own political commitment.

14. René Dumont had spoken rather incautiously about the arrest of the agronomist in a speech in Paris: 'I denounce the fact that an agronomist friend of mine has been arrested just because he helped me'. *Granma* reprinted this statement, and added: 'Raul Alonso Olive (the agronomist), as has been shown, is a confessed agent of the Central Intelligence Agency of the United States.' *Granma* (21 February 1971).

15. J. YGLESIAS, *New York Review of Books* (3 June 1971), p. 5.

16. J. YGLESIAS, ibid; and also HUGH THOMAS, op. cit., p. 1,466.

17. J. YGLESIAS, op. cit., p. 8.

18. For a discussion of law and social control in the Puritan settlement of Massachusetts, *see* K. T. ERIKSON, *Wayward Puritans* (New York: Wiley, 1966).

19. Paul Hollander has coined the term 'survivals theory' in his discussion of Soviet views on juvenile delinquency. The notion is really one of 'cultural lag' transferred to the situation in which (it is alleged) capitalist social relationships have been replaced by socialist alternatives. Cf. PAUL HOLLANDER, 'Juvenile Delinquency in the Soviet Union and the United States, a Converging Social Problem', *British Journal of Criminology* (April 1969), pp. 148–66.

20. *Granma* (9 May 1971).

21. Hollander points to quite the same explanation being used in Soviet Russia in situations where the 'survivals theory' patently does not hold. Cf. PAUL HOLLANDER, op. cit.

22. J. YGLESIAS, *In the Fist of the Revolution* (Penguin, 1970). BARRY REKORD, *Does Fidel Eat More Than Your Father?* (André Deutsch, 1971).

Gail Armstrong City Politics and
and Mary Wilson Deviancy Amplification

For many people – even Glaswegians – their first knowledge
of the Easterhouse area came through the newspapers and
television in July 1968. The peak of this publicity 'campaign'
was reached when Frankie Vaughan publicly announced his
desire to help Easterhouse gang boys 'reform' through involving them in the founding and running of their own youth project. The boys agreed to demonstrate their willingness to co-
operate by taking part in an amnesty – a laying down of
weapons under police supervision. As these events took place
the entire proceedings were given massive coverage by the
media.*

During this period, delinquencies in Easterhouse were given
disproportionate prominence compared to those which
occurred in other areas; a partiality which invited the reader
scanning the paper to assume 'it's all happening in Easterhouse'.
Headlines appearing in the Scottish *Daily Express* included:
'O.K. Frankie, We Will Surrender our Swords, Bayonets,
Knives, Meat Cleavers, and Iron Railings: By Four Gangs';
'Police Called to Clear Hall' (of the project); 'Life is a Night-
mare' (in Easterhouse); 'P.C. Goes Down Fighting'.[1]

Statements suggested that gang warfare was raging in Easterhouse ... 'None of the boys can reveal their addresses in
Europe's biggest housing scheme – I don't want another gang
to find out where I live – that's suicide.'

Vaughan himself was quoted as saying: 'I have heard

* Our own investigation was itself part of the widespread response
evoked in the city (during the summer of 1968) to the area's supposed
problem of gang violence.

61

terrible stories of gang warfare in Easterhouse.' But no space was devoted to any description of gang members.

The project leadership itself was partially responsible for the presentation of this type of view. They sought to 'glamorize' and 'dramatize' the founding of the project. The cooperation of gang-leaders was actively sought as a means of involving the rank-and-file membership; leaders were quickly identified, flown to Blackpool to meet Vaughan, had 'secret' pub-cellar meetings with him and so on. (It subsequently came to light that far from leaders exercising any control over members, it was not even clear who the leaders were. One boy had posed as a gang-leader in order to get a free plane trip to Blackpool!)

The core traits of the gang member were described as a natural and frequent leaning towards violence, coupled with a complete disregard for the pain inflicted on the victim and a lack of motive for the crime.

This whole image on the 'Easterhouse gangster' was highly questionable. While the existence of gangs in the area could not be denied, they were neither as highly organized nor as widespread as the press indicated. Although in a symbolic sense violence was central, actual infractions typically occurred as a result of 'sounding' and 'probing', a function of misunderstanding *between* gangs as well as within them. The suggestion that 'decent respectable folk' had reason to fear for their safety was ill-founded. On the contrary gang boys tend *not* to select their victims randomly, a point which will become clear in the course of this paper.

Nevertheless most of the individuals contacted informally during the early months of 1969 had accepted the content of media portrayal, and even enlarged on it. One waitress in Skye, for example, was convinced that gangs of teenage girls roamed the area forcing passers-by to strip! Nearer home friends and colleagues expressed alarm at our travelling to the scheme alone, while a priest offered the opinion that the area was populated by inferior beings and violent animals who could only be controlled by a superior show of force. Such a reputation also seems to have been accepted 'officially', for during arrangements for a Youth Week in Glasgow reference was made to the need to demonstrate that the majority of youth in the city was not typical of the boys of Easterhouse. On a more concrete level, the housing scheme was officially 'downgraded' by the local authority during 1969 to 1970, often a prelude to the utilization of a housing area as a 'dumping ground' for 'undesirables'. Further evidence of the acceptance of the public reputation is indicated by a test carried out by one of the authors in 1970 to measure discrimination against Easterhouse youth by local employers.

The residents in Easterhouse felt threatened by such media messages and by March 1969 feelings of hostility were running so high that they formed themselves into the 'Easterhouse Fights Back Campaign' – a campaign which gained wide support in the area. Its main purpose was to challenge press treatment of Easterhouse, accusing one daily newspaper of sensationalizing youth violence and of 'planning' to undermine the project.

A meeting of supporters decided to make a formal complaint to the Press Council; local people angrily claimed that living in the area had become an embarrassment to them. They had come to feel like 'slum dwellers', as one commented.

However, press reportage of this first public meeting successfully distorted the feelings expressed there. The banner-headline read: 'Easterhouse Man Tells Protest Meeting "You Can't Ignore the Violence".' [2] Referring to a loudly booed statement made by one member of the audience, the article which followed denied all charges, attempting to discredit the whole campaign by suggesting that the committee consisted of a small group of politically motivated individuals.

Publicity had the effect of making the community an 'object of curiosity' – attracting professional people, students, film crews and many more. The outcome was to sustain the reputation of Easterhouse as a severe delinquent area, by ensuring that it remained a 'talking point'. But more importantly, publicity began to sensitize authorities to the possibilities of 'trouble' there.

What were the objective conditions of delinquency in Easterhouse? Before Easterhouse became publicly exposed as a delinquent area, it was already *officially* designated as such. Yet this shift in status was not a causal one. Nor can objective changes in youth behaviour account for the transition. What is required is an examination of some aspects of the history of social control in Glasgow, and the recent emergence of youth violence as a social problem.

Social Problems in Glasgow: Housing and Violence

Violence is a well-established social problem in Glasgow. Those with official responsibility for control are acutely aware of its long-standing and national reputation as a 'violent city', a matter which has sometimes been the cause of considerable embarrassment.[3] The control of violence in the city has been regularly selected for debate and discussion, especially in the media. Control groups seen as failing to view the situation in a serious light are likely to be accused of incompetence.

The 'causes' of violence have been variously associated with unemployment (the 'razor kings' of the thirties), 'Celtic blood' (which is also held to explain the superiority of Scots soldiers!), and Glasgow drinking habits. More recently, violence has been associated with inadequate social and recreational facilities on the large post-war housing estates.

In the post-war period Glasgow's housing problem was principally one of acute shortage. Four large housing developments on the periphery of the city were consequently completed by the early fifties, Easterhouse being the last and the largest. By the early sixties the housing problem appears to have taken on a different shape. Although there were still too few houses to accommodate those requiring them (as in most large cities), a major concern became the provision of community facilities on the large, isolated post-war estates. It is difficult to explain this concern other than in terms of the disquiet being expressed over 'vandalism' and 'rowdyism' in these areas. In 1967 a Corporation Report on Community Problems notes:

The fact that these problems of violence and vandalism among young people are related to new vast areas of housing development, leaves no doubt in the minds of the Working Party that the situation has a basis in the post-war history of Glasgow.[4]

Particular local conditions may have caused the connection between these phenomena to be made; for example, in the early sixties, a large proportion of residents in these areas would be in the 'delinquent age bracket'. In addition, the notion was currently popular in youth work theorization, and was being incorporated into research projects on delinquency.[5]

Whatever the case, as early as 1965 the Labour administration in Glasgow was looking into ways and means of controlling vandalism, and clearly suggesting the most fruitful strategy lay in the area of community development.

... whatever the causes of vandalism may be, outright suppression by punitive methods is not part of the experiment we are engaged on. On the contrary, the search is for some imaginative alternative ... it would be possible to put to the test one broad generalization which most people would be inclined to accept without much argument – that any area where a sense of community exists has less vandalism in its midst than an area where no-one knows his neighbour or cares much about the place in which circumstances have placed him. ... Further, by bringing good citizens together in neighbourliness, a force is provided, which if only psychological, yet presents some barrier against groups of mischief-makers.[6]

Community consciousness was to be fostered by the provision of certain amenities. Easterhouse and its neighbouring estate, Barlanark, were selected for the 'experiment'. 'Here are two adjoining areas whose decent inhabitants have had to put up with more than their fair share of vandalism.' Although the report is principally concerned with vandalism, a further consideration is that 'rivalry of a *disturbing sort* already exists between the teenage groups of the two areas' [our emphasis]. The solutions forwarded involved the 'painting and polishing' of the community, supplying a 'promenade' as a focal point of interaction and a points system between the two schemes whereby the rivalry would be transformed into healthy competition.

Politics and Deviance

Easterhouse – The Setting

We have noted above the general problems which gave rise to the development of housing estates such as Easterhouse in the post-war period; by the early fifties the scheme was completed and 9,100 almost identical dwellings had been built. It was some years before basic amenities such as schools, transport and shopping facilities were established. Indeed, even at the present time, one could hardly suggest the scheme is adequately provided for in some respects; shopping facilities are minimal, while social and recreational needs are solely catered for by the schools and churches – supplemented by one public house. This 'community', lying five miles from the city centre and housing more than 40,000 people, has neither banks nor public offices.

Four schemes or neighbourhoods are readily distinguishable, which until recently were divided by areas of undeveloped waste land, football pitches and so on. Because amenities are local to each scheme, there is little opportunity – or need – for social mixing to take place *between* them. The result has been for residents of all ages to identify with their own neighbourhood, rather than with the Easterhouse area, the most explicit expression of which has been the 'territory-based' gang.

It would be misguided in the extreme to point to these features of the built environment as *causing* the emergence of the violent gang: many middle-class suburbs are equally deprived yet do not exhibit a similar phenomenon. The street-corner group was evident long before violence involving the use of weapons came to be practised. The importance of the built environment and the local demography lies in the fact that they structured the *pattern* of youth relationships. However the transition from street-corner group to violent gang involves a *qualitative* change in behaviour, and in order to understand this shift it is necessary to refer to the *subjective definitions* of the situation held by the actors themselves.

Easterhouse – Its Youth

In 1966 almost half of this predominantly working-class community was under the age of twenty-one, and for those with little interest in the Boy Scouts or other church activities, the street-corner was the obvious, indeed the only, meeting place. It appears that the large numbers of young people congregating on the street-corners, indulging in what might be termed 'pranks' and minor delinquencies (typical of such peer-group settings), allowed the patrolling policeman, along with some residents, to view the situation with some concern. Certainly 'gang fights' were taking place by the mid sixties:

It was through playing football that it all started. Used to hang about the corner after the game. After I left school there was nothing to do except hang about, you'd just hang about with the same crowd. If anyone got dug-up [usually a *verbal* provocation], you'd all go down; that was classed as a 'gang fight'.

However, it appears that the *meaning* of these encounters completely escaped the patrolling policeman and other onlookers. The following statement typifies the gang boy's view of the matter:

It used to be good going down with them, because you thought you were great. ... Thought you was a big man. Used to go with them and watch the fight, used to stay at the back at first, shout and throw bricks and bottles, you thought it was great. You really enjoyed yourself, it was great entertainment so it was! [laughs].

Asked if there were any casualties:

No, there were no weapons, knives and that; just sticks to bash them over the head. Used to ... [laughs] ... used to be great y'know, everybody used to know each other, say you knew him from school [the person on the other side] or something, used to go 'How's it going?' an' that, but you'd still fling bricks at him! I don't know what really made us do it. There was nothing else to I don't think. We just let off steam that's all it was. It was better than playing football.

Incidentally, up to the present time the boys continue to refer to the gang as the 'team', which is made up of a number of

67

smaller 'squads'. Football is no longer a focal activity amongst these 'teams', but the vocabularies utilized do reflect the violent gang's origins.

In early expeditions or 'raids' on 'enemy' territory, entertainment value was clearly uppermost.

Used to plan our attack and all that ... We used to call [X] the General because he always planned it ... we would hide in the fields, a few of the boys would go down to the Y.M. if there was a dance on, throw in bottles and shout 'Come on! We're the Mental Rebels!' something like that to rile them up. They'd all get mad. Thousands of them would all run out the dance (you know how they've got to be brave to the lassies), so they all ran out. [X] and [Y] would run into the fields, but they run slow so's the Toi [a rival gang] would go 'Ah, we're catching them!' And there's a wee valley in this field and they'd run into it, and the Toi would go 'Ahh!' and they'd [X and Y] fall and all that, and the Toi would get right mad and say 'We've got them! We've got them!' And then we'd all swoop down, y'know, 'Massacre!' an' all that! [laughs].

It is hardly surprising then that policemen with little local knowledge (until 1968 they were based outside the area), patrolling Easterhouse in Panda vans, responded to such scenes with a degree of alarm.

Easterhouse – The Police

Police organization in Easterhouse has undergone two important changes: round about 1965 a mobile plain-clothes unit was introduced in order to 'prevent group disorders', and in 1968 a local police office was opened. Before 1965 police operations in the area were carried out solely by patrolling policemen equipped with Panda vans and were directed by divisional H.Q. some distance away. This meant that the police were rarely able to witness actual acts of law-breaking in Easterhouse, and as one boy put it:

... The police had to come away from Shettleston then; you know everything is finished in about half an hour – by the time they got up, they just got the stragglers. They had to come up through the

Toi, used to get them first! We'd just stand on the top of the hill shouting 'hard luck!' an' that! [laughs].

While attempts at 'prevention' did not elicit the same response:

First they used to patrol the scheme, didn't used to do anything; some of them are too lazy to get out of the van, y'know, they just drew up and when you ran away, that was it.

(What happened?)

Well they just sat in the van, just drew up. Used to stand on the corner at nights, nothing else to do an' that. Used to draw up, you'd run. They used to enjoy it, get kicks out of it, watching you run away.

At this time police experience of youth behaviour in Easterhouse would thus be restricted to a very narrow range indeed, and the use of vehicles to police the area would only serve to increase the distance between police and youth there. These conditions created a situation whereby the policeman's predisposition to view the working-class youth as a potential delinquent could come into play.

According to official sources, each of the city's divisional areas maintains a mobile plain-clothes squad, which is deployed according to current needs. For example, if there was a sudden increase in house-breaking the squad would concentrate its resources in that direction.[7] When the local police office opened in Easterhouse the duties of what became known locally as the 'Untouchables' were described in a police document, 'Police Duties in Easterhouse', by referring to the fact that:

Many anonymous phone calls are received from residents in the area that a number of youths are loitering at a particular locus, and they are usually apprehensive about their future conduct. This is dealt with by the plain clothes squad of Echo 10 or the Untouchables.

Clearly it was envisaged that the Untouchables would fulfill a preventive role in respect of gang activity. In effect, many young people standing at the street-corner came to be viewed with suspicion. Indeed, it became an offence for them to stand there. The widening of police definitions of 'delinquent behaviour', which coincided with the arrival of this squad, had a marked effect on police/youth relations:

... the Riot [Untouchables] started. They used to sneak through the backs and come out ... they used to dress up as workers, boiler suits and ladders and all that. You know, just booked you for nothing, they called it loitering, about twenty of us standing at the close or something ... [we] didn't like it. That was when you really started hating the polis. You weren't doing anybody any harm, standing at the corner, a couple of lassies, a couple of lads having a laugh. Used to get booked all the time by the Riot. There was no problem before then, until these guys started. They really cleaned up the scheme you know.

How did they do that?

Just started booking you, booking you every single night of the week, the only thing you could do was stay in or something.

And later:

I think it's [the Riot] just made the boys more sneaky; they're more cunning now, harder to catch. They got to get more ideas in order to survive. There's still hundreds fighting now, even though the Riot's there.

Such police activity had a marked affect; by colouring youth's attitudes towards the police, by causing more of them to be officially labelled delinquent, and by effecting behavioural changes in the peer group.

In 1968 the police office, a stationary caravan known as 'the hut', was opened. In the long term this has gone some way towards improving relations between police and youths. Nevertheless it seems that the Untouchables had 'set the tone', so that in the early days the local establishment was fraught with feelings of unease.

In December 1967 the Glasgow administration selected Easterhouse as the subject of a Community Problems report specifically concerned with teenage violence. It is feasible that the police manning the new office entered the situation in the expectation of 'trouble'. One of the boys offered the following account:

In Easterhouse it was a different situation [from previous residence], where police didn't stop to talk to the boys, *or* older people at that; there was some type of barrier which was never broken down between police and civies. ... In Easterhouse, if you went down to the shop, which was and still is a mobile van, it could hardly hold two customers, let alone two screws ... But being nowhere to go for the natives, there was also nowhere for police to have a kit-kat and get to know anybody personally. The police situation was, out, do the beat, and back to the hut for a game of cards and a cup of tea ... when the boys got a bit adventurous, the police were just out for any arrest and back to the hut again for some tea and another game of cards.

For the new policeman in Easterhouse there was little opportunity for the routine police duties such as traffic control and the security of business premises. Given this, together with his minimal contact with residents and his awareness of the official designation of the area, it is easy to see that the highly visible and numerous street corner groups in Easterhouse would present an opportunity to fulfill his role in the community.

In 1969, however, the 'unit beat system' was introduced. Whether or not this 'village bobby' idea was adopted through an awareness of the problems outlined above, it certainly had the effect of bringing the police and the community closer together:

... the [Untouchables] don't like the screws [beat police]. The beat police don't like them, they don't want the Touchies out in Easterhouse. They think Easterhouse would be a quiet place if the Touchies went out, and so it would.

Why is that?

Well the Untouchables, they just lift you up for nothing, there's no doubt about it. I mean they're pure pigs. All the beat policemen, well everybody knows them and that. ... Big [X], a policeman on the beat you can say hello to him. ... They don't bother. They come up to the project, give you a lecture about gangs and God knows what else. [X] came up a few times and gave us a lecture, y'know, he's alright, he says he hates the ... [hesitation], y'know they hate the Untouchables, don't like them at all.

Politics and Deviance

However, throughout 1970 the Untouchables continued their 'preventive' activities in Easterhouse.

As early as 1965, then, Easterhouse had been located by the (Labour) administration as being in need of special measures to curb vandalism and redirect 'rivalry of a disturbing sort' into more acceptable channels. Again in 1967 the area was selected as the subject of a Community Problems Report. The reputation, however, did *not* coincide either with the emergence of, or an increase in, gang warfare, *or* with the Corporation's definition of Easterhouse as a 'problem area'. Until the middle of 1968 – the year in which the project was established – these 'disturbing conditions' were not made public. Previously messages about the area transmitted to the public had reflected 'typical' community events, including vandalism and other delinquencies. Reportage was neither prominent, nor persistent enough, nor sufficiently focused in content, to allow the public to evaluate Easterhouse as a special case in terms of gang violence.

The Control of Youth Violence as a Public Issue

During 1967, but more so during the first months of 1968, a debate took place in the City Chambers and in national political circles, over the increases in the rates of violence both in Glasgow and in Scotland as a whole; and this debate received prominent coverage from the newspapers. The debate covered the causes of the increase in violence and 'what to do', and resulted – towards the end of 1967 – in the suggestion that the most threatening aspects of violence was represented by gangs of youths who carried offensive weapons and were not averse to using them on 'innocent victims'. Youth violence was in the process of becoming a full-blown social problem.

While accepting the basically 'political' nature of social problems forwarded by Becker,[8] the case of Easterhouse indicates that in fact, the 'political process' does *not* terminate at the point when some organization 'takes charge' of the problem. It largely depends on who takes charge and how, and the power they have to convince various 'aroused citizens' that *what is being done* is consistent with their interests. Control ideology itself may become the subject of a public debate or issue. There may be widespread consensus over the problematic status of vandalism, for example, but not over a government decision to control offenders by subjecting them to psychiatric treatment. When concern over certain conditions is widespread (as is the case with housing and crime), then interested parties will tend to question or challenge official control strategies from time to time, as was the case with hanging.

Those interested in assuming control of the social problem need to demonstrate the superior effectiveness of their own strategies; thus, public issues are frequently associated with political elections. Elections provide those in power, and competing groups, with an opportunity to present arguments and evidence supporting their own control ideology, and, hopefully, to gain public support.

The measures being advocated by the Progressives in anticipation of the local elections were opposed by the controlling Labour council, who favoured a treatment-oriented policy. The emergence of this debate in fact coincided with the setting up of the Labour Council's committee to study Community Problems. It is arguable that in their anxiety to provide evidence for their own strategies the administration chose Easterhouse since it represented the *lowest* amenity area in the city.

The Scottish *Daily Express* played an agitator's role in the debate to the extent that as well as reporting it in detail and in front-page banner headlines style, it increasingly (and notably in the month before the local elections) devoted a large proportion of space to a series of articles and editorials on violence and youth violence which supported the Progressive/Tory line. Two series of articles explicitly in support of the Progressives' call for an amendment to the 1953 Prevention of Crime Act (to allow new stop-and-search powers) were entitled 'Frisk the Thugs Campaign' and 'Is No-One Safe?' Outbreaks of violence over the Easter weekend that year were covered in the Scottish *Daily Express* by the front page banner headline 'Bloody Easter', and a Conservative M.P. was quoted as saying: 'I shall be using this new outbreak as a further example of what is going on. I don't think Ross [Under Secretary of State for Scotland] will be able to hold out over this much longer.'

Further, the space devoted to 'crime reporting' increasingly reflected turns in the debate itself, rather than in actual crime. Analysis shows significant changes in volume between different categories of crime as the debate moved from vandalism to violence, and finally to youth violence, gang warfare and the carrying of offensive weapons (see graph).

Strong suggestions were made of the incompetence of those in power. During April 1968, in the Scottish *Daily Express* a Police Federation spokesman was quoted as saying: 'The much-wanted powers of arrest and search are being bogged down by politicians.' The same newspaper suggested in an editorial: 'It would not be surprising if people have to look elsewhere than the Secretary of State and his Labour colleagues for a sympathetic hearing.'

In reply to the accusation of political ineptitude it was claimed that the Progressives were attempting to create mass hysteria over the problem, that cool reasoning rather than heated emotions would solve the difficulties, and finally that it wasn't a political problem at all. The Progressives were accused of 'gimmickry'.

However, predictably enough, when statements about Glasgow being a 'city torn by violence' reached much wider publics through television and radio, both sides stood together to reduce this threat to Glasgow's reputation by denying that things were 'this bad'.

When a Glasgow M.P. stated in the House of Commons that 'The Clyde is foaming with blood' he was widely accused of doing the city an extreme disservice. Having gained power in Glasgow in May 1968, the Progressives were now committed to a specific control ideology; and they continued to express their demands – particularly over an amendment to the 1953 Act. One Progressive councillor, in an attempt to bring the 'problem' to the notice of national political leaders, planned to transport and dump at the steps of the Home Office 100,000 questionnaires covering demands for police powers, corporal punishment, etc.

Vaughan's Intervention: The Unintended Consequences of Voluntary Control

During the above debate Easterhouse was not once, to our knowledge, referred to as a problem area. It was not until July of 1968 that the estate became spotlighted. And it must be stressed that official sources have stated that there was *no* increase in gang activity in the scheme at this time, nor did police officials consider the area one of the worst.

We suggest that Vaughan's intervention was highly embarrassing for the local council, especially the group in power. The appearance of a national personality in the role of control agent would clearly be against the interests of *all* parties who had previously expressed disquiet over Glasgow acquiring a national image as a violent city. Vaughan's interest in the area would be seen as providing a further opportunity for attracting unwanted publicity, both for the city's shortcomings over amenity provision, and for the extent of gang violence. In addition he was publicly supporting the 'liberal' ideology which the group now in power had previously condemned. He had presented the gang boy as being responsible and capable of 'good citizenship', thus challenging the stereotype forwarded by the Progressives. Vaughan was openly cooperating with the 'thugs', 'monsters' and 'animals'.

For various reasons Vaughan's project withstood any immediate challenge. For one thing, its sponsor could hardly be accused of incompetence, given his past record of achievement in youth work. Secondly, in view of the recent debate it was difficult to claim there was no need for some sort of large youth centre. Further, it was difficult to refute the presence of gang warfare in the light of media coverage of its general presence in Glasgow, of the amnesty and Vaughan's meetings with self-confessed gang leaders. The police convenor, however, did venture an attack on Vaughan before eventually agreeing to help: he was reported in July 1968 in the Scottish *Daily Express* as having stated: 'This is a piece of bloody nonsense, Vaughan is on a publicity gimmick. I am absolutely astounded that the neds should hold the police to ransom. Vaughan is being carried away with his own importance.'

Although it could be *claimed* that Vaughan's proposals for control could not work, it could only be shown in the long term. It was inconceivable for the Progressives to simply *ignore* these events in Easterhouse, given their apparent concern about youth violence in general, and given the inevitable publicity surrounding an entertainer of national standing.

In looking at the history of the project we can see that initially it was allowed an innovatory status. While the education committee was slow to provide funds, local fund-raising activities were successful, and the *Express*, in covering project events, did not supply the usual stereotype of the gang boy. On 18 July an editorial stated: 'Up with the good work to redeem the wild kids of Easterhouse, up with the sentences for vicious thugs who defy and despise reformation.'

However, a prominent place was reserved for all events connected with the scheme and the project, including any delinquent activities; and a report covering the opening of the project in February 1969 suggested that something was amiss: 'It was expected that many Easterhouse teenagers would attend the ceremony and a special loudspeaker system was installed to relay the ceremony outside the project building. But inside the two army built huts there were many empty seats.'

An incident at the end of March that year where two members of the project were 'bailed out' of gaol on project funds resulted in something of a redefinition of the project. Views were forwarded that a club that allowed funds which had been 'dug out of people's own pockets' to be spent in this way was at the least questionable, and at the most, in the words of the Police Convenor, nothing more than a 'gangsters' recreational hall'. In March 1969 the *Express* condemned this use of funds with the following statement: 'The public put money into Easterhouse to provide youth with facilities and opportunities to keep out of trouble. Never did it cross the public mind that such funds should be used for bail.'

The Police Convenor's subsequent resignation from his trusteeship of the project was supported by this newspaper, and in the following days both he and other trustees and leaders of the project appeared on TV to discuss their differences. Although varying definitions of this and other events were supplied, we contend that their publicity forced the status of the project to shift from innovatory to controversial. The *Express* began to use the latter term in describing the project, and by May Vaughan commented: 'Easterhouse I need as much as a hole in the head as far as publicity is concerned.'

Such reports, followed by others, could be interpreted as evidence for lack of order and/or poor management in the project, an anti-establishment tendency and increasing gang warfare in the scheme.

October of 1969 marked the beginning of close scrutiny of the project by the Corporation and press, subsequent to a 'crisis' which occurred over its leadership during which charges of incompetence were made. The Education Committee set up a special sub-committee to look into the runnings of the project before granting more money. During the first months of 1970 it was clear that the project was in financial difficulties. Late in July, the *Express* claimed that the venture was 'on its last legs' and a month later the Education Committee refused to forward any money until the books had been carefully probed.

The staff of the project were in fact made redundant on 11 August, but the Corporation offered to support it as a local authority venture. The eventual decision was to introduce a policeman, trained in youth work, as the new leader. On 2 January 1971, we read in the *Express* about how – 'Easterhouse once more looks for a new image ... it began in 1968 with the ballyhoo of a showbiz occasion ... but the appeal to the gangs to join in the running of the club didn't work.' And on 4 March: 'P.C. Morrison launches the NEW Easterhouse Project.'

This brief sketch shows how the project came to be redefined and eventually absorbed into the statutory control structure. Those in control in the Corporation had suffered embarrassment over the unwanted publicity it drew, but more importantly through the control ideology it represented. Its public failure as a voluntary organization and its eventual incorporation into statutory control agencies resolved this dilemma.

As the public were informed that the project was not a success, sponsors, leaders and clients dissociated themselves from it, resulting in a crisis of survival.

Throughout the process of redefinition alternative views were being put forward concerning both the conditions of youth violence *and* the effectiveness of the particular control strategies being used. The setting up of the project itself confronted different interested parties with different problems. Those involved in its leadership were faced throughout with something of a dilemma. As a voluntary organization they were largely dependent upon private funds; their problem was to challenge the view that the organization was failing to achieve its aims and was thus misguided in its orientation, but at the same time to persuade a public that the problem was severe enough to be deserving of financial support. They were in the fortunate position of having sympathetic friends in the press and TV, which facilitated the presentation of *their* definition of the situation. Despite this, they were clearly unsuccessful in persuading those who could have helped the project to survive, that it was a viable and effective organization. The leadership was seen as anti-establishment, and at the time of the 'funds' crisis, one of its supporters (a local Labour M.P.), in what seems like a final plea for help, stated in the press in August 1970: 'This was no bunch of weirdies we had here.'

Publicity over the project also created problems for Easterhouse residents who expressed their difficulties via the Fight Back Campaign mentioned earlier. Attempts by residents to offer an alternative view of Easterhouse youth scarcely got off the ground at all; they were greatly lacking in power even to voice their own definitions of the situation, let alone determine their acceptance by others.

The Easterhouse youth were the group with *least power* of all to present their definitions, and conceivably the group for whom the consequences of the reputation were greatest. Their complaints about police activity on the scheme were successfully transmitted to the newly formed Scottish Council for Civil Liberties who duly set up a Legal Advice Clinic in Easterhouse – however, its serious lack of funds for providing representation in the police courts has drastically hindered its activities.

It appears that the groups most successful in solving the 'problem' of Easterhouse were those which had the power to publicize and activate their own definition of the situation – namely the Glasgow administration, who faced the problem of their own control ideologies being discredited by the existence of the project. Once this was absorbed into the official control structure they were able to 'prove' the effectiveness of their policies by introducing a very casual, pipe-smoking police constable as the new leader. On 21 November 1970 the *Express* announced, with a photograph and headline over eight columns: 'When the Law Lends an Arm ... all is well at the Easterhouse Project, Demonstrating how the Law can Lend a Hand to Anything.'

Towards the end of the project's history as a voluntary organization occasional newspaper articles suggested that perhaps the area's reputation was based on misinformation; for example the series which appeared in one evening paper early in 1970 entitled 'The Myth of Easterhouse'. Certainly the press ceased to focus on delinquency in the area once the corporation expressed an interest in taking it over, and at the present we would consider the reputation has, to some extent, been withdrawn. Clearly, the *Express* was preparing to withdraw from the whole controversy when it remarked in October on the new leadership as follows: 'Let officialdom now stick to the book-keeping side of the project. And allow these men freedom to make the most of their experience and knowledge, and the force of their own personalities.'

To the extent that the problems of other groups such as residents were bound up with the area's reputation, its gradual withdrawal has also served to remove threats to their interests.

The Reputation of Easterhouse, and Deviancy Amplification

Prior to the reputation's emergence, the introduction of the Untouchables brought about changes in the objective conditions confronting Easterhouse youth. The appearance of the Untouchables not only coincided with a widening of definitions of 'delinquent behaviour', thereby placing more youth at risk in terms of being officially labelled, it also had the effect of neutralizing what has been termed 'the bind to law'.

David Matza has lucidly described the 'moral holiday' of the subcultural delinquent; a sort of flirtation with both criminal and conventional activity, involving little commitment to either. Matza's observations correspond to our own when he states:

The subculture of delinquency shows antagonism to the law, but this antagonism is primarily directed towards the officials who man the system. Antagonism takes the form of a jaundiced view of officials, a view which holds that their primary function is not the administration of justice, but the perpetuation of injustice.[9]

Such a feeling of injustice clearly accompanied the arrival of the Untouchables in Easterhouse, as the following statements from local boys indicate:

The fighting had just started, and it was just throwing bricks and that, so they brought this riot squad up. And if you were walking out the close they would lift you, go round to somebody else's close and lift them, until they got about eight of you, then do you for breach of the peace, disorderly crowd or that.

You'd see them coming, and you knew the score ... it got to the stage you had to run away from them all the time ... if there was a gang fight, the polis would lift you off the street after it, anybody walking along, and say you were involved in it; even though you weren't, they'd make you involved.

The antagonism expressed by these boys soon became translated into action:

... after they get lifted they're in a bad mood, cursing and swearing an' all that, they're all going like that 'I got done for breach of the peace for nothing, well next time it'll be something!' ... Might as well get the jail for something.

and again . . .

The Touchies make us turn against the beat police, soon as we see *any* kinda polis we start smashing their van up now . . . if they try to chase us we just stand with bricks and just pap the wind-screens in . . . I mean, we don't mean any harm to the beat polis, it's just, there's too many of the Touchies to go about with! [laughs] . . . they go about in about ten, you can't do all of them in!

A policeman who extends his role to include the meting out of punishment (beatings were an allegedly frequent occurrence) was seen as 'fair game' by the disgruntled boys on the street-corner; as one of them put it, 'They have the same language as the gangs.' The bind to law has thus been effectively neutralized. Feelings of fatalism, of being 'pushed around', emerge, and were certainly widespread amongst Easterhouse youth. For the street-corner boy the imputation of delinquent character was difficult to avoid, court appearances and the like were almost seen by them and by some of their parents an inevitable fact of life. 'It can happen to anyone' was a typical response.

Presumably the young people of this area came to acknow-ledge that standing outside a telephone kiosk, for example, constituted infraction of the law; however, we cannot assume that they would accept such a definition of infraction as legiti-mate. Something like a sense of desperation was produced, as the comments above indicate. In the peer-group setting, where manliness is celebrated, to be 'pushed around' is to lose all claim to manly status; what is needed is some dramatic assur-ance that one can still make things happen, and an obvious (though by no means the *only*) choice, is to commit an infraction.

While our evidence acknowledges 'escalation' of gang con-flict prior to the emergence of the public reputation, the latter clearly created further difficulties. For those dependent on the media as their sole source of information, the tendency was to suspect *all* youthful residents as being of delinquent character. Youth certainly *perceived* such threats to their personal iden-tity. The following remarks were made by a non-gang member:

Politics and Deviance

> When I was at work one of the boys [in the personnel depart-
> ment] says 'Where do you stay?' ... I told him the address, he says
> 'Hooligan!' Just like that! ... I goes. 'I'm no a hooligan!' ... If I'd
> told him [when applying for the job] ... he'd have knew me, knew
> I was out of Easterhouse ... Right away, he wouldn't have gave me
> the job.

The situation of 'drift' between 'criminal and conventional
action' aptly describes the morality of the street-corner boy,
but it is our view, that increasingly, and particularly after 1968,
certain areas of 'conventional activity' became blocked to
Easterhouse youths. This occurred both through positive exclusion by various groups *and* through a self-conscious withdrawal by the boys themselves. Indeed, during this period
residence in Easterhouse may be considered a 'stigma'. The
amplifying effects of the reputation are best appreciated by
referring to the gang boys themselves. How did they perceive
the label – and how did they react to it?

For the sake of clarity we can regard the public definition
as operating on two important levels. Firstly it operated in the
wider community amongst a wide range of people socially
remote from the working-class youth of Easterhouse. Of particular significance within this category were those individuals
who set themselves up as controllers of delinquency, including
various 'experts', and of course those officially designated
control agents such as the Glasgow magistrates. Conceivably,
of even greater consequence was the acceptance of the definition by subcultural delinquents resident in *other* parts of the
city. Secondly, the public definition operated locally *within* the
scheme. From the point of view of the gang, the greatest
challenge here came from residents, police and neighbouring
peers. The overall effect was to increasingly restrict the 'delinquent' to his peer group as a source of reassurance that he was
'not really that bad', while at the same time creating a situation
where he is increasingly at risk of indulging in activities likely
to be labelled delinquent. Because of his precarious position
between conventional and criminal culture and thus his awareness of his apparent 'differentness', the chances of his sustaining
positive relationships with outsiders are jeopardized. Although

signification may operate in a very subtle fashion (as opposed to the overt symbolism of the courtroom), it nevertheless does not pass unnoticed. An example which springs to mind is the embarrassment suffered by one of the project boys on being introduced by a leader (to his 'intellectual' friends), as 'the one who reads all the books'. The response of the boy in question was to turn on his heel and leave the room. He later remarked 'What the f— does he think I am? Because I'm a gangster I can't read or something?'

The youth who resides in a delinquent area has a good chance of being labelled delinquent. His moral character may become a question of open debate, and be challenged more frequently. Certain relationships previously of meaning to him may break down:

... each time we get picked up ... it makes you hate them. Sometimes if you're walking up the road with a lassie or your ma, maybe they'll shout you over ... Shouting you by your name. They say [your companion] ... 'Ah, the polis must know him.' If it's a woman up the stair or something, y'know, she'll tell all the neighbours ... 'the polis know him'. Then they all start talking and that ... well your ma will likely hear about it, them saying the police know you ... She'll just ask you 'What were they asking you?' 'Were you doing anything?' Nothing much else, she'll say. 'Don't want you getting into any trouble with them.' That's all.

The likelihood of this breakdown in relationships occurring is further heightened if one considers the difficulties facing a youth resident in a 'delinquent area', in attempting to 'correct' what he sees as the objective basis of his failing. The most obvious remedy available was to change one's address – and a number of Easterhouse boys did from time to time migrate to London – or to quit the streets altogether. By this means an individual may avoid official labelling, but he is still confronted with problems of 'passing' in the wider community. A non-gang member volunteered the following:

One day I went to a friend's house in [a middle-class suburb] and his mother says to me 'Where do you come from?' I says 'Easterhouse ... don't get me wrong, I'm not one of the gang members.' And this is, whenever I introduce myself to anybody, I let them know I'm not a gang member ... Just to assert myself, because I think that people, as soon as they hear Easterhouse, they begin to develop a distrust of you – maybe it's just as though ... Once I was having a party ... I invited people, they says 'Where is it?' I says Easterhouse, and I could see them saying '... Oh!' Y'know? Then I said 'It's cool ... no need to worry.' This was last September, 1969.

Under such conditions, the street-corner 'hangout' presented itself as an area of interaction where there is neither the need to conceal stigma, nor the need to consciously make the cooperative effort to ignore it.

Other writers have noted the tendency for the 'typical' delinquent to be more or less ignored by the mass media, stress being laid on the sensational and dramatic aspects of delinquent enterprise; and Easterhouse is no exception to this practice. The result of media-portrayal (the amnesty and so on) was to create a reputation for the Easterhouse gangs amongst subcultural delinquents in other parts of the city. The result was to extend the battlefield increasing the number of gang fights, although sometimes it was possible to avoid these extra-territory confrontations:

... But we had this big thing about the town, that the ... [hesitates] ... well, I think we were scared to go down the town because of the gangs that came from the South Side, an' that, the Shamrock and all that. Mostly *big* gangs, y'know ... well if you go to the dancing down town you'd this thing about ... well you know they were there, y'know, how to get by them an' that. If there was a big squad of you, you'd just go ahead with them.

And as another boy said:

... say you were down the Barrows, they might come up and say: 'Where do youse come from?' We wouldn't say Easterhouse, we'd say a different place, somewhere ... where there's not so much gangs ... but if you said Easterhouse, you'd probably get battered.

Misunderstandings are generated; the Easterhouse boy, if somewhat reluctantly endowed with his reputation, feels the need to protect it when challenged, and for him such challenges are likely. The consequence is further avoidance of certain conventional areas of interaction:

... You can't go down the town, if you go down the town it's more or less the pictures you go to. You can't really go anywhere else, if you go up the dancing it's a fight. It's a fight all the time unless you're going out with a bird or that.

In the company of peers such confrontations become the subject of discussion. By appreciating the value placed on manliness within the group one can readily predict a full-scale rumble occurring.

... just ... if you're with a lassie they pull you up ... slap you about, and you can't do anything 'cause there's more of them, so you just have to take it ... Well you take her home ... if you meet some of your pals you tell them about it. They say: 'Okay then we'll go down', so ... you meet up with them, start fighting.

Within the scheme itself, the hostility between neighbouring peers was hardly reduced when each could read in the press the horrifying deeds of the other, yet could not discredit such claims by virtue of their own isolation *from each other*.

It would certainly be true to say that most gang boys display a healthy scepticism towards what appears in the press, but nevertheless, within the subculture, national publicity would evoke at least a certain amount of awe. Despite the fact that the tag 'violent thugs' was a source of embarrassment in the context of conventional areas of interaction, when placed in the subcultural world of the gang boy, the connotation is rather more positive.

... I mean, they've got good names as the gemmes, y'know ... they're just as good a team as any of the big teams you hear about ... they'll stand and fight you, they're no idiots or anything.

The publicity surrounding the Easterhouse gangs clearly placed them in the position of having to defend their 'honour'. If Easterhouse was the *worst* area in the city for violent gangs – each of the teams *in* Easterhouse had to demonstrate they were the '*best*' team there. The following indicates the typical prelude to an Easterhouse gang-fight:

... Maybe their saying like that 'the Pak's said they set about all the Drummy' ... you're all standing at the corner ... 'When did they do that?' ... 'they couldn't!' They're all boasting themselves off an' that. 'Come on, we'll go down and see them! Batter them for saying that!' . . . Go down for a fight.

The mutual misunderstandings characteristic of gang-boy relationships are only heightened by media portrayal of atypical and sensational incidents and individuals. While ex-gang members freely admit to falling away from the team on the realization that 'it was all bull', during the period of maximum involvement, a sort of 'mutual distortion society' prevails. This distortion is augmented through the gang boy modifying his self image in the light of outsiders' definitions. From the outside the spiral is reinforced by the readiness to reduce an individual's total range of characteristics and qualities to the simple designation 'hooligan' and to deal with him accordingly. We thus not only participate in the 'mutual distortion society' – but obscure and mystify the meaning membership has for the boys themselves.

Concluding Remarks

The data we have presented on gang boys has been necessarily impressionistic. With a few exceptions (where stated) the information was offered by gang boys and ex-gang boys (for the earlier period) in informal but focused interviews which were tape recorded by one of the authors. We are satisfied that the views expressed in these statements reflect accurately the feelings generated by a high percentage of one of the Easterhouse gangs in early 1970. For several reasons only one gang could be studied at close quarters; some of its members were inaccessible (being detained in various institutions), but a large proportion of those remaining were interviewed. In addition, this gang was observed informally at close range for a period of eighteen months.

We do not wish to present a deterministic picture of the street-corner boy propelled into the violent gang independently of his own volition. At the same time, it is our belief that the events surrounding the emergence of the reputation of Easterhouse youth brought about *objective* changes in the day-to-day conditions of interaction of these boys. The reputation, whilst

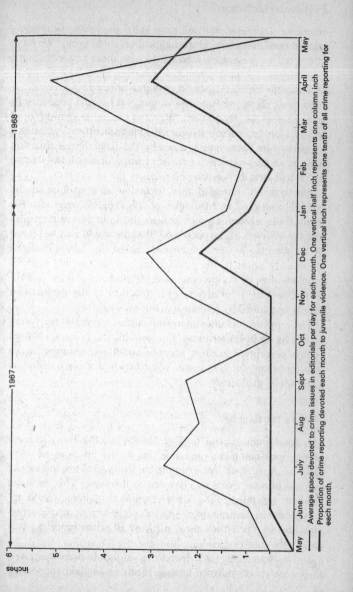

- - - Average space devoted to crime issues in editorials per day for each month. One vertical half inch represents one column inch.
——— Proportion of crime reporting devoted each month to juvenile violence. One vertical inch represents one tenth of all crime reporting for each month.

emerging *independently* of any shift in youth behaviour, created conditions whereby amplification could occur. We have attempted to present evidence as to how these new conditions were viewed by the Easterhouse gang boy, and how his interactions with the outside world were thus affected.

In researching the Easterhouse gangs it became necessary to account for the reputation. We saw this as a spin-off of a political process which developed independently of what was happening in Easterhouse, whereby the Easterhouse situation became an easy vehicle for the expression of a political debate which had already become polarized.

We have not intended this discussion as a critique of the political and control ideologies of the Progressive group. No doubt those advocating such policies did so in the sincere belief that the interests of the people of Glasgow would best be served by their taking power. We have discussed the debate in detail in order to point to the political interests in keeping a social problem alive by taking issue with the running of those institutions established for its control. Reaction to the project can only be explained by reference to this process.

The reputation created many difficulties, especially for young people living in Easterhouse. For not only did it cause changes on the perceptual level, it brought about *real* changes in the conditions surrounding them. What began as a myth ended as a *real* social problem.[10]

Note on the Graph

The graph indicates the 'build-up' in the Scottish *Daily Express* of editorial comment on crime, up to the elections of May 1968. In April 1968, for example, an average of ten inches per day of editorial space was devoted to this issue. This amounts to about one third of the editorial column. A similar 'build-up' is apparent in the amount of space devoted to reporting juvenile violence; in April 1968 three fifths of all crime reporting was to do with youth violence.

From November 1967, increasing editorial space was given to discussion of violence among youth, in implied support of the Tory/Progressive line. The graph shows how space devoted to editorial comment on crime began to vary at this time, along with the quantity of reporting on juvenile violence.

References

1. The Scottish *Daily Express* was selected for analysis in this research because of its high circulation, and also because it was located by Easterhouse people as the newspaper with most responsibility for promoting the reputation. Another Beaverbrook paper, the *Evening Citizen*, was also frequently named. The reports quoted here appeared in July 1968 and in March, April and July 1969.

2. Scottish *Daily Express* (11 April 1969).

3. T. BRENNAN, in *Reshaping a City* (published for the Department of Social and Economic Research, Glasgow University, by House of Grant, 1959), suggests that the decision to commence Glasgow's urban redevelopment programme in the Gorbals area was largely a consequence of the national reputation that area acquired through the publication of the novel *No Mean City*, by A. McARTHUR and H. KINGSLEY LONG (Corgi, 1969).

4. Report by a Joint Working Party on Community Problems appointed by the Corporation of the City of Glasgow and the Under-Secretary of State for Scotland, 1967.

5. See for example, PEARL JEPHCOTT, 'Time of One's Own' (Edinburgh University Press, University of Glasgow Social and Economic Studies, Occasional Paper No. 7).

6. We are indebted to Donald McKenzie of the Scottish Information Office for giving us access to a paper by W. M. BALLANTYNE, entitled 'Good Neighbours Programme: Some Ideas on Ways of Dealing with Vandalism,' and for permission to quote it.

7. Information supplied by Assistant Chief Constable, Glasgow Police Force, September 1970.

8. HOWARD BECKER, ed., *Social Problems: A Modern Approach* (New York: Wiley, 1968). See his Introduction.

9. DAVID MATZA, Delinquency and Drift (New York: Wiley, 1968).

10. A more detailed treatment of some of the themes on this paper may be found in G. ARMSTRONG and M. WILSON (George Allen & Unwin, forthcoming).

Ron Bailey   Housing: Alienation and Beyond

The Housing Problem and Democracy

Politicians of all hues regularly congratulate themselves on their efforts to solve the housing problem; but they convince few people that they have got things under control. Certainly they do not convince the ever-increasing number of people who are homeless or living in appalling conditions. And it is unlikely that they convince those who take a cold hard look at the statistics. There are some three million families (as opposed to individuals) living in places classed as slums. There are more homeless people than ever before actually living in local authority welfare accommodation and hostels, and for every homeless family that obtains shelter in these hostels many more are turned away and often left to walk the streets. The result is that although the number of children in care in 1971 continued the decrease started four years ago, the number in care because of homelessness or inadequate housing actually rose.[1] Rachmanism, harrassment and evictions continue, and the present Government's 'Fair Rents' policy is likely to result in even more legal evictions.

Despite all this the present Tory government claims that its policies are destined to help the slum-dwellers and solve the housing problem, and the last Labour government not only used its Commons majority to defeat a Tory censure vote on housing,[2] but actually then went on to congratulate itself on its record, completely ignoring the fact that they had not even kept their inadequate election promise of 500,000 new homes a year by 1970.[3]

With all this self-congratulation and apparent good intention around it is really quite surprising that everyone does not live in fully centrally heated houses with all mod. cons. Indeed it is amazing that there is a housing problem at all, let alone a worsening one. It would be pleasant for a change to find an outgoing government which frankly said 'We have failed to solve the housing problem.' It is politically necessary to claim that housing policies are succeeding. And so the game of political football goes on, with the sufferers being also the spectators and seeing the same dismal game year after year, administration after administration.

Just as political hypocrisy is part of the system, so are the empty office blocks, the new luxurious town halls, the land speculation where millions are made by those who buy and sell the right lands or buildings at the right times. And so is the private housing development which is very good 'business' but which results in luxury flats and 'town houses' for the middle and upper classes, at the expense of accommodation for those in most desperate need of it. The Royal Borough of Kensington and Chelsea has virtually driven out working-class families by encouraging this policy. Another fact witnessed almost daily is rising rents, whether in the private sector, where the Rent Acts have singularly failed to keep rents down, or in the public sector, where council rents continue to rise. If current trends continue, particularly when the new Housing Finance Bill becomes law, even council housing could become outside the pockets of many people. In Islington recently the local Security Office refused to pay the rents in full of a large number of council tenants because they were deemed 'unreasonable'. Although the matter was finally resolved, its occurrence is an indication of the trend in council rents.

Of course when councils claim that they are forced to put up rents, they are, in strict economic terms, often telling the truth. The problem is not one of rents versus rates (which should subsidize the other?), for rates are also on the increase, but lies rather in the fact that both ratepayers and rentpayers are 'subsidizing' (although this is not the word in general use) those who benefit from the ever increasing interest rates that councils are forced to pay. Such are the priorities of our 'democratic' system, where the people's wishes are supposedly paramount, but where financiers can make millions out of ever-increasing interest rates and thereby place an ever more crippling burden on councils who must borrow from them in order to carry out their duties, and who then, with even the best will in the world, must *within the terms of the system*, pass these on to those on whose behalf they are supposed to act.

Thus the idea of democracy – that ordinary people are important, that they do run things, if not themselves, then at least through their elected representatives – hardly fits the facts of the situation. But if democracy does not exist in the distant and general field of overall control, does it exist in the immediate field for ordinary people – with regard to the actual place in which they live every day?

For the private tenant there is little hope of his having any control over his immediate environment. He lives in someone else's house, and the landlord is the owner, decider, manager. And it is irrelevant whether landlords are 'good' or 'bad'. Even a decent landlord, who is obviously preferable to a bad one, is the manager and controller. The tenant has, at best, to ask *someone else* benevolently for changes or improvements, and at worst to struggle bitterly for them. The landlord also decides the type of tenant he wants, the size and nature of the accommodation he provides, the rent he charges, the amenities available. In theory the tenant can refuse to accept what is offered, but in practice this means throwing away an opportunity of at least finding somewhere to live (a very difficult thing especially if a family has children), or rejecting one 'choice' for an identical one three roads away. In a situation where accommodation itself is scarce, and the person providing it makes all the decisions, choice is a theoretical luxury only, and many people are forced to accept crumbling accommodation, insanitary conditions, overcrowding and high rents. Even such legal restrictions on the landlord as minimum building standards, overcrowding regulations, public health legislation and the Rent Acts do not alter this situation, for two basic reasons.

Firstly, there is widespread and large-scale avoidance and flouting of the regulations. This is because tenants themselves seldom know (all) the regulations and thus if they see a breach they cannot recognize it as such, and because even where tenants do know their rights they are very often afraid to complain for fear of being turned out either legally or illegally. Secondly, *even where the regulations are enforced*, these simply restrict the landlord; they do not give the tenant control of his home, any more than the Factory Acts give the workers control of the factories.

Council tenants also have a similar lack of control. Are people on housing lists ever asked their views on design and layout when new homes and estates are being built 'for them'? Are actual tenants ever asked to comment on the advantages or disadvantages of the places they live in? And would such comments have any effect anyway? Do housewives ever have any say over what are, after all, their working conditions? What say do electors have about the layout of estates, or about rules governing tenancies? Who decides when the rates go up and how they are spent? Certainly tenants are not consulted, or even when they are it is usually bogus consultation involving the local council saying to residents 'this is what we have decided; now you can discuss it'.[4] Indeed the councils themselves, consisting anyway of members more answerable to their party whips and caucuses than to those who elected them, often have little control over what they can and cannot do for the reasons already outlined. They put rents up when interest rates tell them they must. The types of houses or estates they can afford to build are governed more by the money they can borrow and the charges they must pay for this, than by even their wishes, let alone their tenants' wishes. On top of all this, council tenants are often told either directly or indirectly how lucky they are to live off the community on their subsidized rents – hardly the type of message that is designed to lead tenants to believe that they have any right to exercise, or attempt to exercise, any control over their immediate environment.

What, finally, of owner occupation? This is the ultimate goal of many people who yearn for freedom and independence. While it is certainly true that owner-occupiers do have more freedom than tenants, it is worth considering just how far this extends. Who decides the final price they pay, their contract or the rising interest rates on their mortgage? Their choice about the type of house they wish to buy is strictly limited: a house with 'two up, three down' in one street is probably virtually identical to another with 'three down, two up' half a mile away. The kind of house a buyer can purchase, and even the location of it, is decided by the amount of mortgage he can raise rather than by free choice. And thus the area in which an owner-occupier can live is largely beyond his control. All these factors limit severely the freedom which owner-occupiers have.[5]

There exists therefore a dual, but related, housing problem. There is the obvious scarcity and the shortage of decent housing at the price people can afford. In addition there is the problem of control and management. In no sense, either on general policy or concerning their immediate environment, do working-class people, whether living in slums or in what is described as adequate accommodation, have any control over their lives. They are thus completely alienated from decisions which affect their lives. Years of being shunted from one room to another, years of promises by politicians of better things to come but which have borne little or no fruit; years of never being asked to comment on (except by their cross every five years), let alone exercise any control over, their housing conditions, have all produced a situation in which the homeless and badly housed are probably the most downtrodden section of society: they feel disenfranchised because they are disenfranchised. 'Yes I agree it's terrible here, dear, but there's nothing we can do about it' is a common feeling among the homeless, and badly housed, millions. And to a large extent this feeling is thoroughly correct. If people keep to the channels provided by the system there are virtually no ways in which they can alter their lives. Most people therefore are disillusioned; they play no role in politics because they see no reason to do so; they are what is generally described as 'apathetic'. And the very people who bemoan this apathy – the politicians and the 'concerned' liberals *et al.* – are the very people who cause it to continue both because they are continually urging people to become involved in the futility of party politics and because they are amongst the first to condemn any real attempts by ordinary people to affect their own environment. The involvement these people want is involvement on their terms; but every success in achieving this leads only to more apathy in the future, for once again people see that their action has changed their lives very little; the rent continues to rise, the ceiling still leaks, the decision makers are still as distant.

There is however one way in which ordinary people can affect their lives, alter their immediate environment and reject decisions allegedly made 'on their behalf' and that is by taking direct action. But it is just this kind of action that those who bemoan apathy condemn or at best try to steer back into the normal (non) channels. In short then, the kind of involvement that the political line pluggers want is only involvement in those channels that they decide are 'right'. Ordinary people, on the other hand, are coming more and more to realize that if they are to affect their lives, the only way to do this is by rejecting the system and taking direct action.

It is the development of one direct-action movement – the hostel and squatting campaigns – that the next part of this paper outlines and discusses.

It will be seen that this movement has reacted to both the scarcity and the control aspects of the housing situation, and that ordinary people have, implicitly at least, taken actions which have said 'no, you will not decide – we will'. It is these people's attempts to affect their lives that are the most meaningful actions in society today.

Direct Action and Housing

In spring 1965 the Daniels family were evicted because the owner of their flat wished to to sell the house. As they had children they could find no alternative accommodation, so being homeless they ended up in the Kent County Council homeless family accommodation, King Hill Hostel (a former workhouse), at West Malling. At least Joan Daniels and the children ended up there; the rules only permitted Stan to visit the hostel during the day, at weekends. Under no circumstances was he allowed to remain with his family overnight. This was the way in which the Kent County Council Welfare Department carried out its legal obligation under Part III s 21 (1) b of the 1968 National Assistance Act to provide 'temporary accommodation for persons in urgent need thereof'. Husbands were separated from their wives and children. In addition, the council defined the word 'temporary' to mean three months. At the end of this time the wives and children were required to leave, and if they had not found anywhere else to live, the children were taken into care. By the end of July, therefore, the Daniels were due to be evicted from the hostel, their three months being up. It was at this point that Stan Daniels decided to defy the rules. When the welfare officials arrived to evict Joan and take the kids into care they discovered that not only was she refusing to go, but also that Stan had moved in with her. All attempts by the welfare officials to remove the family – which included turning off the services – failed, so they retreated in order to obtain further instructions. The Daniels's action sparked off a campaign of defiance that was to last for twelve months. Other husbands, equally fed up by the forced separation from their families, also moved in, and all families decided to ignore the three-month rule. For the first time, the 'right' of the council to make the rules was questioned. The council reacted aggressively and announced that such defiance would not be tolerated, legal action to end it would be taken and the newly formed King Hill Hostel Resident Committee would not be accepted as a negotiating body. The families organized a campaign to force the council to change the rules, and were supported in this by two small left-wing groups – Solidarity and Bromley Socialist Action. Marches to the County Hall in Maidstone, pickets of welfare offices, and 'sleep ins' by husbands were held to publicize the struggle. The council replied by seeking a possession order against the Daniels family, and by seeking injunctions against the husbands, restraining them from breaking the rules.

The injunctions restraining the husbands from entering the hostel out of visiting hours were obtained and the men had to give undertakings to obey them. These were however withdrawn by two husbands and soon there was open defiance by over twenty men. The council therefore enforced the injunctions and had two men sent to prison for contempt of court. By this time the campaign had achieved a good deal of publicity, and the jailing of Roy Mills and Brian Lomas only added to the council's problem, particularly as on their release the two men immediately showed their contempt for its inhuman rules by immediately returning to live at the hostel. By enforcing the injunctions the council had achieved nothing – except a large amount of adverse publicity and an even more determined resistance at the hostel.

The attempt to obtain a possession order to evict the Daniels family also proved more difficult than the council had bargained for. Stan Daniels decided that two could play at legal games and he started studying the National Assistance Act. He discovered that there was nothing in the Act which said that 'temporary' should be three months. He further discovered that under the Act the local authority had to submit a scheme to the Ministry for approval, outlining how they intended to discharge their duties. Had Kent submitted a scheme? Was their practice in accordance with it? Did the then Labour government therefore approve of the separation of families and the three-month time limit?

A local by-election enabled the families to really push this last point. Labour candidate Jim Wellbeloved was asked, as he spoke about the Labour Party bringing freedom from eviction, what was his government doing about evictions at King Hill? Did they approve of the Kent scheme for temporary accommodation? When no answers were forthcoming there was uproar. The Minister of Health and Welfare, Kenneth Robinson, was then picketed. Two families even held a fast outside his home. He expressed 'sympathy' but he could not help the families. The families were on their own, supported only by their own determination and the two small left-wing groups mentioned above. The might of the Tory council, ably supported by the Labour minority, was thrown at them.

As the injunctions had failed to crush the resistance, and the possession order case was finally referred to the High Court (which would mean considerable delay), the council tried other tactics. They expressed themselves to be 'sympathetic' to the King Hill families but refused to discuss things while the 'outsiders' were around and while the defiance of the rules continued. This trick fooled no one and the campaign continued until the council again had two men jailed for visiting the hostel out of hours. By this time however the councillors were sick of the whole struggle, and despite eventually obtaining their possession order against the Daniels in July 1966, one year after the campaign had begun, they gave in. Husbands were allowed to live at the hostel, the three-month limit was ended, conditions were improved. A small group of working-class families had by defiance and cunning defeated the might of the County Council, which was backed up by the state machine and its laws.

The struggle demonstrated both to those involved and to a wider group of people who had followed it, that ordinary people, by relying on their own strength and determination and having no illusions about politicians, could take direct action to change their lives – and win. They had achieved this victory not by becoming 'involved' in the political party system, nor by relying on the 'sympathy' of Ministers, nor by listening to the political pundits, but simply by real involvement – in direct action. And this, to both the Labour and Tory councillors of Kent,[6] was anathema, for the struggle clearly developed from one against the imposition of workhouse rules at King Hill to one about even more basic matters – who had the right to decide. And this matter had been determined by a show of organized strength from the families of King Hill Hostel.

Following the King Hill struggle, a number of other authorities changed the rules at their hostels; the government issued two circulars urging them not to split families and not to impose time limits; and generally Welfare Departments became more defensive about conditions in their temporary accommodation. The Poor Law, which officially had been repealed by the 1948 National Assistance Act, but which still existed all too often in practice, was beginning to be eroded. The concern generated by the struggle, and by the showing of *Cathy Come*

Home in November 1968, led to the formation of Shelter, a body which has played an important role in continually publicizing the facts about the housing situation.

The wariness of local authorities after King Hill enabled other homeless families to launch successful campaigns for better conditions. At Abridge hostel in Essex a campaign developed in September 1966, just a few months after the King Hill victory. This hostel was perhaps the worst I have ever seen – and I have visited about 200 – and here again husbands were barred. Indeed it would have been impossible to let them live at the hostel, for it consisted simply of two long, open dormitories – one sleeping room and one day room – in which the fifty women and children occupants lived and died. There was no privacy whatsoever. The husbands petitioned the Essex County Council for better conditions at the hostel, and they too received the support of a few believers in direct action, some of whom had been active at King Hill, and who staged demonstrations in defiance of the rules. On one occasion husbands and supporters moved in with materials and tools to convert the hostel into self-contained units to enable the husbands to live there. Eventually they withdrew and gave the council one week to act and threatened to return in greater numbers if nothing was done. Three days later the council announced that the hostel would be closed and converted into family units, and the families would be rehoused – despite the fact that they had previously claimed that they were unable to do this as they were not a housing authority but only a welfare authority. Under pressure they discovered that they could do all kinds of things, rather than risk another King Hill. Again it was the determination of ordinary people that had won this victory – not reliance on the channels provided by successive Labour and Tory administrations of Essex County Council.

This pattern was followed in December 1966 and January 1967 in Birmingham, where widespread publicity led to considerable changes in the hostels; in autumn 1967 in Wandsworth, where a campaign at Durham Buildings forced the Labour council to quietly forget about a nine-month limit they had attempted to impose; and more recently a number of hostels and 'halfway houses' – Chaucer House in Southwark, Beechcroft Buildings in Tower Hamlets, Duncan House in Hackney, Louise Court in Lambeth, Plumstead Lodge in Greenwich, and others – have all formed residents' associations to campaign for speedy rehousing, better conditions and the closure of the old workhouse and tenement blocks. The results have been that in London and most of the home counties the practices of separating families and imposing time limits have been ended; families are rehoused considerably quicker; conditions have improved and one after another, councils are being obliged to close down the old Victorian tenement ghettoes and instead use empty houses for homeless people.

This latter policy had also been a very direct result of the squatting movement which developed from the hostel campaigns, at the end of 1968. The hostel struggles had brought together a number of people who had decided that their most useful role as committed revolutionaries was to support and encourage direct action by ordinary people on issues that immediately affected them and so demonstrate that badly housed and homeless people have got the power to act and win and are capable of organizing their own lives. It was considered that this was the only way to develop the disenfranchisement and apathy that people felt into active and organized opposition. Thus the people who had participated in the hostel struggles looked for ways in which to push the campaign one step forward.

During a number of the hostel struggles the idea of squatting had been voiced by some of the families involved. At Abridge and Durham Buildings, families expressed their readiness to squat, and it was only the speedy success of those campaigns that made this unnecessary. During another campaign in the summer of 1968 the idea of squatting was again voiced and likely targets were even picked. This was a campaign that developed at Coventry Cross, an insanitary, rat-infested and overcrowded Greater London Council block of flats at Bromley-by-Bow, E.3. The tenants formed an action committee to protest at the conditions which, they claimed, were a danger to health. The G.L.C. were forced onto the defensive – a good case could be made out that the flats were insanitary, particularly as the drains *were* a danger to public health. The council were thus portrayed as the guilty party, and so in September 1968 they announced that all 190 families would be rehoused and the flats would be closed for modernization. So squatting again became unnecessary.

In November, however, a group of people who had been active in these campaigns met and decided to take the direct action of the hostel campaigns a stage further by starting the London Squatters. We knew that amongst some sections of the homeless there was sympathy for squatting, and we hoped that our initiative would cause this to erupt into widespread action. After a few 'token squats' we were ready, in February 1969, to install homeless families in empty property owned by the London Borough of Redbridge. The mixture of defiance and cunning learnt during the hostel campaigns was to be the main factor dictating tactics. Local authority houses were picked on so that our propaganda could put the opponent legally as well as morally on the defensive. Redbridge was both a welfare authority, with obligations to provide temporary accommodation, and a housing authority, with obligations under the 1957 Housing Act to consider the needs of the people of the district and provide housing accommodation. How, we claimed, could they be said to be properly fulfilling their obligations when they were acquiring perfectly good houses and leaving them empty in preparation for a redevelopment plan that was not due to start for years?

We also studied the law, both to avoid arrest and so that we would know how to frustrate any attempts by the council to evict the squatting families. We discovered that squatting itself was not a criminal offence – the numerous signs saying that 'trespassers will be prosecuted' are wooden falsehoods. We learnt that if we used no force in entering a house, nor stole anything, nor damaged the place, then we could not be arrested for squatting and the police could not get involved. We also learnt how to thwart the council's attempts to remove us from the houses and in particular we discovered that the Statute of Forcible Entry of 1381 made it a criminal offence for anyone forcibly to enter property in the possession of another without a court order. Even if the owner has a right of entry he must not assert that right forcibly but must have recourse to the courts. Thus if the council wanted to evict us they would have to go to court – and we were ready for that.

In February 1969 three families occupied houses in Ilford that were scheduled to remain empty for years. The local council's reaction was to seek injunctions against the organizers to restrain us from continuing our trespass on their property. These never worried us because our main concern was for the families in the houses and any outside helpers that needed to visit the houses could always be those that were not restrained from doing so. In practice the injunctions were virtually ignored, as we considered that after Kent's experience the local council would not have people imprisoned for contempt of court. Thus, we thought, they would be even more reticent about obtaining injunctions against the families and having them sent to prison, and again we were right.

After the injunctions had failed to stop squatting, the council then attempted to use an archaic procedure under the Forcible Entry Act of 1429, which gives to local magistrates the power to clear property of all occupants and hand it back to the owner, providing that they are satisfied that there has been a forcible entry or a forcible detainer (holding) of the property. Redbridge Council admitted that there had been no forcible entry, but claimed that as we had erected barricades, this constituted a forcible detainer. We claimed that in law barricades did not constitute a forcible detainer, and the magistrates refused to act. The council then applied to the Queen's Bench Divisional Court for an order to compel the magistrates to act, but this also failed, so the council was left with their final and proper remedy of applying to the County Court for a possession order against the squatting family. As expected, they easily obtained this, and the family were ordered to vacate the premises by 15 April 1969. We had prepared for this and the family obeyed the order and left and squatted in another house. Meanwhile another family was installed in the first house. Legally, therefore, the council had to start again.

The council were taking a beating legally and also in terms of publicity. Every court hearing received more publicity and this was helped by marches, leaflets and various other demonstrations. Furthermore the council's high-handed act of sending their workmen into empty houses that might have had years of life to smash them up with pick-axes incensed a large number of people. The squatters' family-swapping was the last straw – 'they've gone too far this time', said the local deputy housing manager – and the council leaders met to decide what to do next. As the legal way of getting rid of squatters had got them nowhere they agreed to dispense with legal niceties, and on 21 April about a dozen private bailiffs were employed to evict three squatting families without a court order. These men smashed open the doors of the houses with iron bars, forced the squatters and their children out of bed, swore at them and removed them and their furniture from the houses. One friend of the squatting families was beaten up so badly that he spent the next two weeks in hospital with a broken jaw. These actions were blatantly illegal – not only did they constitute a breach of the Forcible Entry Act but they also amounted to a riotous assembly at common law, and the assault causing the broken jaw was clear *prima facie* evidence of grievous bodily harm. And yet the police, whose legal duty it is to arrest those who commit crimes, and who have a strict statutory obligation to arrest rioters, stood by and did nothing. Barking magistrates also refused to enforce the law when applications for summonses to commence private prosecutions were turned down without reasons being given. Redbridge Council, therefore, in attempting to crush those who denied them the right to leave houses empty for years while there were nearly 5,000 people on their housing list, was allowed to get away with serious criminal acts. One can only marvel at the mental gymnastics that the upright and respectable councillors of Redbridge must have used to justify their brutal actions to their Christian consciences. Unfortunately for the council, these actions did not stop the squatters and more houses were occupied and the publicity greatly increased after the evictions. Some ratepayers

103

even objected to the District Auditor about ratepayers' money being wrongfully spent.

But as at King Hill, reason now played little part in the thinking of the local authority: they had to assert their right to decide at all costs, and so the private army of bailiffs was again brought to Ilford in June 1969. This time, however, the squatters were more prepared, and a minor skirmish on June the 23rd was simply a preliminary to the amazing battles of June the 25th.

At 5.30 a.m. on that day some twenty men crept into Woodlands Road, Ilford, dressed in steel helmets, carrying dustbin lid shields, ropes, ladders and bricks and launched a brutal and illegal attack on the house occupied by squatters (needed for redevelopment in 1977). The occupants were woken by bricks and bottles crashing through the windows and by the sight of ladders being set against the house for the final assault. Again the police stood by and watched this riot take place, but this time it was not successful and the squatters repelled the army of bailiffs. A similar battle then followed in Audrey Road, Ilford, and again the bailiffs were repelled, but again no arrests were made. Redbridge Council and their private army seemed to be above the law.

However, these disgraceful incidents really backfired on the council. Pictures of steel-helmeted bailiffs throwing bricks at the houses appeared in most national papers, and eye-witness accounts of the attacks were also printed. Town Clerk Kenneth Nicholls's statement that 'the legal processes have been too slow, so it has been necessary to ignore them' (*Ilford Pictorial*, 2 July 1969) did not exactly help the council's image. The council had got themselves into an impossible position: they had failed to defeat the squatters legally and now, after some initial success, their illegal methods had also failed.

Despite the fact that some councillors still wanted to 'use tear gas on the swine' the leading members realized that some peace offering would have to be made, particularly as the council's immunity from the law appeared at last to be at an end. Barking magistrates had at last been pressurized into granting private summonses alleging riot against the bailiffs for their actions of 25 June.[7] Public pressure, and the fact that their previous refusal to grant summonses had been taken to the High Court, overcame their reluctance to act.

During July therefore there were negotiations which resulted in a settlement. The council agreed to rehouse the squatters and review their policy of leaving houses empty. In addition they agreed to explain the reasons to the squatters if they decided to leave any houses empty in the future. In return the squatters agreed to call off the campaign. The final result of the settlement was that Redbridge Council changed its policy and started to use more of its empty houses for its homeless families. Further negotiations in 1970 resulted in some houses that were still empty being handed over to a housing association for use.

After the whole redevelopment plan was scrapped by the Department of the Environment in July 1971, more recently acquired houses were handed over or used by the council, and now only a small number are empty. More pressure is now needed to get these opened up, but there is no doubt that the squatters forced Redbridge Council to change their policy, and also persuaded them to act far more 'reasonably'.

The Tory–Labour alliance against those who used the only method open to them – direct action – to force the council to use the houses, was defeated by the strength and determination of a few ordinary people. It was not traditional political manoeuvring that achieved this – indeed this had been tried before the squatters ever set foot in Redbridge – but action. And it was this action that all the councillors [8] – even those who claimed to want to see the houses used – bitterly opposed, and in their desire to see the squatters crushed they consented to house wrecking and the employment of private armies.

However much, therefore, politicians may squabble amongst themselves, they will close their ranks and unite to try and crush any real attempts by ordinary people to affect their lives. At the same time they will call for 'involvement' and bemoan apathy.

The defeat of Redbridge Council was quickly followed up. Lewisham backed down immediately when confronted with squatters, and not only allowed them to stay in occupation, but also handed to the squatting group in question a hundred other empty houses for them to use. In return the squatters agreed to vacate the houses when the time came for demolition, as they had no wish to hold up the council's house-building programme. The council also agreed to determine squatting families' housing positions on the basis of their pre-squatting accommodation so that the better conditions of a squatting house would not prejudice a family's chance of securing a permanent council house, and so make them perpetual squatters.

Since this agreement was finally concluded in December 1969, the Lewisham squatters have squatted over 150 families in houses in the borough. This situation was brought about by direct action and not by any involvement in the party political system. Indeed those who think working people should vote Labour looked pretty silly in Lewisham, as it was the Labour minority on the council that called the deal with the squatters a 'sell out to the law of the jungle'.

The Lewisham victory was followed in summer 1970 by the G.L.C. itself deciding to hand over empty houses both to the squatters and to housing associations. This policy was brought about, as housing chairman, Horace Cutler, admitted, as a result of a squat in Gomm Road, Bermondsey, S.E.16. Thousands of houses have been opened as a result of this decision. In September 1970 the London Borough of Tower Hamlets opened negotiations with the squatters, following the long squat in Arbour House, Stepney, which had been going on since the previous September. The negotiations were eventually finalized in January 1971, and that borough then became the first Labour borough to hand over houses to the squatters. During 1971 council after council conceded and decided to hand over empty houses to squatting groups. Some gave in quickly when confronted with direct action – Lambeth and Ealing, for example – whilst in others a mere approach by the squatters plus the knowledge of Redbridge and also of the trouble that Southwark Council had brought upon themselves by trying to oppose the squatters, proved sufficient.

Thus by the end of the year, in addition to the boroughs already mentioned, Greenwich, Wandsworth, Islington, Camden, Brent and finally Southwark had agreed to hand over houses to self-help groups of working people. And in Redbridge the Department of the Environment had successfully been approached for empty houses.

The long struggle in Southwark deserves particular mention, as this borough presented a prime example of a council falling down in its obligations under the National Assistance Act. Also the statements of its Labour council are classic examples of how the idea that ordinary people should run their lives is absolute anathema to politicians. The battle began in September 1970 when two homeless families were refused temporary accommodation and left to walk the streets. With the help of some of the Lewisham squatters these families occupied empty houses owned by the borough of Southwark in Harders Road, Peckham, S.E.15, and two days later they were followed by a third family. All the councillors were then circularized and asked to reach an agreement with the squatters along Lewisham lines, but although the council owned over 1,600 empty properties in the borough, many of which were due to stand empty for years, and although there were 9,000 families on the borough's housing waiting list, the council turned down the idea of such a scheme, and without even meeting the squatters to discuss the matter. Court proceedings were then initiated to evict the families.

The intricate details of the Southwark struggle cannot be described here, except to say that the usual tactics of marches, pickets and appeals were used by the squatters to publicize their case and nearly forty families took up occupation. In addition, certain confidential council reports were obtained and published, and these revealed facts that the council tried to keep from the public about the number of empty houses in the borough and the council's policy of smashing up the interior of many of these. (So much for democracy: how can councillors be accountable when they do not give the public the facts upon which to judge them?) The squatters also appealed to well-known Labour politicians to help them but, with the exception of Richard Marsh, M.P., who did go and see Southwark Council, no help was forthcoming.

Legally, Southwark Council were able to obtain possession orders much more quickly than Redbridge, as the authorities had altered court procedure to enable this to be done; in fact, however, skilful delaying tactics and genuine appeals on points of law by the squatters meant that it still took the council nearly five months to obtain its eviction orders. At that point the squatters commenced the usual game of musical chairs.

Perhaps the most important factor in the whole struggle was the attitude displayed by the councillors. They desperately tried to find reasons not to hand over houses to the squatters, and when all their arguments were refuted they could only dig their heels in and claim that the squatters were not responsible people because they had taken direct action, which was outside the normal channels. Their *ideological* opposition to ordinary people running their own lives was made perfectly clear in their first press statement on squatting, issued on 24 September 1970. They argued that if they accepted the squatters' proposals for the use of empty houses they 'would be put in the position of having to share the administration of [their] housing policy and the management of [their] properties' with ... people who 'have a special interest in the matter'. Finally however, after a twelve-month struggle, they were manoeuvred into handing over empty houses to a self-help group; in addition the council had been forced to repair houses themselves at an amazing rate in an effort to weaken the squatters' case.

This has been an important effect of the squatting movement and it links up with the demands of the campaign at hostels for the homeless. While the latter have campaigned for the closure of the old tenement ghettoes, the squatters have forced councils to use more short-life houses. Thus it is now the norm in many boroughs for homeless families to be accommodated in empty houses, and the pressure that brought about this change came from the movement that started at King Hill and which has developed into the thirteen London squatting groups.

So far in this account I have mainly documented how direct action has affected the scarcity aspect of the housing situation and has led to better conditions and policies. Even here, though, the issues of who controls and who decides have emerged quite clearly. The stands taken by Kent, Redbridge and Southwark councils were as much stands of principle as anything else: with few exceptions the members of these councils could not accept the idea that ordinary people had a right to a say. The existence of the squatting groups, however, also demonstrates another vital point – that such people *are* quite capable of organizing their lives. Squatting 'shows' that the mysteries of housing management are mysteries developed and perpetuated by the system, and in reality ordinary people are more capable of organizing their own lives than any trained housing managers. This was never more clearly demonstrated than when Lewisham housing manager Dennis Yates criticized the squatters in October 1971 for having internal problems, but was then forced to admit that in using the short-life houses as they had the squatters had done a job that the council was not capable of doing.

The squatting groups are run by the people living in the houses. At their weekly meetings they make policy and elect any committees that they feel they need. They decide collectively what rent they should pay, how it should be spent and whom they should employ. There have been many problems, but these have not been brushed under the carpet and ignored; they have been dealt with in a responsible way. Every group is also a power base in its borough. They have demonstrated to some of the disenfranchised badly housed people that they *can* have a voice; they have shown that there is a way forward from apathy and that people can organize and change their lives. The groups have become effective action and pressure groups on welfare departments (in forcing them to accept homeless families that they have turned away), public health departments (in getting them to do their job better and give additional housing points for bad conditions) and housing departments (in requiring them often to re-assess people's housing positions and in pushing forward people for rehousing). Illegal evictions have also been fought.

These are a few of the ways in which organized groups of

badly housed people have shown that they can exert pressure. And the message from all this is very clear: working people can have a say and a voice – by taking direct action and organizing themselves. The more that message is got across the nearer will be any kind of revolution. Squatting is but one small move in that direction.

References

1. *Children in Care in England and Wales* (H.M.S.O., 1970, Cmd 4559).

2. 'The Conservative censure motion on the Government's housing policy and its failure to fulfil the election pledge of 500,000 houses by 1970 was rejected in the Commons.' *The Times* (30 January 1970).

3. 'A motion congratulating the Government on its housing achievement . . . was then carried.' ibid.

4. JAMES FEARNLEY, 'Newington Man Slams Council', gives an exposé of the consultation games of Southwark Council, which he calls a 'complete fraud and an expensive exercise in community conning'. Published in *Walworth Compass* (mid August 1971; obtainable from Gerry Williams, c/o Cambridge House, 131 Camberwell Road, London S.E.5). See also TOM WOOLEY, 'The Politics of Community Action', *Solidarity*, Vol. 6, No. 9 (available from 53a Westmoreland Road, Bromley, Kent).

5. Much of this information on housing control has been taken from JOHN REYNOLDS, 'Democracy and Housing', *Solidarity*, Vol. 2, No. 10.

6. With the notable exception of the Tory Member for Ramsgate, Kenneth Joseph, who consistently supported the struggle.

7. The result was that two bailiffs were sent for trial accused of riot. The Director of Public Prosecutions then took over the case and did a deal. They pleaded guilty to affray and the riot charge was dropped. But the point had been proved – the eviction attempts were illegal.

8. Again with one exception – Labour Councillor Tony Young.

Simon Maddison Mindless Militants? Psychiatry and the University

One is struck very forcibly by the external appearance of students with regard to hygiene, clothing and C.N.D. badges. You only have to look at them to tell they are unstable.[1]

In recent years there has been a steady growth in the demand by organizations, ranging from child-care agencies to industrial corporations, for psychiatrists to use their understanding of human behaviour to help what are seen to be complex organizational and social dilemmas. Universities are one form of organization in which psychiatrists have already attained a generally accepted position. Following the American example, British universities have set up Student Health Services, many of which have been explicitly founded upon, or have moved towards, a 'psychological orientation'. Either psychiatrists are appointed to these services, or G.P.s with some knowledge of psychology help to shift the facilities away from first aid provisions and towards a concern with mental health of students.

This study will look at the role of psychiatrists and student doctors in an attempt to show that in both their traditional role of treating patients, and in their new concern with screening and consultancy work, they are undertaking decisions based not on medical, but social, political and moral determinants. In doing so they are helping universities to achieve their organizational goals by the use of psychiatry as a managerial instrument.

University Goals

If one surveys the reasons given by doctors and psychiatrists for the setting up and extension of student health services and then places these alongside the expressed concerns of administrators and politicians about the nature and place of universities in contemporary society, a remarkable coincidence of emphasis emerges. What exactly are the goals which policy makers proclaim for universities?

Economic

Since the 1950s, the debate surrounding the expansion of higher education has been largely concerned with the economic value of education to the nation, rather than its educational value to the individual. The Robbins Report of 1962, an essentially liberal document in its conception, was the first systematic attempt to relate the structure of higher education to the needs of modernized capitalism. Its proposal was:

> To review the pattern of full-time higher education in Great Britain and in the light of national needs and resources to advise Her Majesty's Government on what principles its long term development should be based.

The rationale behind its recommendations for the expansion of higher education was:

> The growing realization of this country's economic dependence upon the education of its population has led to much questioning of the adequacy of present arrangements. Unless higher education is rapidly reformed, it is argued, there is little hope of this densely populated island maintaining an adequate position in the fiercely competitive world of the future.[2]

The government, well aware of the importance of feeding the economy's need for qualified manpower, welcomed the Report. However, the economic system, with its increasingly intractable problems, has forced successive governments – unconcerned to radically change the system in favour of educational and other priorities – to maximize their 'return on investment'. While maintaining the rationale behind the recommendations, almost every basic argument in Robbins about the structure of higher education has been discarded for the sake of education on the cheap, the binary system being the favoured weapon to economize while obtaining more student places.

It is in this vein that Mr Van Straubenzee, Under-Secretary of State for Education and Science, says that British universities can be proud of their record in keeping down student wastage, yet warns against complacency because by one estimate the cost is still about £4 million a year.[3]

The concern to minimize 'student wastage' and the loss of 'society's most precious asset',[4] which is said to 'add to the economic burden of our educational system',[5] is equally uppermost in the minds of student health officers. Research into this area is the subject of regular reports in the professional journals, the results of which are carefully monitored by the University Grants Committee.[6] Although concern from the medical profession does acknowledge that the cost of failure to the individual has to be considered, the economic goal is given equal prominence.

Contemporary society cannot afford to waste any of its intellectual elite, not only because there is not enough of it but also because it is too expensive to do so. A student in the U.K., for example, costs, in terms of capital investment, fees, maintenance and tuition, some £2,000 a year, and if anyone should fail for reasons that might have been averted, then that failure represents a considerable and tragic loss to the economy.[7]

Such sentiments are by no means untypical; The Report of the Princeton Conference on World Student Mental Health gives weight to its recommendations with a similar statement.[8]

One way to eliminate student wastage (which has not escaped educationalists) would of course be to exclude potential 'wasters' from university in the first place, the double economic advantage of this being that other students 'who might have made better use of the places available' would not be excluded.[9] Under the sway of these economic arguments, Dr Farnsworth of Harvard advised that 'if signs of probable failure were overwhelming in spite of plenty of intelligence, the applicant should not be admitted' (one of the signs suggested is 'a history of short cuts in ethics to gain desired ends').[10] Debate within the profession as to whether prediction should be for the purposes of exclusion or not has declined recently in the face of research which showed that whilst 'neurotic introverts' had a higher chance of breakdown, they were also likely to show high academic achievement.[11] Faced with this dilemma and the likelihood of excluding what were seen to be future 'good students', the profession is awaiting a better test. Several of these are being worked on, one, at Aberdeen University, supported by the Social Science Research Council. It seems highly probable that with the continuing economic cutback in education, the use of such tests for exclusion will revive with the discovery of an 'accurate' test.

Academic

The corollary of this concern to minimize 'wastage' and 'failure' is to maximize 'success'. Robbins argued that 'estimates should be made of the "need" for different types of skilled manpower at successive stages of the expected expansion of the economy and that the educational plan should be based on these'.[12] For a student to be eligible as one type of skilled manpower, education must no longer be an end in itself but become relegated to the means of acquisition of a certain commodity of great value in the educational market – namely a degree. The crude definition of 'success' is the completion of a course and the passing of exams.

However, to fail on the basis of this definition does not reflect on the system by which the student is being judged, as Dr Gunn says of those suffering from examination anxiety: 'it is not that they are incapable, or that the examination system is unfair, but rather that they have failed in some way to adjust and adapt to the continuing demands of maturing.'[13] 'Maturing' then means an acceptance of the egg-grading system of exams which define what education is concerned with; otherwise it is said by Gunn that a student suffers from 'poor motivation' or 'failure to accept the responsibility to undertake a career'. Despite the occasional plea for academic flexibility, the dominant concern of student health officers is to work within the present manpower production educational system geared to the commercial market; after all, as one states, 'specialization is an essential aspect of a sound identity'.[14] Meanwhile, as one of the ways to produce less wastage and appease the policy makers, it is suggested that 'top-class sportsman may be nurtured academically and eventually be "given" a "pass" degree'.[15]

Socialization

As well as a waste of invested time, money and effort, the argument runs that society loses 'respected and valuable citizens'.[16] But how can we be sure they will be 'valuable citizens'? One of the official goals of universities is the socialization of students into their future place in society. The Robbins Report talks of 'the transmission of a common culture and common standards of citizenship' and the acceptance that it is a 'proper function of higher education, as of education in schools, to provide in partnership with the family that background of culture and social habit upon which a healthy society depends'. Students who might have questioned the dominant nature and purpose of education (as outlined above) had to be prepared even in the quiet days of 1954 to be themselves an object of research to those concerned about the 'next generation'.

Students after all, are potential leaders of the next generation, and the pattern of development in their rather hot-house environment must be observed and absorbed by anyone who hopes to help in bringing stability to their lunatic fringe.[17]

Similarly, The Group for the Advancement of Psychiatry, in a paper on 'The Role of Psychiatrists in Colleges and Universities', places most emphasis in its argument over the need for psychiatry on the:

generally recognized [fact] that college graduates form a high percentage of the leaders in any community, and the more maturity they display in their leadership the better it is for the welfare of the community. The emotional health and maturity of this influential two per cent of our population who are enrolled in our colleges and universities thus becomes of prime importance.[18]

One of the problems, as seen by such sources, was that many 'emotionally handicapped' students did *not* drop out but graduated and then carried their 'maladjustment' into professional and community life. The psychiatrists' services in the university were thus to help develop 'constructive citizens'.

The attributes of such a 'constructive citizen' are not listed but are unlikely to be those of a student who questioned the élite conception of the university as guardian, repository and inculcator of certain values; the 'constructive citizen' was sent forth into the world properly equipped to discharge his duty as social, political and moral leader and did not encourage people to self activity against existing élites. According to this conception, health officers were there to help bolster up and perpetuate a hierarchical educational system and society.

It is only rarely that the student as an individual and his development as an autonomous person ever get to be the focus of attention. Even when they do it is usually within the perspective Malleson adopted as British representative at the Princeton Conference, when in arguing for student health services as one of the agencies to help students, he maintained that 'left to himself the average student is unlikely to make the best use of what the university offers him', and therefore: 'In filling this role the university physician has left aside his old ideas of detecting and treating disease and is concerning himself with the efficient and harmonious adjustment of the individual to the needs of a particular society.'

In the case of those students who do leave university before getting, or without, a degree, the adjustment role of the psychiatrist is again called upon to help 'cool them out'.[19] Psychiatrists both participate in, and advise sympathetic trained personnel to hold, 'exit interviews'. While American universities often do this to maintain their goodwill with people who may become members of the legislature that controls the budget of the university that 'flunked them out',[20] the main aim of this exercise is to relieve feelings of resentment and discontent by smoothing the path of entrance into a lower niche of society. Dr Gunn, despite an admirable concern that society should not compound the failure of a 'drop-out' by stigmatizing him, finds the ex-student a 'tragic, but, at times, dangerous, figure'.

Rarely does the ex-student prove himself or herself with feats of great endeavour in the commercial world perhaps because if they had the energies for that, or a strong enough motivation for personal profit, then they would not have failed anyway. More often they become the 'chip-on-the-shoulder' types and blame themselves, their parents, society or university for their predicament. There is often an unchannelled bitterness which may be eruptive or smouldering and it does little to help them with adaptation.[21]

So the individual student must be adapted, not the situation from which he dropped out, or the one he is about to enter; these are assumed not to need changing. The chip-on-the-shoulder is seen as unjustified, the bitterness should be channelled into oneself, the drop-out can be helped to drop out but 'with less antagonism and resentment for our social system'.[22]

Control of Social Deviance

The minimizing of student wastage, and the production of future leaders and well-adjusted citizens, necessarily involve the university in controlling and dealing with any social deviance it encounters. The university is a situation of competing definitions, particularly in such areas as respect for property and sex, where non-conformist behaviour challenges the acceptable image of how the correctly motivated, mature student should behave. Ryle poses the question which university psychiatrists are concerned to answer; 'what kind of meaning is to be attached to students' various non-conformist behaviours?' Sociologists would agree with the style of this question in that meaning does not automatically announce itself, but rather has to be read into all events and situations. But what are these 'non-conformist behaviours' in the first place? There is nothing self-evident about them; the recognition and definition of particular actions as non-conformist or deviant depends upon social evaluations. The answer is that behaviour which is viewed as problematic in terms of the goals we have described is similarly viewed by university psychiatrists. The identification of such behaviour as indicative of mental instability quite clearly shows the psychiatrist acting as a moral entrepreneur.

Farnsworth presents the following list as 'examples of behaviour that suggest the presence of emotionally unstable persons'.

Library vandalism, cheating and plagiarism, stealing in the college and community stores or in the dormitories, unacceptable or antisocial sexual practices (overt homosexuality, exhibitionism, promiscuity), and the unwise and unregulated use of harmful drugs.[23]

Psychiatrists are seen by other authors as particularly helpful in dealing with phenomena such as vandalism, for 'it is an especially trying problem for any academic community and helping some students to develop respectful attitudes toward property is a very difficult task'.[24]

Ryle includes the homosexual in his list of 'abnormal personalities', while Sim prefixes a list of undesirable sexual habits from transvestism to masturbation (the latter is 'evidence of underlying mental disturbances and referral to the physician is urgently indicated'), with the view that when one meets problems of sex and morals,

one feels justified in abandoning a neutral position as regards irresponsible pre-marital intercourse. The present trend of uninhibited sexual behaviour in the young is not one which anybody who is familiar with the physical and psychological problems can condone. As a social phenomenon it should be amenable to manipulation or influence and I am in no doubt on which side the tutor should be.[25]

Doctor or Double Agent?

In assisting the university in the curtailment of such defined deviant behaviour and helping it to achieve the other goals outlined, psychiatrists and student doctors sometimes operate openly in the formal decision process; however, this is not always the case. Examples of breaches of confidentiality and suspension and alteration of the Hippocratic Oath in ways that are not revealed to the student can be found when the psychiatrist is operating within the traditional doctor/patient relationship. Farnsworth commenting on the case of homosexuals says 'exchanges should remain confidential *unless* the patient indulges in further unacceptable social behaviour', and again, 'nothing that the patient divulges during the course of the medical interview may be used by the physician without the patient's permission *unless* the welfare of others is directly at stake.' [26] It is statements of this sort that have led Szasz to depict the psychiatrist as a 'double agent' and demand that 'we must remove psychiatry from its hiding place, the infirmary.' [27]

Not all psychiatrists in universities act in these ways. Professional pressures and codes of ethics operate to curtail the grossest practices of this type. Many American psychiatrists would reject out of hand such an attempt to involve them as was made at one university, where psychiatrists were asked to assist the administration and a zealous police division in what proved to be a large-scale effort to 'ferret out nests of suspected homosexuals'. Once suspects were rounded up, the psychiatrists would examine each to discover if they *were* homosexuals. [28] Certainly the English literature on students does not contain examples of this sort of collusion of agents of society that David Cooper has described as one basis of 'real (as opposed to mythical) violence in psychiatry'. [29]

In fact there is no need for psychiatrists to expose themselves to criticism in quite such stark and blatant ways, for there is a second and more powerful way in which psychiatry is a social and political exercise and can work in the university to achieve that institution's goals, and in so doing enhance rather than discredit its reputation, respect and following.

Psychiatrists do not even have to enter the formal decision-making process to act in a social and political way. As sociologists of psychiatry and mental illness have forcefully argued, the very use of the traditional medical model of practice, with its implications of an unfolding disease process similar to a physical illness, has social and moral implications. For unlike a physical illness, recognition and definition of mental illness depends not upon expert diagnosis, but on social evaluations of specific behaviours which are the property not of an in-

119

dividual but of an interaction situation. The real nature of the psychiatric doctor/patient relationship is the attribution of meaning to 'problems of living'.[30] By implying that he is like the non-psychiatric doctor, when in fact he deals not with the disease of a sick person but with the social problems of a university, the psychiatrist in a second and more insidious way misrepresents himself to the student/patient.

The actual use of psychiatrists in various organizations has accompanied an increasing tendency to interpret all kinds of social and political problems through a psychiatric framework. Many aspects of crime are seen mainly as reflections of family instability and personal maladjustment; communist bureaucracy and certain kinds of political behaviour are analysed as reflections of distorted relationships to parents. The growth of this sort of explanation, together with criticisms of basic features of society formulated in terms of the 'neurotic conflicts of our times', has been described by Riessman and Miller as a 'new psychiatric world view'.[31] The universities have not been immune to this; the development of psychiatric definitions and their extension into areas of educational life has been part of this process. The implications of this are far reaching and must now be discussed.

The Crisis of Legitimation

The growth of alternative life styles and sets of values as expressed in the philosophy of hippies and in the political radicalism of students is seen as deeply threatening by the university authorities. One headmaster, addressing members of the British Student Health Association, feels that 'our schools and universities are faced with the problem of finding a means of maintaining their structure in the face of disruptive influences'; because parents do not give moral guidance these days, there is a 'need to restore the built-in stabilizing factor', as 'we are in the presence of a breakdown of this built-in control system'.[32]

An ex-secretary of the London School of Economics, H. Kidd, addressing the same conference on 'Student Unrest' expresses great concern over the 'extremists' adept in 'engineering situations, [and] in manipulating the larger body of students'.[33] He identifies the current of thought among students that is particularly 'apt to respond to the extremists' message and leadership' as that of 'questioning authority'. Radical politics take root when the older generation is discredited, has lost its moral standing, and lost the legitimacy of its authority. As Kidd's argument is that we do need authority to preserve freedom or else we have the rule of the strongest, the ability of extremists to 'assist the process of delegitimization' must be checked while clear motivation must be given to the 'moderate' students, rendering them less receptive to the 'extremists' ideas.

Dr Davies, at a later stage of the conference, presumably feeling it might be illiberal to deny revolutionary ideas any room at university, came up with the reassuring proposal that such ideas be regarded as a normal step in development if they occur in the student's first year, as fortunately he then has 'time to learn the next lessons' which are:

that revolution is impracticable, even if it were desirable, that the most that can be hoped for is reform in certain respects, that in order to achieve reform he has to be equipped with knowledge and skills, and that the university provides him with opportunities to prepare himself in this way.

A look at how psychiatrists and student health doctors not only treat but interpret behaviour which threatens legitimate authority is instructive. It is the drug taking of the hippie and the challenging activity of the political radical which are regarded with the most concern.

Drugs

The approach taken to drug taking relies upon a psycho-pathological model based on psycho-sexual development. Ryle states that the psychopathology of the drug taker is 'most often related to unresolved Oedipal problems or to early deprivation'; further, 'the split between the bad world of reality and the good world of the drug cult may reflect, and come to perpetuate, an inner split in the personality'. Sim is almost hysterical in his defence of the *status quo* and denunciation of drugs.

Drug taking as a cultural habit represents the attitude of the lotus eater and fosters indolence and the constant pursuit of sensuality. In a leisured society these experiences, it has been argued, are essential; but we are a leisured society because we are an industrial society and still a relatively efficient one. The philosophy of the lotus eater may be acceptable to some artists, vagrants and the work shy but it is out of harmony with our present culture where mastery of anxiety is the main impulse to achievement.

The assumption throughout is that there is something that is commonly thought of as reality which exists for everyone. The alternative idea that reality is a set of conceptual frames and assumptions, and that there are a number of competing versions of reality just as there are of 'total identity' and 'harmony with our present culture', is not considered. The drug taker's claim that drugs thrust man more intensely *into* reality is not open to debate. When the student is considered to be emotionally disturbed, such a claim can be dismissed as merely further confirmation of his unresolved Oedipal problems and the like. Management of these students then becomes 'humanitarian', treatment for sickness rather than punishment for sin. Thus Linken makes an 'alternative case for a student health approach to disciplinary problems with the use of student health facilities as a form of probationary service'.[34]

Political

Political behaviour is similarly viewed. Blaine and McArthur state:

A college psychiatrist is frequently involved in the management of those persons who converge upon the office of the President and other high places in the university with bizarre ideas and behaviour that may seem frightening but usually are only annoying. Such people are likely to be emotionally disturbed and, in some instances, psychotic. It is a very welcome service when the psychiatrist manages to steer these patients into treatment and end the trouble and discomfort they have caused.[35]

One such student diagnosed in an illustrative case by Ryle as suffering from 'affective psychosis – a hypomanic attack' is in the psychiatrist's hands because: 'during her first term [she] invaded the room of the Senior Proctor and refused to leave; she was trying to persuade him to abolish his office because it would no longer be necessary now she had discovered the power of love.' The student's ideas may have been utopian, but the very idea of any political motivation is not considered by Ryle. Instead he relies upon a psychiatric perspective and notes how two months later she was 'much preoccupied with her own inadequacy and insignificance' and that therefore she was suffering from a 'mild depressive illness'. Again the idea that this might be a realistic reaction following the failure of a political mission is not considered, rather Ryle finds it necessary to back up his original diagnosis with what he sees as confirmatory evidence – that despite the fact she functioned normally, 'her responses to ideas and people continued to some extent to show a tendency towards polarization into extreme, either/or concepts'. This is not considered to be her continuing political perspective.

The extreme position of this type of analysis is stated by Sim, who after condemning gambling in students in terms of the 'feeling of winning being like an orgasm and that of losing to symbolic castration', looks for the 'deeper mechanisms' involved in student violence because in his view, 'organized violence at a time of universal education with free tuition for the needy, seems so illogical [and] exasperation over the existing order is not a convincing answer'.

He finds a 'convincing answer' in the discovery that students demonstrate in order to get hit by police batons and that the 'need for punishment is usually based on profound guilt feelings', further that the 'most intense guilt feelings in our culture are derived from sex guilt'. The argument develops that the majority on demonstrations are the perpetual protesters, but that these are also the same people who take drugs, 'have generally renounced the morality of society', and are more 'permissive' about sex. The next step is for him to explain why permissive students in past generations did not demonstrate. This presents no problem for Sim, who finds that they were able to fulfil their 'strong desire for sex experience' with prostitutes – people of a lower social class who, having already 'debased themselves', could be 'held in low regard, which would tend to lighten guilt feelings'. Alas, however, present students have sex with their peers in intelligence and social class, and as these partners are very close to their own brothers and sisters 'such relationships reactivate early taboos and engender strong feelings of guilt'. So – exit all lefties to get a dose of police brutality to lighten such morbid feelings.

The Power and Politics of Labelling

The use of a psychiatric explanation to name student behaviour as sick has political implications. While clinical and scientific objectivity are claimed, the action is discredited, reduced to both a symptom and the cause of pathology, the moral and wilful character of the behaviour is neutralized. Goode has shown this in his article on 'Marijuana and the Politics of Reality' where he terms such naming a 'strategy of discreditation'.[36] Young has similarly argued that the use of the 'sick' label tends to 'deny the legitimacy and in fact the very existence of norms and values which are different from that of the definer'. He continues that the total mystification of the relationship between the society and the so-called deviant/mentally ill person, is achieved amongst other ways by the 'denial of authenticity'; that is, of the meaning the individual gives to his acts; the 'denial of personal integrity', where actions are ascribed not to the emergence of alternative standards but to personal failings; the 'denial of freedom', by which the individual is said to be impelled by forces beyond his control which can only be fully understood by the expert – our friend the university psychiatrist – and finally, 'denial of aims', whereby the real aims and attitudes of the individual are systematically misinterpreted and others are substituted by the experts.[37]

For the deviant, in our case the student defined as mentally ill, to contest the definition imposed on him is seen by the psychiatrist as further validation of his diagnosis; agreement with the psychiatrist is the first step on the way to a successful 'cure'; resistance is a sign of being a difficult case, having a bad prognosis, or of getting worse.

Ryle amply shows this process in the case of the student he diagnosed as having an 'acute identity crisis with some psychotic features' because as a chemistry first-year he took twelve days' time out to write a play in blank verse in a hotel in North Wales. He refused to enter into what Scheff has termed the 'negotiation situation',[38] in that on being persuaded to return and reluctantly attend the Student Health Centre, he mocked the interviewers: 'when offered a single suggestion or interpretation, he would accept it with an exaggerated deference. When offered a choice of interpretations he would mime at picking an answer out of a hat, before replying with one of them.' Such behaviour is seen by Ryle as validation of the original diagnosis rather than as a realistic reaction to what the student perceived as a situation in which he was powerless. The fact that he said that 'inside all was clear to him, his only concern for the time being was to complete the play he was writing ... and that the journey away from university had been a search for necessary privacy in which to come to terms with himself' is dismissed by Ryle as an inadequate explanation – his authenticity is denied. The fact that the themes of the play were 'pity, the falseness of most lives (which should be recognized but could not be changed) and the need to acknowledge what could not be understood', are regarded as further symptoms. Ryle then has to scurry around delving into past behaviour to unearth *one* rebellious episode at boarding school to clinch the diagnosis, concluding weakly that the student later withdrew from the university and graduated elsewhere with a degree in English literature, there being no further episodes of psychiatric instability. The same approach is used in the case of the student diagnosed as 'anxiety state: conflict over masculinity', an example of the psychiatrist operating with a student problem not obviously threatening 'legitimate authority'. Here Ryle included in his account the following interpretation of non-cooperation by the student in the treatment situation: 'In therapy he had first challenged my authority, but later he expressed both lack of trust in my concern (an inadequate father) and fear of my power (a potential rival).'

The doctor/patient relationship in this context is one based on power, the student has no right to question the motives of the psychiatrist nor of the university administration or teaching staff whose values the psychiatrist upholds. He upholds them in that he is involved in questioning certain motives and defining and treating certain behaviours. Those that he does concern himself with are not chosen arbitrarily but stem from a value position in the university, made up of ideas about what the educational process is, how it can be best achieved and how the university should fit into the wider society. When the dominant conception of what a university is all about is questioned, when it becomes clear that some sections of the university view the world differently, and, further, act in ways concomitant with an alternative viewpoint, a serious problem is posed for those members of the university who have vested interests in stability and in the legitimacy of their own special version of reality.

Where behaviour violates value biases and perceived interests it is felt necessary to construct interpretations; however, not just *any* interpretation will meet the purposes of the dominant group, for as Goode has said, the 'problem becomes a matter of moral hegemony, of legitimating one distinctive view of the world and discrediting competing views'. Goode continues:

This process (of achieving moral hegemony and mystification) must not above all be seen as whimsical and arbitrary; it must be grounded in the nature of reality itself. The one selected view of the world must be seen as the *only possible* view of the world; it must be identified with the real world. All other versions of reality must be seen as whimsical and arbitrary and, above all, in error.

This paper seeks to argue that the psychiatrist is one of the principal people available to help those interests in society that profit by the maintenance of the *status quo,* and who need to conserve their increasingly attacked moral hegemony as a part of this. The attack is not limited to particular incidents such as occupations or the pulling down of gates; these are simply the occasions when the underlying and continuous conflict take a highly visible organized form. The crisis of legitimation is a constant feature of contemporary university life. 'Nothing has greater discrediting power today than the demonstration that a given assertion has been "scientifically disproven". Our contemporary pawnbrokers of reality are scientists.'[39] The psychiatrist claims both the cloak of medical and scientific objectivity; his usefulness to the university is his ability to label what is seen to be threatening behaviour as manifestations of mental illness. Thus discredited, it calls for 'treatment', not debate; social order is preserved by the attempt at internal controls rather than by resort to overt external legal sanctions. The strategy is ideological but is not seen to be so because the whole process de-ideologizes the power struggle of social groups.

Spreading the Net

To actually achieve this the psychiatrist has to extend the acceptability and usage of the psychiatric explanatory framework. He must both see as many students as possible in order to explain to them the 'real' basis of reasons for their attitudes and actions and persuade the deviant to believe in the 'scientific treatment of a medical illness'; and he must persuade other members of the university, administration and teaching, to evaluate students in the same way. This is done in several ways, which have resulted in an increase in the ability of the psychiatrist to impose his definition of the situation on events that happen in the university.

Psychiatrists have, for example, derived indications of proneness to mental illness from questionnaires sent out to accepted university applicants. Such questionnaires request information on family and personal history of mental illness, on past study problems, and in one university, on sporting interests; if no sporting interests are indicated, it is assumed you will probably get lonely and will therefore be prone to mental illness. Students identified in this way are asked to come for an interview in the first few weeks of term. The theory behind this is that awareness of your likely clientele, coupled with periodic checking and intervention, will enable successful treatment at an early and favourable stage in the development of mental illness. In this practice, no awareness is shown of the potential self-fulfilling prophecy effect such a presentation of a way of seeing oneself to the student might have. The approach assumes that it is better to err on the side of illness than of health, that an individual continues to be vulnerable in different environments and that psychiatric assessment even in the absence of obvious illness or symptoms never does any harm.

More importantly, in this approach, the initial interview is seen as crucial in emphasizing the Health Service's approachability and accessibility, so that the student himself will return, should he have problems of any kind, and also so that he will advise other students about the doctor who can help them if they go to see him. University psychiatrists are aware that their ability to reach as wide a section of students as possible depends on their accessibility as a help source, and indeed a help source for *any* perceived problem. Dr Still expresses pleasure at the growth of consultations for explicitly social rather than medical reasons saying that at Leeds University: 'The majority of those consulting the doctors do so to obtain guidance, or a standard by which they may judge their actions, or decisions, or a reassurance that their actions and plans are reasonable.' [40] This projection by university psychiatrists of themselves and their services is part of a conscious attempt to build what Kadushin has termed a 'community of the friends and supporters of psychotherapy and psychoanalysis'.[41] Evidence of some success in this venture, I believe, is shown by the considerable increase in *self*-referral to the university psychiatrist by students in universities where the student health service has projected itself and worked in the above ways. In one university, the Chairman of the Freshers' Conference viewed the work of the Student Health Officer as so important that, on his own initiative, he offered him the forms on which new students had marked which societies they were interested in, saying that he knew the sports forms were used to try to detect vulnerable students and thought that the information he had might help in this detection.

Another way the extension of the psychiatric framework of evaluation is achieved is by the psychiatrist contacting both academic and administrative staff to alert them to what he perceives to be student problems and signs of disturbance. The Princeton Conference (referred to earlier) discussed at length the compilation of lists of symptoms which would aid personnel in referring students. For dormitory counsellors, advocates of the list suggest that the following items be included, 'problems of acting out; anti-social behaviour; disciplinary cases; withdrawal and isolation; undue anxiety; and too-frequent advice-seeking'. For athletic coaches, the items were 'avoidance of athletic competition; students who break down in competition; undue anxiety in competitive athletics'. Formalized lists of this sort do not yet appear to be extensively used, but people are encouraged to refer whenever they are in doubt. Ryle is concerned that tutors 'refer students with academic problems for psychiatric assessment, even in the absence of obvious psychiatric illness'. He continues:

the critical need in my view is to build up a system of easy access and of access by various routes, so that students, tutors and others, once alerted to the signs of trouble, *however manifest*, are able to seek prompt help for it. [My emphasis].

In this way a 'lay referral structure'[42] is built up in the university. This is a network of people, usually turned to for help, who impose a form on the seeking of help, mediating between student and psychiatrist and channelling him to the 'expert'. Personal observation of regular meetings set up by the Student Health Officer at one university in which chaplains, tutors and others discuss student problems, in *theory* to get the 'combined mental powers of the group' to understand the problems, in *fact* turned out to be sessions at which the doctor interprets and labels cases presented by tutors, etc., in a pseudo-psychiatric way and suggests the best way to handle them. Through this process, a student seeking advice on any matter from various sources in the university is very likely to enter a situation where his motives, behaviour and feelings will be interpreted in a pseudo-psychiatric framework, where his own definitions of the situation will be under great pressure to change and where he may find himself placed firmly on the path which leads to the psychiatrist. In Scheff's words, a 'psychiatric public' is created 'which takes for granted the *reality* of mental illness' and in which a medical definition of personal problems and other behaviour is sustained.[43]

Conclusion

In this paper I have attempted to show that the psychiatrists' purposeful search for clients in the university and their extension of the psychiatric framework of evaluation and explanation has increasingly led to those students who pursue actions which threaten the university's structure being discredited and channelled into 'safe' medical treatment. The motives, attributes and values of students that are not questioned are those of the person Riessman and Miller have called the 'New Hero'. With a nice twist of the use of psychiatric labels, they say he suffers from the 'Pathology of Moderation'.

The adjudication of the competing definitions about aspects of the university and the meaning of student behaviour takes place in a situation of power, one in which the university authorities have power and legitimacy; and dissenting students, in a situation of mystification, have little chance of resisting the label of mad rather than bad. Their ability to resist in future will depend upon their ability to throw off the cloak of science which covers the process I have described, and to consciously use and extend alternative frameworks of evaluation that recognize, and allow for, the meaning the individual attributes to his actions. However, such an attempt will be at a time when there is increasing use of the psychiatric label to explain and denounce simultaneously. As more students challenge the existing social order, so will the technical expertise of psychiatry be increasingly used to eliminate more of these 'undesirable' students.[44] Its attractiveness to the university authorities is increasing, for if a part of the social control apparatus is invisible or disguised, society and the university can 'maximize a stable, predictable social order while maintaining the appearance of a high devotion to personal freedom (and even to a benevolent, humanitarian concern for its "disabled" members)'.[45]

The sociologist should concern himself with the 'kinds of explanations a society fabricates about behaviour in its midst ... It should be regarded as extremely significant that deviant behaviour seems to have attracted explanations which activate a principle of psychological abnormality.'[46] I would suggest that these explanations reveal a society that is concerned primarily with individual, non-social methods of change. They emanate from universities rooted in a class society where the educational system performs functions which are determined by the social relations on which that society is based. These are not just the training in skills for the commercial market, but also the inculcating of standards of behaviour and values designed to uphold that society while ensuring subordination to authority. Psychiatrists and student health officers sometimes consciously, sometimes unwittingly, cooperate in this exercise.

The question arises as to whether this need be the case. D. Cooper, R. D. Laing and others have shown that psychiatry can work in other ways than that of covert representative of the ongoing social and political order. The psychiatrist in the university could work to 'free the student into his self-education'[47] and help convert universities into educational institutions operating in a different relationship to society, and concerned to change that society.

Students do have emotional problems, but psychiatrists, or others concerned with student mental health, rarely conceptualize these in terms of institutional and administrative failures; they prefer to look for the causes in their intra-psychic life and ignore the social-system pressures that might be affecting them. When psychiatrists deal with the problems of students that do not immediately threaten the university in a directly political way, the same approach is taken. Thus Still, in listing the factors he identifies as operating to produce an illness or breakdown, states that (apart from emotional disturbances connected with a love affair and difficulty in adjustment for overseas students) in a large number of the 'more severe' cases 'there are seriously disturbing features in the family history and in the family environment from which the student comes'. Since he feels that by themselves, examination or academic stresses are only comparatively infrequent causes of illness, for all other cases the cause lies:

not so much in the actual stresses of the academic situation, as in some flaw or weakness or defect inherent in the student's own personality ... The situation in which the student finds himself in the university is not one which would give rise to mental ill health were it not for the presence of some such weakness or idiosyncrasy.[48]

Similarly in the analysis of Ryle – one author who does show some awareness of the impact on the student of the university environment – we find the statement that:

This complex and competitive situation can allow rapid growth and development in those with adequately firm inner resources, but for others, particularly for those with disturbed family backgrounds and unresolved conflicts, the situation is dangerous.

The remedial procedures are then determined by this concept of adaptive failure and the assumption that the university has not contributed to the students' problems.

University psychiatrists, student medical officers, and counsellors have shown little sign of awareness of their entrapment in institutional values; I have shown, in fact, many share these same values. One author has made the plea that the university counsellor

should detach himself from the values of the status quo and from his obligation to adjust the student to it. He should strive to grasp the vision of radical change that the intelligent and activist youth are struggling to formulate. He should use a sociological perspective to reconceptualize students' problems in the light of both campus politics and the larger society's urgent needs.[49]

132

Mindless Militants? Psychiatry and the University

For those who would answer this plea it may be necessary to build a power base outside the established hierarchy which will allow them to operate independently of the university and its aims. Until this is achieved, students might be well advised to take up the American trade union leader's suggestion that, 'if those employers start hiring psychiatrists, our unions are just going to have to get their own psychiatrists.' [50]

References

1. Dr J. SCOTT, in discussion following C. B. KIDD, 'Research into Emotional Disorders in Students', *Proceedings of the British Student Health Association* (1963), henceforth referred to as P.B.S.H.A.

2. *Higher Education Report* (H.M.S.O., 1963, Cmd 2154), p. 1.

3. *Hansard*, Vol. 18 (H.M.S.O., 4 March 1971).

4. A RYLE, *Student Casualties* (Allen Lane: The Penguin Press, 1969), p. 15.

5. Dr J. PAYNE, 'Review of the Literature on Student Wastage' (P.B.S.H.A., 1969), pp. 52–8.

6. UNIVERSITY GRANTS COMMITTEE, 'Enquiry into Student Progress' (H.M.S.O., 1968).

7. Dr A. GUNN (1), *The Privileged Adolescent* (Medical and Technical Publishing Company, 1970), pp. 63–4.

8. D. L. FUNKENSTEIN, 'The Student and Mental Health; An International View', *Proceedings of Princeton Conference, World Federation for Mental Health* (1956), p. 221.

9. J. WILSON, ' "Success" May Be the Key In New Studies of Student "Failure" ! ', *New Academic*, No. 2. (13 May 1971), p. 152.

10. Dr D. L. FARNSWORTH (1), *Mental Health in College and University* (Cambridge: Harvard University Press, 1957), p. 152.

11. R. P. KELVIN, C. J. LUCAS and A. B. OJHA, 'The Relation between Personality, Mental Health and Academic Performance in Students', *British Journal of Social and Clinical Psychology*, 4 (1965), pp. 244–53.

12. Lord Robbins in a speech, 'Recent Discussions on the Problem of Higher Education in Great Britain', quoted in 'L.S.E.: What It Is and How We Fought It', *Agitator Publication* (L.S.E. Socialist Society, 1967), p. 18.

13. Dr A. GUNN, 'Students Under Stress', *New Society*, No. 443 (25 March 1971), pp. 485–7.

14. Dr D. R. DAVIES, 'The Unrestful Student', P.B.S.H.A. (1970), pp. 46–53.

15. Dr A. GUNN (1), op. cit., p. 136.

16. A. RYLE, op. cit., p. 13.

17. R. H. BOLTON, 'The Student Health Services, The National Health Service and the University Medical Officer', *Universities Quarterly*, Vol. 19, No. 1 (November 1954).

18. COMMITTEE ON ACADEMIC EDUCATION OF THE GROUP FOR THE ADVANCEMENT OF PSYCHIATRY, 'The Role of Psychiatrists in Colleges and Universities', Report No. 17 (Kansas: published by authors, September 1950).

19. B. CLARK, 'The Cooling-Out Function in Higher Education', *Education, Economy and Society*, ed. A. H. Halsey, J. Floud and C. A. Anderson (New York: Free Press, 1961).

20. Dr D. FARNSWORTH (1), op. cit.

21. Dr A. GUNN (1), op. cit., p. 130.

22. Dr A. L. LINKEN, 'Management of Drug Missuse in a University Setting', P.B.S.H.A. (1970), pp. 73–8.

23. Dr D. L. FARNSWORTH (2), *Psychiatry, Education and the Young Adult* (Springfield: Charles C. Thomas, 1966), quoted in T. SZASZ (See Note 27).

24. G. B. BLAINE, and C. C. McARTHUR eds., *Emotional Problems of the Student* (New York: Appleton-Century Crofts, 1961), p. 12.

25. M. SIM, *Tutors and Their Students – Advice from a Psychiatrist* (E. & S. Livingstone, 1970), p. 42.

26. Dr D. L. FARNSWORTH, (1) and (2), quoted in T. SZASZ (See Note 27).

27. T. SZASZ, 'The Psychiatrist as Double Agent', *Campus Power Struggle*, ed. H. S. BECKER (New York: Transaction Books, No. 1, 1970), pp. 153–70.

28. Reported in S. L. HALLECK and M. H. MILLER, 'The Psychiatric Consultation: Questionable Social Precedents of Some Current Practices', *American Journal of Psychiatry* (August 1963), pp. 164–9.

29. D. COOPER, 'Violence in Psychiatry', *Phalanx*, No. 2 (winter 1969/70).

30. T. SZASZ, *The Myth of Mental Illness* (New York: Hoeber-Harper, 1961). T. J. SCHEFF, *Being Mentally Ill* (Chicago: Aldine, 1966).

31. F. RIESSMAN and S. M. MILLER, 'Social Change Versus the Psychiatric World View', *American Journal of Orthopsychiatry*, 34 (January 1964), pp. 29–38.

32. F. LANGLEY, 'Attitudes to Authority – Changing Pattern in Schools', P.B.S.H.A. (1970), pp. 45–7.

33. H. KIDD, 'Student Unrest: What Has Been Going on? An Administrator's View', P.B.S.H.A. (1970), pp. 20–29.

34. Dr A. L. LINKEN, loc. cit.

35. G. B. BLAINE and C. C. McARTHUR, op. cit., p. 12.

36. E. GOODE, 'Marijuana and the Politics of Reality', *Journal of Health and Social Behaviour*, Vol. 10. No. 2 (June 1969), pp. 83–94.

37. J. YOUNG, 'The Zookeepers of Deviancy', *Anarchy*, No. 98 (April 1969), pp. 101–8.

Mindless Militants? Psychiatry and the University

38. T. J. SCHEFF, 'Negotiating Reality: Notes on Power Assessment of Responsibility', *Social Problems*, Vol. 16, No. 1 (summer 1968).

39. E. GOODE, loc. cit.

40. R. J. STILL, *The Mental Health of Students* (University of Leeds, 1966), p. 22.

41. C. KADUSHIN, 'Social Disturbance between Client and Professional', *American Journal of Sociology*, 67 (March 1962), pp. 517–31.

42. E. FREIDSON, 'Client Control and Medical Practice', *American Journal of Sociology*, 65 (January 1960), pp. 374–82.

43. T. J. SCHEFF, 'Users and Non-Users of a Student Psychiatric Clinic', *Journal of Health and Human Behaviour*, Vol. 17, No. 2 (summer 1966), pp. 114–21 (Scheff's emphasis).

44. See the case at Washington University described in I. L. HOROWITZ, 'The Brave New World of Campus Psychiatry', *Change in Higher Education*, Vol. 2 (January/February 1970), pp. 47–52).

45. R. LEIFER, 'Involuntary Psychiatric Hospitalization and Social Control', *International Journal of Social Psychiatry*, Vol. 13 (winter 1967), pp. 53–8.

46. E. GOODE, op cit.

47. J. R. SEELEY, 'In Defense of the College Psychiatrist', in *Where Medicine Fails*, ed. A. L. STRAUSS (New York: Transaction Books, No. 4, 1971).

48. R. J. STILL, 'The Prevention of Psychological Illness Among Students', *Universities Quarterly*, Vol. 17, No. 1 (December 1962).

49. J. STUBBINS, 'The Politics of Counselling', *Personnel and Guidance Journal*, Vol. 48. No. 8 (April 1970), pp. 610–14.

50. Quoted in S. L. HALLECK and M. H. MILLER, loc. cit.

Jerry Palmer   # Thrillers: The Deviant
                     Behind the Consensus

When I gave a version of this paper recently to the Deviancy Symposium I was asked whether I considered the reading of thrillers a deviant activity. My reply should have consisted of a quotation from Rex Stout, an American thriller writer: 'My theory is that people who don't like mystery stories are anarchists.' Another way of putting it would be to refer to the back cover of an early English paperback edition of Mickey Spillane: 'The author with 70,000,000 sales!' In short, no, I don't consider the reading of thrillers a deviant activity, and I don't see any way in which such a majority pastime could meaningfully be called so.

It is perfectly true that the thriller is based upon the description of deviant acts – murder, rape, burglary, espionage, etc. In the rather genteel thriller of the interwar years (Agatha Christie, Ngaio Marsh, etc.) deviant acts were clearly reprehensible, and only performed by the villain of the piece, whereas the hero was the model of probity. There seemed to be good reason for Howard Haycraft to say that thrillers flourish when the population is on the side of law and order.[1] But in later writers, the hero's acts are just as 'deviant' as those of the villain; what difference is there, George Orwell asked, between the policeman and the criminals in *No Orchids for Miss Blandish*? 'It is implied throughout *No Orchids* that being a criminal is only reprehensible in the sense that it does not pay. Being a policeman pays better, but there is no moral difference, since the police use essentially criminal methods.'[2] If the reader is expected to approve of the representation of deviant actions, even to derive pleasure from them, why is the reading of them not deviant? The answer is that in the modern thriller the representation of deviant acts is used to construct a component of the consensus. It is probably for this reason that the descriptions of sadistic brutality that abound in the pages of – for instance – Mickey Spillane are unlikely to be made the subject of prosecution for obscenity, despite the fact that, as a recent article in the *Justice of the Peace and Local Government Review* argued, 'the community, particularly the impressionable young, are far more likely to be "depraved and corrupted" by scenes and descriptions in 'respectable' books, films, television and radio of horrific brutality, lustful sadism and indiscriminate slaughter'.[3] The thrust of the present article is to show that such representations are quite literally eminently respectable, because they are there to lend support to values that are absolutely central to modern Western civilization. Magazines like *Oz*, on the other hand, are prime targets since they use sexually explicit material in an attempt to make a criticism of major institutions, such as the family, work, etc.

The manner in which the description of deviant acts contributes to a consensual view of the world can only be understood on the basis of an analysis of the ideology proposed by the thriller: the world is portrayed in a particular light and its problems are solved in a particular way by a particular kind of person. What it is necessary to demonstrate at the outset is that the categories of 'deviancy' and 'consensus' are appropriate for the discussion, for it is certain that the notion of a moral and rational monopoly inherent in the notion of a 'consensus' is largely a myth; and if 'consensus' goes, then 'deviancy' accompanies it, for the latter can only be defined in terms of 'consensus'.

The concepts are adequate to a discussion of thrillers in this respect: many of the hero's acts are explicitly presented as 'deviant', but simultaneously as justified, since they help to preserve society:

I knew why I was allowed to live while others died! I knew why my rottenness was tolerated and kept alive and why the guy with the reaper couldn't catch me and I smashed through the door of the room with the tommy-gun in my hands spitting out the answer at the same time my voice screamed it to the heavens!

Politics and Deviance

I lived only to kill the scum and the lice that wanted to kill themselves. I lived to kill so that others could live. I lived to kill because my soul was a hardened thing that revelled in the thought of taking the blood of the bastards who made murder their business. I lived because I could laugh it off and others couldn't. I was the evil that opposed other evil, leaving the good and the meek in the middle to live and inherit the earth.[4]

Ian Fleming presents a similar assessment of James Bond:

This underground war I was talking about, this crime battle that's always going on – whether it's being fought between cops and robbers or between spies and counterspies. This is a private battle between two trained armies, one fighting on the side of law and of what his own country thinks is right, and one belonging to the enemies of these things. ... But in the higher ranks of these forces, among the toughest of the professionals, there's a deadly quality in common – to friends and enemies. ... The top gangsters, the top F.B.I. operatives, the top spies and the top counterspies are cold-hearted, cold-blooded, ruthless, tough, killers ...[5]

The body of this article is devoted to resolving this paradox: why is it necessary that the hero should perform acts that are explicitly presented as deviant in order to qualify as the hero?

Professionalism

The world of the thriller is inhabited by sets of contrasting pairs of character-types: the good girl and the bad girl, the hero and the villain; one of these pairs is the amateur and the organization man.

The presence of the total amateur in the thriller is not immediately obvious. It has often been pointed out that the thriller is analogous to the medieval romance in that here too the 'damsel in distress' is rescued by the 'gentil parfit knight', albeit from a fate that nobody, and least of all thriller heroes, any longer imagines is worse than death. The girl whose lack of adaptation to the world of spies and gangsters makes her ideal material for a hostage is indeed a common figure in the thriller, and it is she, above all who incarnates the total amateur. There is a perfect instance in Donald Hamilton's *The*

Removers, one of the Matt Helm novels that were made into a successful film series, imitating the Bond/Sean Connery success, and staring Dean Martin. Helm is held prisoner with his ex-wife and her present husband; he has tried to indicate to her that she should attempt to seduce the frustrated and obviously oversexed villain, but her sense of decency seems to obtrude. Helm reflects:

I mean, she was obviously going to be raped anyway. It had been inevitable since early that morning when she'd let them take the shotgun from her. I'd assumed she'd known it – hell, all she had to do was *look* at the guy – and was planning on it, figuring how best to make use of the fact that she was female, for the common good. ... I guess the fact is that I'd been counting on her as I'd have counted on a good female agent in the same spot – or any woman with courage or good sense, for that matter. ... But it was fast becoming obvious that the thought hadn't crossed her mind, or that if it had, she'd dismissed it as something too horrible to be seriously considered. A provocative glance or two, maybe, even a smile, perhaps, but if anybody seriously expected her to go into that room with this vile man and entertain him ... Well! How disgusting could you get, anyway? I wasn't going to get any help from her, that was abundantly clear.[6]

Typically, when the amateur is confronted with a crisis situation, he is unable to *do* anything; or if an attempt is made, it is stupid, worse than useless – amateurs are essentially passive participants in the world of action that the thriller portrays.

Diametrically opposed to the total amateur is the organization man, the bureaucrat of crime. The plans that Blofeld, the master-mind of SPECTRE, describes at the beginning of Fleming's *Thunderball*, typify this version of the villain:

'The Corsican section,' he said softly, 'will put forward recommendations for the replacement of No. 12. But that can wait until after completion of Plan Omega. On this matter, there are certain details to be discussed. Sub-Operator G, recruited by the German section, has made an error, a serious error which radically affects our timetable. This man, whose membership of the Red Lightning Tong in Macao should have made him expert in conspiracy, was instructed to make his headquarters at a certain clinic in the south of England, an admirable refuge for his purposes. ... Unfortunately this foolish man took it upon himself to become embroiled in a hotheaded fashion with some fellow patient, at the clinic. ... This will involve an irritating but fortunately not a serious delay in Plan Omega. Fresh instructions have been issued. ... The date of his flight will be communicated to Sub-Operator G and he will by that time be recovered and will post The Letter according to plan. The Special Executive ... will read just their flight schedules to Area Zeta in accordance with the new operational schedule.[7]

The characterization through the use of bureaucratic terminology is precise: 'Plan Omega', 'Area Zeta', 'Sub-Operator G', and so on. The whole tone of voice is redolent of company chairmen and senior civil servants: it is, in Fleming, the voice of the villain, of the man with meticulous plans, who will not tolerate any interference with their machine-like precision ('this foolish man', 'irritating delay').

Analytically, the polarization between the amateur and the organization man can be summarized thus: in a world which has, as it were, rules of play, the amateur is chronically out of place; since he knows none of the rules, he improvises, with the inevitable result that he merely makes things more difficult for the hero. The bureaucrat, on the other hand, tries to foresee and forestall all possible contingencies: he has a perfect knowledge of the rules and the gambits because he makes them. As a result, he is often incapable of improvising, and when a contingency that he had failed to foresee arises, he is completely lost. Fleming's Dr No, for instance, puts Bond through a 'programmed' confrontation with death, the final stage of which consists of Bond being catapulted from a great height into an enclosed inlet inhabited by a 50-foot-long squid; no one, the doctor is quite certain, could possibly survive, and the course is designed solely to see how long the victim can endure – the doctor is 'interested in pain'. Bond, however, does survive, takes Dr No by surprise as a result, and kills him without difficulty.

The mid-point between these two alternatives, the point occupied by the hero, consists of professionalism. Matt Helm is an excellent incarnation of this, as we saw in his assessment of his ex-wife's views; there is an even clearer representation of it in his earlier confrontation with a rather inept thug hired by the villain:

'All right for you, Buster,' he said in his best, menacing tone. 'You want it here, you can have it here, the full treatment!' He started forward.

I took my hand out of my pocket and gave the little snap of the wrist that flicks that kind of knife open if you keep it properly cleaned and oiled and know the technique. Opening it two-handed is safer and more reliable, but it doesn't impress people nearly so much. Tony's eyes widened slighly, and he stopped coming. This wasn't supposed to happen. When you pulled knives on suckers and squares, they turned pale green and backed off fearfully; they didn't come up with blades of their own.

He hesitated, saw that my cutting implement was only about half the length of his, regained confidence, and came in fast. I was tempted to play with him a bit, but it was hot, I was tired and sleepy, and when you start playing cat-and-mouse with human beings you deserve trouble and sometimes get it. I sidestepped his clumsy thrust, moved inside the knife, clamped a good hold on his arm, and made one neat surgical cut. The knife dropped from his fingers.[8]

The sequence develops with the inevitability guaranteed by the hero's ironical description of his opponent, and this representation of his superiority is an intrinsic part of the reader's enjoyment of the situation.

Another instance occurs in Bond's defeat of Red Grant in *From Russia, With Love*. Grant describes, with obvious relish, how Bond has fallen completely for the programmed trap designed for him by SMERSH's planner, a chess Grand Master and – anachronistically, one hopes for the sake of the U.S.S.R. – a Pavlovian psychologist; the detail which especially interests Bond is that he is to be killed with a single bullet through the heart at the exact moment that the train they are in enters the Simplon Tunnel. In the interim, therefore, Bond slips his cigarette case between the pages of his book and, at the appropriate moment, places the book over his heart. The ruse works, Grant believes he is dead, and Bond, profiting from his carelessness, manages to kill him after a brief struggle.

This is professionalism, not only in that it is skilled – bureaucratic planning has its own skills – but in that it represents a combination of improvisation and programming. At the outset of his mission Bond is given a specially constructed briefcase:

> In each of the innocent sides there was a flat throwing knife, built by Wilkinsons, the sword makers, and the tops of their handles were concealed cleverly by the stitching at the corners. ... More important was the thick tube of Palmolive shaving cream in the otherwise guileless spongebag. The whole top of this unscrewed to reveal the silencer for the Beretta, packed in cotton wool. In case hard cash was needed, the lid of the attaché case contained fifty golden sovereigns. These could be poured out by slipping sideways one ridge of welting.
>
> The complicated bag of tricks amused Bond, but he also had to admit that, despite its eight-pound weight, the bag was a convenient way of carrying the tools of his trade, which would otherwise have to be concealed about his body.[9]

His assessment of the 'bag of tricks' is ironical, but when it comes to the crisis, he utilizes this careful preparation; he organizes his sham death in such a way that he falls at a point only inches from 'the little attaché case – within inches of the lateral stitching that held the flat-bladed throwing knives ... that he had mocked when Q branch had demonstrated the catch that held them.'[10]

His defeat of Grant depends on a combination of planning for just such contingencies, and the ability to improvise. Pure planning would put him in the position of Grant, unable to respond flexibly to unexpected situations because – according to the plan – there are no unexpected situations. Mere improvisation would leave him defenceless, for through lack of experience and training there would be no *expected* situations. His ability to assess the possibilities of the situation calmly, given the high probability of imminent death, to make a rapid contingency plan, and – above all – to fight, hand to hand, is the result of years of practice; but at the same time the years of practice have not dulled his capacity for fresh thought.

Spillane's heroes are similarly professional. At the end of *The By-Pass Control* Tiger Mann hunts down a Soviet spy in the middle of a tract of deserted sand-dunes:

I stoppped long enough to study the topography, trying to choose the exact spot he would have picked for the ambush.

There was one, a peculiarly shaped dune that seemed to have a dish-shaped back that covered all fields of fire and could hide a man completely from anyone making an assault . . .

I started up the incline.

Above me the low flying gull wheeled suddenly and made a startled ninety degree turn toward the water, flapping in to land beside the sandpipers.

It was enough. The gull had seen him first.

That dune was a clever trap. It was the spot I'd look for. There was only one other left.

The waiting was over. I ran.

He was half buried in a hollow he had dug for himself, secure in the knowledge that he controlled the action . . .

He had it too, that feeling for the *thing*. He knew I was there when I came over the rise . . .[11]

His opponent too is a professional, but this does not alter the reason for Tiger Mann's victory: he is able to out-think the other, and his near-instinctive assessment is based, like Bond's plan, on a combination of experience and a capacity for improvisation.

This combination is also reflected in Spillane's style. Undoubtedly one of the sources of his success is the unflagging pace at which his novels move, and this is due more to the narrative style ('tough style') than to the multiplication of incidents such as murder or sexual encounter that are dramatic *per se*. The particular elliptical quality that is responsible for the attraction of Spillane's style is intended to incarnate the hero's capacity for understanding of and intervention in the world. For instance: Mike Hammer is spotted by a girl 'in a dress that was too tight a year ago . . .'; she 'decided I could afford a wet evening for two and walked over with her hips waving hello'. The incident is presented in such a way as to make it dramatic, but at the same time the choice of phrase demonstrates that the hero understands the situation perfectly; thus when she speaks to him, he knows how to answer her. Similarly: 'He snapped a light off, threw a couple of switches and picked up the slugs. While he was running the photos I walked to the window ...' Again the mundane has been dramatized, and the choice of term used to represent the actions suggests that the hero is thoroughly familiar with this kind of operation. On occasions it is clear that the choice of term used is intended to suggest that an action is so much the product of a learnt-by-rote process that it has become a technique that could as it were be applied without thought: 'I ran through a list of names in my head and couldn't place it'; 'I put it through my mind again, nodded, and said ...'; 'I said, "If you want me, leave a call at Donniger's". His mind closed on the name ...' What occurs is that the hero applies a standardized technique to new information, 'processes' it.[12]

In Spillane's style one sees very clearly all the features that characterize professionalism: the incidents are dramatic, but the hero, because of his years of experience coupled with the ability to assimilate new information and to react in a flexible manner when the occasion demands, is perfectly capable of dealing with them.

The professionalism of the hero betokens a man who is responsive to socialization (as opposed to the total amateur) but who manages to retain his individuality, incarnated in initiative (as opposed to the bureaucrat). In him the demands of society and of individualism are reconciled. His professionalism is also skill, and it is a skill in acts that are presented as deviant, not recommendable for the majority of the population; the reason why his superior skill should be incarnated in deviant acts will become clear later.

Conspiracy

The professionalism of the hero is dedicated to a confrontation with conspiracy of one kind or another. It is probably the sense of moral outrage provoked by this attempted subversion of the 'normal' world that provides one of the fundamental components of the thriller.

Fleming and Spillane form an excellent contrast in this respect. In Fleming's novels the conspiracy is identified with the character of the villain, a person who is certainly non-British, frequently the result of miscegenation (Dr No, Red Grant, Blofeld, etc.), and invariably endowed with moral characteristics calculated to alienate the reader's sympathies; witness these comments by Largo, one of the villains of *Thunderball*, discussing the 'interrogation' of his girl-friend, whom Bond has persuaded to defect:

'I brought her back to consciousness and questioned her, she refused to talk. In due course I shall force her to do so and then she will be eliminated. ... I see no reason to be dismayed by this occurrence. But I am in favour of a most rigorous interrogation.' No. 5 turned his head politely in Largo's direction. 'There are certain uses of electricity of which I have knowledge. The human body cannot resist them. If I can be of any assistance ...'

Largo's voice was equally polite. They might have been discussing a seasick passenger. 'Thank you. I have means of persuasion that I have found satisfactory in the past. But I shall certainly call upon you if the case is an obstinate one.[13]

This bureaucratic attitude towards human suffering is nauseous.

In Spillane, on the other hand, the conspiracy is usually anonymous; the villain is either a shadowy figure with a central European name, who appears only through the traces of brutal killings, and – eventually – in a face-to-face confrontation with the hero in a remote and unlikely location, where he is killed; or the villain is someone whom the hero trusts implicitly and knows well, in 50 per cent of the novels the girl the hero was sleeping with: in Spillane the essence of villainy is treachery.

In any event, the reader must be made to feel that the security of a world-order that he values is threatened by a conspiracy: not the open antagonism of another nation that declares war, but the covert attacks of thieves, murderers, spies: deviants and perverts of every kind. The theory of deviancy in its early manifestations (deviancy=social pathology) is very similar to the cosmology of the thriller, for both rest upon the identification of a given social order with the *natural* order of things, and disruptions are therefore *unnatural*. Hence the presence of such caricatural villains as Balek in James Mayo's *Let Sleeping Girls Lie*:

Balek was over six feet tall, taller than Hood, his body and legs thin and almost rod-like with none of the form of muscles. The forehead receded rapidly with lank hair hanging straight back over it and, between the eyes, a great dark hooked horny protuberance emerged like a beak. The unblinking eyes were staring at Hood's like a bird's. The skin was dark; there was a tiny mouth underneath the great beak. The man – if you could call it a man – wore a sort of smock and was barefoot. Hood was aghast.[14]

Balek is literally an unnatural irruption into the world; Largo is only 'morally unnatural'. In either case the reader is intended to feel a sense of outrage similar in kind to that felt by Mike Hammer in the passage quoted earlier from *One Lonely Night*.

The threat that the conspiracy constitutes must be averted by the superior professionalism of the hero. This superiority consists of more adequate adaptation to the world in which the action is placed, the underworld. The hero thus has to use the means of the underworld – violence, deceit – and is fully justified in suspending the norms of 'justified suspicion' or habeas corpus, since the conspiracy is aimed precisely at establishing some sort of tyranny where these democratic luxuries would all disappear. It is for this reason that the hero is normally someone whose connections with normal law enforcement agencies is tenuous; a P.I., a spy, an undercover agent of some sort.

When the hero uses violence he does so in hot blood (Bond, on various occasions, expresses great aversion to killing in cold blood) and the passion involved in large part exonerates the hero in the eyes of the reader: this personal hatred fuses with the sense of moral outrage provoked by the behaviour of the conspirators, and the sense of exclusion from 'our' world that is projected onto the villain makes his death seem more than justified; for its justice is never questioned.

Competition

It is self-evident that the hero must prove himself superior to the forces of evil that threaten the world in order to emerge the hero, not only morally, but also in his practice: he must win. (The exception is John le Carré, where the hero is a tragic figure). What is less obvious is that the hero also has to prove himself superior to the world he is saving. This is manifest in his relationships with his colleagues.

Despite the fact that he is basically a lone wolf, the hero enjoys the support of a 'back-up team': Bond has the Secret Service and friends such as Leiter, Mathis, and Tanaka; Mike Hammer has Velda and Pat Chambers. However, this support is rarely much use to him: in the last resort the hero is nearly always solely responsible for victory, and if anyone else is present it is usually in a passive, helpless capacity. The ending of Spillane's *Bloody Sunrise* is typical: the villain, as so frequently in Spillane, is the girl, Sonia, Tiger Mann was sleeping with and protecting; she and her associates trap Mann, his fiancée, Rondine, and two others in a deserted house and leave them, inextricably trussed, with a time bomb; by pretending to admit defeat, however, Mann has managed to make Sonia careless, and she takes, along with the incriminating statement in his own handwriting that she has made him sign, the ballpoint pen he used, which contains a powerful, miniaturized, silent time bomb; escaping painfully from his bonds he renders the time bomb left to kill them harmless, and he and his friends hear the explosion that kills Sonia.

It is no exaggeration to say that the role of the support team is to show how superior the hero is, in other words to demonstrate that he is, in the full sense of the word, the hero. The closing sequence of Carter Brown's *The Body* is another instance.

Carter Brown's hero, throughout his series, is Al Wheeler, an 'unorthodox' police lieutenant previously employed by military intelligence. To solve this case Wheeler provokes the villain, Rodinoff, into shooting someone in his presence, but with no other witnesses, and then shoots him. The solution is, to say the least, of dubious legality, and he tells the Sheriff that Rodinoff committed suicide in his presence; his boss is unimpressed, since the story will sound thin in court and anyway he had had a tail on Rodinoff for days and would soon have apprehended him by more regular means. He then notices that Wheeler is wounded (there was a brief exchange of shots that ended in Rodinoff's death) and the true story emerges:

> It was my turn to stare. 'Then what made you suspect Rodinoff?'
>
> 'I didn't suspect Rodinoff,' he said coldly.
>
> 'Then why put a twenty-four-a-day tail on him?'
>
> 'Dammit!' he roared. 'I didn't! That was fiction. I couldn't stand listening to you any more. I have my pride, though what use it is to me I'm not sure! You think I liked standing here listening to you telling me how I'd fallen down on my job! I had to say something!'
>
> He grinned at me suddenly. 'I should resign and give you my job, Wheeler. But I won't, of course!' he added hastily. 'You had every moral right to kill Rodinoff, even if you had no legal rights. The story of the suicide will stick.' [15]

Not only are the support team there to demonstrate, by their own deficiencies, the hero's superiority, but also to provide support for the hero's perspective on the action, his sense of right and wrong, just as the Sheriff does for Al Wheeler in this passage. Similarly, in Spillane's *One Lonely Night* Hammer is castigated in court by a judge who sees him as no better than the criminals he has killed. Hammer's view of events, that the end justifies the means, is supported by Velda and by Pat Chambers, Hammer's fiancée and police captain friend:

> 'Mike ... that judge was a bastard. You're an all-right guy. ... You know it as well as I do. You read the papers. When you're right you're a hero. When you're wrong you're kill happy. Why don't you ask the people who count, the ones who really know you? Ask Pat. He thinks you're a good cop. Ask all the worms in the holes, the ones who have reason to stay out of your way. They'll tell you too ... Mike you're too damn big and tough to give a hang what people say. They're only little people with little minds, so forget it.' [16]

However, the hero's tendency to overlook the norms of the law can result in disagreement with his support team. Velda never questions the justifiability of Hammer's methods, but Pat Chambers does, even though he invariably admits in the end that Hammer was justified; in the long run the Sheriff always backs Wheeler against recrimination and bureaucratic interference, but this support has to be constantly renegotiated, for

Wheeler's unorthodoxy is a permanent bone of contention. Similarly, in *Murderer's Row*, Helm decides to disobey the orders sent to him from Washington:

'I got your message.'

'Yes, sir.'

'Independence is a virtue, I'm told, but there are arguments in favour of discipline. We will discuss the matter later. .... What did the little Michaelis girl have to propose?'

'She has hired me to assassinate Mrs Louis Rosten in a discreet way. Twenty-five hundred down, twenty-five hundred on delivery. I've only collected five C's so far, but I'm getting the rest tomorrow after she's been to the bank.'

It silenced him briefly. I'd hoped it might. He asked at last, 'What are your plans?'

I said, 'I thought the deal was that no questions would be asked.'

'That was in another connection. You can't very well ...'

'Can't I?' I asked. 'How important is this machine of Dr Michaelis? The last I heard the fate of the world hung in the balance.'

'But ...' I heard him swallow at the other end of the line. He thought I was needling him, but he wasn't quite sure. Well, I wasn't quite sure, either. He called my bluff. 'Very well. Use your judgement.' [17]

Put simply, the support team basically have the same perspective on events as the hero, but just as they are incapable of solving the mystery without him, so politically, or morally, they are never quite certain about how far they ought to support him; his practical capacities, the need they have for him, enables him to command support; but this support has to be constantly renegotiated. This aspect of heroism was long ago the subject of a perceptive comment by Ralph Waldo Emerson:

Heroism works in contradiction to the voice of mankind and in contradiction, for a time, to the voice of the great and good. Heroism is an obedience to a secret impulse of an individual's character. .... Therefore, just and wise men take umbrage at his act, until some little time be past; then they see it to be in unison with their acts. ...

Self-trust is the essence of heroism. It is the state of the soul at war, and its ultimate objects are the last defiance of falsehood and wrong, and the power to bear all that can be inflicted by evil agents. [18]

Politics and Deviance

It is clear that the hero must be a competitive person in order to be the hero: he has to demonstrate that he can always go one better than even the people closest to him. It is the contention here that in the thriller competitiveness is always seen as intrinsically bound in with isolation.

Isolation

Nowhere is this isloation seen more clearly than in the hero's sexual relationships. In Fleming, Bond's relationships with women are clearly demarcated, in true public-school fashion, into the twin categories of companionship and sex. The category of companionship applies to the secretaries at Secret Service headquarters:

> She [his secretary] was tall and dark with a reserved, unbroken beauty which the war and five years in the Service had lent a touch of sternness. Unless she married soon, Bond thought for the hundredth time, or had a lover, her cool air of authority might easily become spinsterish ...
> Bond had told her as much, often, and he and the two other members of the 00 Section had at various times made determined assaults on her virtue. She had handled them all with the same cool motherliness (which, to salve their egos, they privately defined as frigidity) ...
> But the new [secretary], Mary Goodnight, an ex-Wren with blue-black hair, blue eyes, and 37–22–35, was a honey and there was a private five-pound sweep in the Section as to who would get her first.[19]

It is difficult to imagine anyone running a sweepstake on the heroines of the novels, or Bond 'making a determined assault upon the virtue' of any of the women he actually sleeps with: the schoolboyish notions are a mark of the impossibility, or undesirability, of sexual relationships with these women.

The relationships with the heroines, on the other hand, are of course entirely sexual. What is less obvious is that their premises are antagonism and hostility.

Two instances: Tiffany (*Diamonds Are Forever*) and Tracy (*On Her Majesty's Secret Service*). Tiffany is a diamond smuggler, and Bond poses as a small-time crook who wants to join the gang; when they meet her attitude is blatantly hostile:

> The girl raised her eyes from looking at her face and inspected him in the mirror, briefly and coolly.
>
> 'I guess you're the new help,' she said in a low, rather husky voice that made no committment. 'Take a seat and enjoy the music. Best light record ever made.'
>
> Bond was amused. He obediently took a few steps to a deep armchair . . .
>
> 'Do you mind if I smoke?' he said . . .
>
> 'If that's the way you want to die.'
>
> Miss Case resumed the silent contemplation of her face in the mirror . . .[20]

The calculated indifference continues throughout their first meeting, but as they meet more often her attitude changes, and eventually, aware that Bond is on the other side, she helps him to escape from the gang who have beaten him up, and they sleep together; the end of the novel promises happiness for both, but by the beginning of the next in the series she has left him and married another man.

Similar hostility is found in Bond's meeting with Tracy. They have raced each other through the countryside and she has won, eventually disappearing from sight. By coincidence they go to the same hotel, where Bond finds out who she is, and later meet in the local casino. She gambles beyond her means, and Bond, to save her from the disgrace of blacklisting, pays her debts, and goes to have a drink with her:

> She looked at him gravely, considering him. Then she also drank. She said. 'My name is Tracy. That is short for all the names you were told at the reception in the hotel. Teresa was a saint. I am not a saint. The manager is perhaps a romantic. He told me of your enquiries. So shall we go now? I am not interested in conversation. And you have earned your reward.'
>
> She rose abruptly. So did Bond, confused. 'No. I will go alone. You can come later. The number is 45. There, if you wish, you can make the most expensive piece of love of your life. It will have cost you forty million francs. I hope it will be worth it.'[21]

The hostility is, of course, overcome, in nearly every case, but if happiness is the result, it is invariably temporary. Bond may, at the end of *Diamonds Are Forever*, be very happy with Tiffany, and he may even marry Tracy in the final chapter of *On Her Majesty's Secret Service*: Tiffany leaves him and Tracy is shot as they drive off on their honeymoon. The conventions of the thriller demand that the hero be sexually alone at the beginning of any novel.

The second aspect of Fleming's sexuality that is significant is its therapeutic value for the girl. The great majority of the heroines are, in one way or another, below par when Bond meets them, and the relationship with Bond has an improving effect upon them: Vesper, Solitaire, Tiffany, Tatiana, Pussy, Domino persuaded to abandon their allegiance to Communism or gangsterism and to collaborate with the Secret Service; Tiffany, Honeychile, Pussy, Tracy, Kissy, Vivienne all cured of Lesbianism or frigidity. To point out that in the Bond world it is the male who is dominant is to underline the obvious.

Spillane is in some ways a contrast, for although on the surface his heroes totally dominate their women, this domination overlays fear. One passage will illustrate this:

... directing every essence of her nudity towards [me] in a tantalizing manner as if an impenetrable wall of glass separated [us] so that she could taunt and torture with immunity, laying a feast of desire before a starving man who could see and smell and want, but couldn't get through the barrier...

She came closer to the invisible wall, tempting me with her delights, daring me, and when she couldn't fathom my response became even more abandoned in her offering.

It was she who broke the barrier down. She had laid the feast but had given way to her own hunger and knew that the prisoner was really herself and threw herself across the space that separated us with a moan torn from her own throat, then she was a warm, slithering thing that tried to smother me with a passion she could no longer suppress.[22]

This is a remarkable passage. The man remains aloof, retaining control over his own sexuality until the woman has abandoned herself to what is presented as an animal appetite ('warm, slithering thing'); sexuality is a 'feast', but a feast that arouses a hunger that is incompatible with self-control, a hunger to which one becomes a 'prisoner'. It is because sexuality is seen in these terms that the man is only willing to abandon himself after the woman has done so; and it is because sexual appetite is incarnated in woman that woman constitutes a threat to the male ego: the temptation is to self-control, and it is the role of the ego to impose this control. This is no doubt also one of the reasons why the hero's mistress is so frequently the villain of the piece. Moreover, even when treachery does not occur, each of the two main heroes has the obsessive memory of a woman who betrayed and attempted to kill him years before: this narrative convention is an excellent portrayal of the threat that the hero feels from any woman.

The heroes' permanent companions (Velda, Rondine) constitute a measure of exception, since they are absolutely to be trusted, and the relationship that the hero has with them is sexual: Hammer breathes heavily whenever he sets eyes on Velda, but never sleeps with her as he wants to marry a virgin; Tiger Mann, being a hero of the sixties, does sleep with Rondine. However, it is questionable to what extent their roles as companion and as sexual partner fuse together, for whenever they are in the role of sexual partner, their behaviour and the hero's responses are evoked in the same terms as the confrontations between the hero and other girls. In so far as sex exists in Spillane's world, it is an aggressive and fear-based sexuality.

In neither Fleming nor Spillane can there be the kind of reciprocity and solidarity that is the basis of everyday adult sexual relationships in the real world, for the hero has to be constantly on his guard, constantly aware of the antagonisms between himself and the girl; the nature of the fear and the antagonisms are different in the two authors, but the distance and the isolation are constant.

This sexual isolation is only the most striking example of a general isolation that results from the hero's irregular institutional position (P.I., spy, etc.) and from the necessity to prove himself superior to his support team.

It is hardly the case that the sexuality of thriller heroes is, in any very meaningful sense of the word, 'deviant'. But it is certainly presented as unusual: the sexual encounters, which are intended to titillate the reader, gain their dramatic impact from the implicit contrast with the daily experience of their readers – a *Sunday Times* reviewer, quoted on the cover of *On Her Majesty's Secret Service*, suggested that Bond was 'what every man would like to be and what every woman would like between her sheets'. As with the hero's professionalism in violence, the fact that he is glamorously unusual is essential.

The Contribution of Thrillers to Ideology

It is possible to argue that the hero's qualities and behaviour are an eminently rational response to the nature of the world in which he finds himself; this is perfectly true. However, thrillers are fiction, and there is no guarantee that the world is really like this at all. It may be that the world is portrayed in thrillers as hostile and conspiracy-ridden solely in order to justify the hero behaving in the manner in which he does. Or – to put it more accurately – the hostile world and the aggressive, competitive, isolated hero are a symbolic pair, each of which is only defined in terms of the other; moreover, the world is only the rotten place that it is in the thriller because everyone else behaves in the same way as the hero, or tries to.

Thus the focal point of the thriller, its central contribution to ideology, is the delineation of a personality that is isolated and competitive and who wins because he is better adapted to the world than everyone else. This superiority is incarnated in acts that are deliberately and explicitly deviant, and yet justified. The individuality, the personal worth of the hero is presented as inseparable from the performances of actions that in any other circumstances would be reprehensible; yet at the same time the 'circumstances' are a fictional construct, designed to justify the pleasure that the reader derives from the representation of such acts. Individualism is inherently anarchic, the thriller asserts, but this is palliated by the objective effects of the hero's actions, the saving of the world. It would appear that only in the performance of such acts is the hero able to assert both his individuality (isolated and competitive) and his sociability (to save the world). It is for this reason, too, that his professionalism is important: the amateur is chronically ectopic, totally anarchic by default of personal capability, and the bureaucrat is over-socialized; the hero has the best of both worlds.

What the thriller does, essentially, is explore the various ramifications of the proposition, common enough in our society, that the individual must be competitive in order to be an individual:

True equality, so conceived, is incompatible with the recognition of quality, not only in the shop-keeper's sense of special excellence, but also in the philosopher's sense of distinctive character. For all diversities between one human being and another ... involve some superiority and some inferiority, actual or potential. Differences distinguish and divide: they make possible, and ... inevitable, the hierarchies and hostilities that give rise to so great a proportion of the suffering we see around us. ...

In a civilized society, then, men cannot – at any rate, as long as human differences flourish uncurtailed – enjoy to the full the benefits both of freedom and of equality; they must either consent to inhibitions on the development of their natural selves or accept inequality with all its unhappy consequences. Therefore, if you want people to develop freely within a social system and also to escape the evils that inequality entails, you must prevent or neutralize as far as you can those differences that set some men against and above their fellows: you must anticipate the equality of the grave by perpetuating ... the equality of the cradle and the womb.[23]

References

1. HOWARD HAYCROFT, *Murder for Pleasure* (Appleton-Century, 1941), p. 316. I have chosen to deal exclusively with the area of the 'tough thriller' in this article on the grounds that it is now this version that is the commoner of the two in popular entertainment – when one of Dorothy Sayers's Lord Peter Wimsey novels was serialized recently on TV, it was the period nostalgia that was the source of entertainment rather than the tension associated with thrillers nowadays. Given that this restriction is imposed, it is reasonable to concentrate on the most successful writers in the genre – Spillane and Fleming – since others tend

to imitate these, for good commercial reasons. In practice it is perfectly possible to integrate into the paradigm both the polite thriller, deriving from Sherlock Holmes, and the 'tough thriller' of the 1930s – Chandler, Hammett, Macdonald – with only superficial alterations. Lack of space prevents this here, and the reader is referred to my forthcoming book *Ideology of the Thriller*, which deals with everything from Hoffmansthal and Poe onwards.

2. GEORGE ORWELL, 'Raffles and Miss Blandish', *Collected Essays* (Mercury Books, 1961), p. 258.

3. Quoted in *The Times* (9 August 1971).

4. MICKEY SPILLANE, *One Lonely Night* (Corgi, 1961), p. 207. References are not to the first editions of any of the thrillers quoted, but to a standard English paperback edition. Since the format of paperbacks changes every now and again, page references can be taken to refer to the edition cited.

5. IAN FLEMING, *The Spy Who Loved Me* (Pan, 1967), pp. 169–70.

6. DONALD HAMILTON, *The Removers* (Coronet Books, 1966), p. 153.

7. IAN FLEMING, *Thunderball* (Pan, 1963), pp. 58–9.

8. DONALD HAMILTON, op. cit., p. 83.

9. IAN FLEMING, *From Russia With Love* (Pan, 1959), pp. 91–2.

10. ibid., p. 197.

11. MICKEY SPILLANE, *The By-Pass Control* (Corgi, 1968), pp. 210–11.

12. Quotations taken from, respectively: *The Big Kill* (Corgi, 1960), p. 7; *Day of the Guns* (Corgi, 1966), p. 126; *Bloody Sunrise* (Corgi, 1966), p. 8; *Kiss Me, Deadly* (Corgi, 1961), p. 143; 'Man Alone' in *Killer Mine* (Corgi, 1965), p. 100.

13. IAN FLEMING, *Thunderball*, pp. 203–4.

14. JAMES MAYO, *Let Sleeping Girls Lie* (Pan, 1967), p. 71.

15. CARTER BROWN, *The Body* (Four Square, 1963), p. 125.

16. MICKEY SPILLANE, *One Lonely Night*, pp. 19–20.

17. DONALD HAMILTON, *Murderer's Row* (Coronet, 1966), pp. 58–9.

18. RALPH WALDO EMERSON, *Essays*, First Series, No. 8 (Macmillan, 1911), p. 206.

19. IAN FLEMING, *Moonraker* (Pan, 1959), p. 30.

20. IAN FLEMING, *Diamonds Are Forever* (Pan, 1958), p. 30.

21. IAN FLEMING, *On Her Majestey's Secret Service*, pp. 34–5.

22. MICKEY SPILLANE, *The Death Dealers* (Corgi, 1967), p. 110.

23. JOHN SPARROW, *Times Saturday Review* (23 January 1971).

Paul Walton*

The Case of the Weathermen: Social Reaction and Radical Commitment

A new Weatherman catchword was 'barbarism'. The Weathermen see themselves as playing a role similar to that of the Barbarian tribes, such as the Vandals and the Visigoths, who invaded and destroyed the decadent, corrupt Rome. (Some Weathermen even suggested changing their name to the Vandals.) This would have a double meaning, first a reference to the barbarian tribe; second a reference to the line from Bob Dylan's 'Subterranean Homesick Blues' – 'The pump won't work 'cause the vandals stole the handle'. The name Weathermen comes from a line in the same song – 'You don't need a weatherman to know which way the wind blows.' [1]

Despite the rapid spread of militant political deviancy in the U.S.A. and the U.K., there is little indication that sociologists are seriously attempting to study or analyse the phenomenon. With a few notable exceptions, the emergence of groups like the Weathermen and Mad Dog in the U.S.A. and the Angry Brigade in Britain has led merely to shoulder-shrugging, easy dismissal, or such theoretical gems as the statement that these deviants are either 'out of their caps', or 'financed by C.I.A.'.

Indeed, despite the emergence of a mass student revolt in May 1968, despite the rise of violent revolutionary youth movements, anecdotes and speculation still tend to guide one in the study of political deviancy, and this crystallizes the objections which many radical deviancy theorists have felt

* I would like to thank Jock Young, Ian Taylor, Laurie Taylor, Graham Murdock and Paul Rock, for their helpful advice and criticism even where ignored. I must stress that whatever theoretical originality this paper possesses is in part derived and dependent upon collaborative work which will appear in Ian Taylor, Paul Walton and Jock Young, *The New Criminology: For a Social Theory of Deviance*, Routledge and Kegan Paul, 1973.

towards social theory – that it is unable to deal with the unorthodox except in a trivial manner.

Much of even the very best of recent American theorizing in fact looks mundanely like 'common sense' when faced with the task of analysing political radicalism. An example here is Lemert's clear statement of the Social Reaction perspective. He notes the turn away from the belief that crime and deviance give rise to social control and he states: 'I have come to believe that the reverse idea, i.e. that social control leads to deviance, is equally tenable and is potentially a richer premise for studying deviance in modern society.' [2]

This is of course hardly new to anybody who has looked at the radical left, where the recognition of the repressive existence of social control and its consequences has always been ideologically very central. At its crudest, the position of radicals has always been that social control prevents social change, and that therefore social control leads to the need for social revolution, or political deviation. Of course Lemert meant much more than this by his statement – as the rest of his work indicates – yet some of the most advanced social reaction positions do little more than indicate that the powerful have a virtual monopoly over the way in which social action is defined and treated. Moreover, when Howard Becker stated the following, he was dealing with yesterday's papers as far as the left was concerned:

> The question of what the purpose or goal (function) of a group is and, consequently, what things will help or hinder the achievement of that purpose, is very often a political question ... if this is true, then it is likewise true that the questions of what rules are to be enforced, what behaviour regarded as deviant and what people labelled as outsiders must also be regarded as political. [3]

How can we, then, apply deviancy theory to the understanding of a deviant group whose perspectives and reflexivity are often as developed as, and in some cases, superior to, the framework which is intended to explain them? It is not surprising, as Stuart Hall has indicated, that political deviancy does not figure prominently in the study of deviant behaviour. He states:

Becker suggests that this is because, in many forms of social deviancy, 'the conflicting segments or ranks are not organized for conflict; no one attempts to alter the shape of the hierarchy'. This, despite the fact that the definition of deviancy as a 'social problem', the labelling process, and the enforcement of social controls all contain an intrinsically political component. Horowitz and Liebowitz argue that 'deviance has been studied by employing a consensus-welfare model rather than a conflict model'.[4] This has tended to suppress the political element in deviant transactions with straight society.[5]

The intention here is to show that the problem goes deeper than the choice of appropriate models, and that it can force us to re-examine some of the salient assumptions of deviancy theory. I wish here to use an analysis of the Weathermen to repeat and develop one or two criticisms of existing theory which have appeared elsewhere,[6] for precisely this purpose of examining assumptions.

Recent developments in deviancy theory have rid us of the ridiculous. By the ridiculous I mean the kind of social theorizing which wrote off much deviant behaviour as clinically pathological or irrational. It has, for example, rid us of the need to take seriously statements like the following which reflect little more than the ideological prejudices of the psychiatric profession. Writing on 'Why Students Protest', Seymour L. Halleck asserts:

... there can be no true understanding of such a complex human phenomenon as protest without examining *the specific psychological needs* * of individual protesters. Psychiatrists often find that a patient will join a protest movement immediately following a failure in school or a rejection by a close friend. *In such cases, activism must be understood as something more than an intellectual or idealistic commitment.* There appears to be an inverse relationship between teaching of despair and activism. At the time of Berkeley Free Speech controversy, admissions to the student psychiatric clinic dropped markedly. I have noted similar trends at the Universtiy of Wisconsin. During a massive protest of the draft which resulted in a sit-in, three of my patients cancelled their therapy hours. In each case they remarked that psychotherapy seemed meaningless when there were so many important things to do.[7]

* Unless otherwise stated, all italics are the author's.

Politics and Deviance

Deviancy theory teaches its students to distrust psychologizing and to seek analysis which is truer to the deviant phenomenon; but whether it can really move beyond this is questionable. Its attraction and success so far depend on its superiority over the comments of professional psychiatrists, psychologists, and criminologists whose theories take flight into mysticism. Deviancy theory looked radical, for it enabled its students to mock those who resorted to a language similar to that of their paymasters. 'Those bums at Berkeley' as President Nixon would have it, or, in the words of a departed Minister of Education, Edward Short, '... it is high time one or two of those thugs were out on their neck ... they are just a mixed group of wreckers, some Maoist, some just Brand X revolutionaries'.[8] In a context of this kind, deviancy theorists have obviously looked radical in their explanations. But have they adequately described the political and structural contexts in question?

The Social Reaction Approach

There is no a-theoretical approach to some 'real' world: the world is situated, understood and located via our theory, and, in this sense, there are only two types of theory: the good and the bad. Some of it *is* bad – and indeed much deviancy theory perpetuates 'reification'; this is, it accepts an estranged society as normal, and deviances from such a society as 'abnormal'. But in the under-studied area of political deviance the limitations of doing this are clearly exposed. As Horowitz and Liebowitz note in their seminal article, written in 1968:

The traditional distinction between social problems and the political system is becoming obsolete. Behaviour which in the past was perceived as social deviance is now assuming well-defined ideological and organisational contours, while political marginals are adopting a deviant life-style. This merger of social deviance and political marginality creates a new style of politics, based on strategies that are traditionally considered illegitimate. The result of this trend is estimated to be an increase in the use of violence as a political tactic, and the development of a revolutionary potential among the expanding ranks of deviant sub-groups.[9]

These insights have been rapidly confirmed – for the end of the sixties and the beginning of the seventies have indeed witnessed an increase in the use of violence as a political tactic, which has in consequence forced some of us to transcend our Ivory Tower theories. In England, the first really cogent attack on deviancy theory was produced by Taylor and Taylor in their radical article 'We Are All Deviants Now', in which they suggested that much deviancy theory is underpinned by little more than a conservative theory of values. They argued that:

The 'magic' words in this type of theorization are values, goals, norms and status; individuals in society are seen as playing a gigantic fruit-machine; but the machine is rigged and only some players are consistently rewarded. The deprived ones then resort to kicking the machine or to leaving the fun-palace altogether (e.g. attacks on property or involvement in drug-taking sub-cultures). Nobody appears to ask who put the machine there in the first place, and who it is who takes the profits. Criticism of the game is confined to changing the pay-out sequence so that the deprived can get a better deal. What at first sight looks like a major critique of society (that is, anomie theory) ends by taking the existing society for granted. Much of the same may be said about labelling (or transactional) theory which also attracts its share of radical adherents. This concentrates on the way in which those who accidentally or unintentionally break the rules governing the playing of the machine are dealt with by society, by describing the way in which people are defined by others (by social reaction) as delinquents, drug addicts, or mental patients. In other words, it is concerned with those who by their actions turn others into social problems. Again, what starts out as an attack upon the official and unofficial power-holders in society (e.g. probation officers, teachers and policemen) emerges as a complex theoretical edifice with arguable psychological assumptions and considerable political ambiguity. Of course there are definers and defined but what do the definers represent? What interests are they defending? How do their actions reinforce the existing nature of capitalist society? No answers to such questions are provided: the definers are a group of free-floating 'baddies'.[10]

So labelling theory, which appeared to many of us to offer a radical promise, seems to fall short. We must know why.

The short answer is that whilst it acts as an explosive demystifier of cruder, more reified theories, labelling 'theory' is not in fact so much a theory as a method. Labelling theorists or transactionalists have merely *informed* the study of deviancy by borrowing from phenomenology. They have insisted that a definition or label is a meaning placed on an action by others and that it is not the action itself. They have thus insisted that the same action can be endowed with several meanings, and that these may vary. But if it is true that certain social meanings are only acceptable in certain social contexts, then the social meanings of acts and the choice to commit them are not as variable as many of these theorists would have them be.

In this way, we are forced to confront one of the central assumptions of this 'theory' – encapsulated in the statement of Howard Becker's that '*deviance is not a quality of the act the person commits*'.[11] Becker's statement can only be true of physical action; that is, an action to which no social meaning has yet been given. I would suggest that deviants, like every other actor, frequently endow their action with meaning; and that, further, this meaning is not re-invented on each occasion that individuals engage in physical action. Rather, it is derived from a fairly constant stock of social meanings which exist to describe physical acts. It is only by crudely opposing physical to social action that the transactionalists, or more especially Becker and Lemert, can claim that an action is only deviant when so defined by others. Their approach is, almost unwittingly, focused on the definition arising in the minds of others. But where is the bank-robber, for example, who is unaware that he is engaged in the social act of stealing? Taking an object (a physical act) without the owner's permission will always be described as stealing in societies where the institution of private property exists.

A central objection, then, to the transactionalist position is that we do not act in a world free of social meaning. With the one exception of 'new' behaviour, it is often clear to people what actions are deviant and what actions are not. In contrast to transactionalist theorists, I would assert that *most deviant behaviour is a quality of the act*, since the way in which we distinguish between behaviour and action is that *behaviour* is merely physical, and *action* has meaning that is socially given. In the now classical example of the marihuana smoker, it is obvious that this activity is motivated by hedonism – but there is a fundamental difference between engaging in an action for pleasure which is approved by everybody, and engaging in a pleasurable act which is regarded by large numbers of people as deviant, and in this case, as illegal. The awareness that an act is deviant fundamentally alters the nature of the choices that an individual makes.

We have here shifted the focus away from the view of the deviant as a passive, ineffectual, stigmatized individual (what Gouldner has called 'man on his back') towards that of a decision-maker who actively violates the moral and legal codes of society. This is obviously of the utmost importance in the case of political deviancy, for our theory must allow of a creative, but purposeful, deviant who consciously decides to transgress law and order. The reliance and dependence by much recent deviancy theory upon the cruder phenomeno-logically-derived arguments has not been adequate in the explanation of such acts of deviance. The processes by which social obligations become defined and established is not viewed by such theorists as involving a process of struggle between large, competing groups, interests and structural positions. And for this reason, the outcome – the everyday conception of what is right, the commonsense world in which both normals and deviants live – is not seen as having been shaped by entrenched positions of power and interest. And, moreover, if indeed it is legitimate to view deviance as a challenge to authority at either the instrumental or oppositional level, it also follows that it must be viewed as ultimately predetermined by struc-tural inequalities and ideological consensus, *no matter how complex the mediatory variables*. From this viewpoint, struc-tured inequalities, preserved and protected by the powerful, act as causal forces preventing actors from pursuing their interests except via deviant means. It is my contention here that much deviance – both 'political' and 'non-political' – *must* be viewed as a struggle or reaction to normalized repression, a breaking-through, as it were, of accepted, taken-for-granted, power-invested common-sense rules. My view of this repression follows Gouldner's statement in *The Coming Crisis of Western Sociology* that:

> The powerful are both ready and able to institutionalize compliance with the moral code at levels congenial to themselves. *Power is amongst other things this ability to enforce one's moral claims.* The powerful can thus conventionalize their moral defaults. As their moral failures become customary and expected, this itself becomes another justification for giving the subordinate group less than it might theoretically claim under the group's common values. It becomes, in short, *normalized repression.*[12]

Whether or not deviants merely neutralize this moral code in order to justify their break-through, or whether they develop an ideological opposition to the code will of course be an important feature in any explanation or classification of deviancy. But, most importantly, to approach deviance in this way has the great virtue of enabling us to identify the missing element of power in the creation of deviancy. If we examine the creation of deviancy and reaction in this way, that is, we do not end up with a completely indeterminate picture: we see that the institution of private property in a structured and inequitable society divides men from men as owners and non-owners. It is in the light of this division that the activities of thieves, police, magistrates, and property-owners become explicable.

Alvin Gouldner came very near to this kind of criticism of modern deviancy theory when he argued that,

> Becker's school of deviance thus views the underdog as someone who is being mismanaged, not as someone who suffers or fights back. Here the deviant is sly, but not defiant; he is tricky but not courageous; he sneers but he does not accuse; he 'makes out' without making a scene. Insofar as this school of theory has a critical edge to it, this is directed at the caretaking institutions who do the mopping-up job, rather than at the master institutions that produce the deviant's suffering.[13]

Gouldner's criticisms are too narrowly focused, however, for the social reaction perspective on deviance would be one necessary element in any fully developed theory; what follows in this paper is an attempt to examine its difficulties and weaknesses in the light of the rise of deviant phenomena which seriously threaten its working assumptions. Modern deviancy theory should not reject the labelling perspective out of hand; it needs, however, to be incorporated into a political sociology of the state.

Deviancy and the Dialectics of Commitment

In the following examination of the Weathermen I have attempted to lay bare the ideological road along which the Weathermen have travelled. My intent is not to criticize but rather to document the self-conscious shifts in their outlook and practice. In tracing the emergence and development of one form of political deviancy, both the utility and the shortcomings of the work of Becker and Lemert are implicitly demonstrated.

The brief history of the Weathermen that follows is startling, for their emergence was both rapid and improbable. The impact of the Weathermen upon the average American was aptly summed up by a Chicago police chief who explained the inability of the police to contain the Weathermen during their 'Days of Rage' by alluding to the fact that, up until then, there had always been a gap between what the radicals said they would do, and what they did in practice. The gap between words and deeds was closed.

But the Weathermen are also useful illustratively in that they present (in an extreme form) a self-consciousness and awareness amongst individuals defined as 'deviant' which much deviancy theory would seem to be incapable of analysing. At present, behaviour which in the past was conceived of as deviant is now assuming well-defined ideological and organizational contours. The politicization of groups such as drug takers and homosexuals is only the most obvious manifestation: any attempt to resist stigmatization, manipulation in the name of therapy, or punishment, is a self-conscious move to change the social order, and in any conception of the political process in terms other than looking at such matters as voting figures, these activities are political. On the other side, political marginals such as the Yippies, the Weathermen, the Situationists, the Black Panthers, are creating new styles of political activity based on strategies traditionally considered criminal.

That is, the Weathermen are important not only in their powerful impact upon American society, but also in their reconciliation of marginality, criminality, and deviancy within an explicitly political grouping. We can in fact use our data on the Weathermen, and political deviants in general, to indicate the direction that criminology and sociology will have to take if it is to rise above mere ideology. The Weathermen provide both empirical *and* theoretical evidence for treating sceptically some central propositions of the social reaction perspective; for they are a self-conscious group of revolutionaries culturally rooted in their recent experiences of American society. Their very name celebrates the youth culture from which they sprang, a youth culture whose many contradictions have found frequent expression in the work of Bob Dylan. They quote Dylan's metaphor, that 'you don't have to be a weatherman to know which way the wind blows', and elevate it to an analysis of political trends. Like the Yippie, Jerry Rubin, they insist that one must *DO IT*. Unlike Rubin, they do not believe that revolution can be fun. And as a self-conscious group of criminal revolutionaries they have experienced the full force of social reaction.

In examining them we shall be examining deviancy theory in two ways. Firstly we shall use their talk, their ideology, to counter the view of all criminals as creatures who are sadly determined by external forces. As one critic of the social reaction approach put it:

One sometimes gets the impression from reading this literature that people go about minding their own business and then – 'wham' – bad society comes along and slaps them with a stigmatized label. Forced into the role of deviant, the individual has little choice but to be deviant.[14]

Anybody who examined the Weathermen would be foolish to write theories that pictured the deviant as a subject in need of pity. We only have to listen to Weathermen rhetoric which deliberately and explicitly sets out to justify criminal positions, not in terms of neutralization but in terms of oppositional imperatives.

In the words of a leading Weatherman, John Jacobs, ex-Columbia University student (speaking at a Weatherman Conference shortly before going underground), the history of today's youth begins with the beat generation in a world which can best be explained via a 'white Devil' theory of history, taking up the need to be 'crazy violent motherfuckers'. 'JJ', as he is known, declared that the Weathermen's position was that 'We're against everything which is good and decent'.[15] At this same conference Bernardine Dorhn stated that the leadership of Weathermen, the Weatherbureau, approved of Charles Manson,

Dig it, first they killed those pigs, then they ate dinner in the same room with them, then they even shoved a fork into a victim's stomach 'Wild'.... In between such raps, the people sang a medley of weathermen songs, high camp numbers such as, 'I'm Dreaming of a White Riot', 'Communism is what we do', and 'We need a Red Party'. Spirited chants broke out too. 'Women's Power', 'Struggling Power', 'Red Army Power' ... 'Charlie Manson power', 'Power to the People', 'Off the Pig'.[16]

Unless one holds to some notion of collective insanity (and one assumes social theorists would reject such an explanation) it is impossible to understand such statements unless we accept that beliefs are choices. For there is no set of determinates known to sociologists which would *force* deviants to talk and act the way the Weathermen do.

The second criticism of social reaction theory which emerges from a study of the Weathermen is bound up with the social psychological assumptions of such theory. Most of their theories of deviance are decontextualized. That is, the importance of the deviants' world view, the meanings which the deviants themselves attach to their initial actions, are seen as unimportant or abitrary, unless they are the result of social reaction. But this assumes society stops and starts; that the interplay of action and social reaction are separable. In fact they are dialectically related. Deviants are part of society all the time. The transactionalists or labelling theorists are not transactional enough. We cannot understand deviant action and the consequent social reaction unless we grasp the role of deviant beliefs in relation to the beliefs of larger society. In this sense the social reaction perspective has been very mechanical in failing to see that deviant beliefs may bring about different kinds of social reaction. There is a difference between being revealed as a homosexual who believes he has genetic faults and being revealed as a homosexual who argues that 'gay is good' and that it is liberating. Again the traditional social reaction perspective has failed to grasp the acceptance of, and seeking for, social reaction, which much political deviancy involves. A clear example of this occurred during the May 'events' in France in 1968, when students reacted to the accusation that they were under the influence of the 'German Jew' Daniel Cohn-Bendit by parading through Paris under banners emblazoned with the slogan 'We Are All German Jews'. This embrace of the deviant label served not only to highlight the spurious (in this case, irrelevant) nature of the label; it also helped to solidify the movement in the face of attempts at a stereotypical dismissal. Even a superficial look at the discussions and objectives within the Weathermen group will enable us to see that political deviancy at least involves the deviant in careful consideration of the image he projects onto society, and the importance of this for his future actions in view of likely social reaction. As one Weatherman convert put it:

The Chicago National Action was conceived by the Weather Bureau as an anti-imperialist action in which a mass of white youths would tear up and smash wide-ranging imperialist targets such as the Conspiracy Trial, high schools, draft boards and induction centres, banks, pig institutes and pigs themselves. The main reason why we chose such a wide range of targets was our desire to project the existence of a fighting force that's out, not primarily to make specific demands, but to totally destroy this imperialist and racist society.[17]

Perhaps the most lucid exposition of the Weatherman view of this action is put by the same convert who importantly was not new to the American movement. He describes the self-criticism sessions on the bus to Chicago in a fashion which reveals a clear attempt to come to terms with possible reaction:

The heaviest part of our struggle on the bus was the discussion on what 'winning' meant in Chicago. Why in past street actions, when we could have offed a pig, did we hold back? Why are we afraid of escalating the struggle and of winning? Why are we, in short, afraid of pushing out our politics and our struggle to the very limit in each tactical situation? Without answering this question, and without successfully overcoming this fear, we would not be able to fight in Chicago.

As the struggle on the bus developed, we realized the reason for our fear. *We were afraid winning in a particular tactical situation would entail the escalation of the struggle*; that is to say, the ruling class and their pigs would increase their attack on us. It would mean that the next time, we would have to fight much harder on a higher level.[18]

Part of the problem with labelling or social reaction theory stems from its confusion concerning the role of thought. In erecting decontextualized psychological theories it has *unnecessarily* limited itself. The centre of this confusion lies in those theories erecting a fairly spurious distinction between primary and secondary deviation. For this distinction blurs the role of beliefs in commitment to a deviant role or identity. The Weathermen on the bus to the Chicago action discussed and fought out the necessity of 'escalating the struggle' in terms of whether it was a correct strategy – a belief question. The debate was not simply over 'how do I see myself' but rather over 'can I take what others are liable to do to me next time'. One suspects that many non-political criminals and deviants ask themselves similar questions. That is, much commitment to a deviant identity does not resolve around 'Am I really a Weatherman?', or rather 'am I really a homosexual or thief?' etc., but rather 'are my objectives worth what I am risking?'. In short, commitment must be a function of a set of beliefs tested against reality, as much as it is a function of social reaction. Yet it is precisely this question which is hidden in the psychologism of much present transactionalism.

We shall examine the context in which the Weatherman believed 'the system' emerged more closely and then return to an examination of deviancy theory.

The American political tradition is full of gaps when compared with the European. It has no real history of Social Democracy or Communism and its radical tradition is more populist, derived from the Wobblies; it is a violent, racist, wealthy society with the richest working class in the world. It has within it millions of young, moderate, middle-class college students, directly affected by the Vietnam war, affluence and the black movement. The consciousness of recent American radicalism bitterly embodies these contradictions. The Weathermen emerged out of the S.D.S. (Students for a Democratic Society), which in 1962 was a liberal college-based integrationalist movement. The S.D.S. moved to the left as 'normalized repression' and consequent political impotence led it through support for sit-ins, draft resistance, conspiracy trials and Black power. Against this background the Weathermen appeared.

The 'phenomenology' of the Weathermen is the attempt to refute pessimism, and is a struggle to engage in meaningful activism. The Weathermen captured part of the leadership of S.D.S. early in 1969 with a reasonably plausible perspective on American Imperialism, at the biggest National Council Meeting that S.D.S. had ever seen (with over 1,200 delegates and members present). About 300–400 of the delegates were allied to a group called Progressive Labour (P.L.), an American Maoist organization whose caucus in S.D.S. was called W.S.A. (Worker–Student Alliance). In a sense, Progressive Labour condemned itself in that whilst it opposed all nationalism, it refused to recognize the special and particular oppression of the Black people. The National Collective of S.D.S. opposed P.L. and called them chauvinists. As one defender of the Collective put it to P.L.: 'You are a white American chauvinist, not an internationalist', 'you must look to the world proletariat. The American working class is bourgeosified, it is no longer relevant.' [19] During this conference P.L. were expelled from S.D.S., which itself fell into two factions, R.Y.M. I

(Revolutionary Youth Movement) the Weathermen, and R.Y.M. II, who eventually split, leaving the Weathermen by themselves. By 11 September 1969, the following philosophy was emerging from Weatherman leader and S.D.S. Educational Secretary, Bill Ayres. In an article curiously entitled '*A Strategy to Win*', he said,

> ... if it is a world-wide struggle. if Weatherman is correct in that basic thing, that the basic struggle in the world today is the struggle of the oppressed people against U.S. Imperialism, then it is the case that nothing we could do in the mother country would be adventuristic. Nothing we could do because there is a war going on already, and the terms of that war are already set.

Later in the same article, Ayres elaborates: 'But the more I thought about the thing, "fight the People", it's not that it's a great mass slogan or anything but there's something to it.'[20]

Weathermen beliefs spring not from some insane genetic or psychological distortion, but from that thinking which Norman Mailer has characterized as the 'inevitable logic of the next step' (cf. *Armies of the Night*). Even their most horrendous statements can be seen to follow logically from their analysis of American society as a society based on 'White Skin Privilege', in itself not a difficult analysis to accept. For the Weathermen this belief propels them into constant action to smash 'white honky-tonk pig racist Amerika'. They see themselves as agents of the Vietcong, 'bringing the War home'. At their last conference in Flint, shortly before they went underground, the *reductio ad absurdum* of their viewpoint was expressed by the late Ted Gold, who died with two other Weathermen when their Greenwich Village bomb factory-house was blown up on 6 March 1970. At that conference Gold stated that, 'An agency of the people of the world' would be set up to run the U.S. economy and society after the defeat of the U.S. imperialism abroad. A critic spoke up:

> 'In short, if the people of the world succeed in liberating themselves before American radicals have made the American revolution, then the Vietnamese and Africans and the Chinese are gonna

move in and run things for white America. It sounds like a John Bircher's worst dream. There will have to be more repression than ever against white people, but by refusing to organize people, Weatherman isn't even giving them half a chance.'

'Well,' replied Gold, 'if it will take fascism, we'll have to have fascism.'

Weatherman – virtually all white – continues to promote the notion that white working people in America are inherently counter-revolutionary, impossible to organize, or just plain evil – 'honky bastards', as many Weathermen put it. Weatherman's blank view of the post-revolutionary world comes from an analysis of American society that says that *'class doesn't count, race does'*.[21]

A Weatherman's *commitment* to an extreme deviant position vis-à-vis society's belief system flowed from societal reaction only in a negative sense. For before the 'Days of Rage' in Chicago they were not hunted, wanted men: they deliberately worked towards Chicago because they were committed to the belief that 'blacks were going up against the wall alone' and that it was wrong to allow this to happen. This viewpoint, coupled with the belief that white youth were potentially re-volutionary whilst the mass of society was reactionary, led them to decide that doing serious damage to property and the state would demonstrate that they could win, that they were a serious force, and that it would turn social reaction away from blacks on to blacks and whites.

This kind of history of commitment to deviant acts directs attention to the dialectical interplay between deviant beliefs and deviant actions in a situated context; whilst a social reaction analysis of radicalism would emphasize a much more static view of deviant commitment. Lemert, for example, attempted to confront the question of a self-commitment to deviation by pointing to the inadequacies of the structural approach advanced by Merton and others. He suggested that there are two kinds of research problems in the study of deviation.

(i) how deviant behaviour originates,
(ii) how deviant acts are symbolically attached to persons and

effective consequences of such attachment for subsequent deviation on the part of the person.[22]

In his work, Lemert utilizes the distinction between what he terms primary and secondary deviation. For Lemert primary deviation is,

assumed to arise in a wide variety of social, cultural and psychological contexts, and at best to have only marginal implications for the psychic structure of the individual: it does not lead to symbolic reorganization at the level of self-regarding attitudes and social roles.

Whereas secondary deviation is conceived as: 'deviant behaviour, or social roles based upon it, which becomes a means of defense, attack or adaptation to the overt and covert problems created by the societal reaction to primary deviation'.[23]

The significance of this distinction is its concern to give some description of the process of commitment. At the level of primary deviation, deviation has to be explained in different terms from those in which secondary deviation is dealt with. The causes of primary deviation for Lemert, are wide and varied, or as Becker puts it: 'There is no reason to assume that only those who commit a deviant act actually have the impulse to do so. It is much more likely that most people experience deviant impulses frequently.'[24] But secondary deviation is seen as different. 'In effect, the original causes of the deviation recede and give way to the central importance of the disapproving, degradational and labelling reactions of society.' [25]

In short, the secondary deviant *internalizes* and is committed to deviancy for reasons different from his original action. This analysis of commitment to deviancy seems faulty and unproven, and is certainly ridden with unjustified psychological assumptions. As a recent critic of this approach has stated:

to see the full irony of this possibility – that social control can lead to deviance – interactionist analysis has been directed towards examining the *social-psychological implications* * of official registration. Unfortunately, the *theoretical* * links between social con-

* My italics.

trol and further deviant behaviour have never been completely forged, let alone subjected to adequate empirical testing.[26]

Moreover the same critic suggests in looking at the distinction between primary and secondary deviation:

The distinction between the two is either in terms of etiology or the extent to which the offender has a deviant identity. Thus Lemert suggests that secondary deviation refers to a 'special class of socially defined responses which people make to problems located by societal reactions to their (primary) deviance', and it is committed by people 'whose life and identity are organized around the facts of deviance'.[27]

These distinctions are unworkable in theory and unproven in practice. In the case of political deviancy, it is clear that the 'original causes of the deviation' in no way 'recede' simply because of social reaction. Indeed it may be argued with more justification that social reaction to radical ideas, in the form of 'normalized repression', is the cause of initial commitment to political deviation. Futhermore it is by no means clear, except perhaps in the case of political deviants and organized criminals, that there are many deviants 'whose life and identity are organized around the facts of deviance'. Most deviants are not full-time deviants. What appeared initially to many deviancy theorists to be a radical theory is revealed as a totally inadequate account of commitment to deviancy. Indeed it seems that the concern of much of this approach avoids the question of initial deviation and drives it towards a dubious stress on the psychological impact of social reaction. It is perfectly possible to conceive of deviants who never experience the kind of social reaction described by Lemert and Becker, yet who constantly commit deviant acts, who are engaged in smoking pot, stealing, agitating, engaging in sexually deviant acts, etc. Implicit in the social reaction approach is some peculiar fascination with the attempt to erect *a priori* explanations of why some people become 'hard core' criminals and deviants and others do not. But explanations of this kind will only be revealed by looking at social contexts and beliefs.

We have indicated the social reaction approach as un-social

and psychological; in doing this, the claim is not being made that social psychology is unnecessary but rather that such explanations must in no way be ahistorical. If we substituted the term socialization for deviation, it would become immediately apparent that contextually embedded beliefs and experiences are not necessarily primary determinants of commitment. Anyway, what would primary as opposed to secondary socialization mean *unless* we had some theory which clearly differentiated between them? The 'social reaction theorists' have no real theory to explain why secondary deviation is more important in commitment to deviancy than is initial deviation.

Let us return to the Weathermen to examine this question. Until the 'Days of Rage' in Chicago, the Weathermen were an open, extreme radical group whose emphasis on the importance of the blacks was influenced by the powerful and relatively successful Black Power movements like the Black Panthers, who they saw to be taking the brunt of repression in American society. Their decision to 'bring the war home' to Chicago was a result of the beliefs that led to their 'initial deviation'. The events at Chicago, discussed at their conference in Flint, Michigan, shortly afterwards, led the Weathermen to reject any mass white support.

As Harold Jacobs has suggested:

Prior to the 'Days of Rage', the Weathermen still retained its faith in the revolutionary potential of the white working-class youth. But rather than criticizing itself for the low turnout in Chicago, it instead began to turn its back on white people ... Much of Weatherman's political activities after this reflected a despair at organizing white people. At Flint, Weathermen decided to become nothing but a support group for the blacks and the Vietnamese.[28]

Chicago was a turning point for the Weathermen, for it marked their isolation from the rest of society. Their own tactics drove them underground. A non-Weatherman, John Gerassi, describes Chicago as follows:

The first major Weatherman battle was fought last October in Chicago. Weatherman has expected thousands to show up for the declared objective to break up the Loop (Chicago's rich business district). Firearms were forbidden although they knew the fighting would be heavy and deaths likely. Only 500 scared, self-conscious collective members arrived. They were outnumbered by the police almost ten to one, with the National Guard on call nearby. 'Well,' shouted a Weatherman leader, 'You know why we came, and what we said we'd do. This is only the beginning. Whether it's also the end or not depends on us, now. So let's do it!' And they charged. The fighting was probably the hardest yet in the history of the New Left. Thousands of police, with tear gas and clubs and then with guns against a wild but tightly disciplined group of white kids, protected by helmets, boots and steel genital guards, using lead pipes and chains. The city watched in amazement as the Weathermen, meekly at first, then increasingly stronger, pushed through, dispersed, regrouped, dispersed again and got through from their staging area to the Loop where they did as they had said – smashed windows and wrecked stores. More than 200 Weathermen were arrested and eight were shot (none died), yet the next day, they were back. This time, the main thrust was to come from the Weather women. There were only 65 of them, surrounded by 150 cops. The girls were more scared than the day before, feeling more isolated. Then Bernadine Dorhn, a 31-year-old former lawyer and member of the Weather Bureau, told the women 'the fear that people feel in this demonstration has to be put against the hunger, fear, death and suffering of black, brown and yellow people in this country and all over the world'. Then she led them out of Grant Park across from the Hilton Hotel and into the police lines waiting. The Weather women fought well too, and downed many cops, but they were stopped. Still, they were back again the next day, and so through the week. At the end, 284 were in jail with bail of $1,000,000.[29]

Chicago failed for, following it, most Weathermen went underground, with their support in America minute; and their actions are described by other Left groups as 'insane'. The development of an outlaw viewpoint soon emerged, with its culmination in the 'bomb the bourgeoisie' thesis. The philosophy was simple:

Look, even when we lose we win. We know how the Man is. The Man is repressive. The Man is fascist. The Man would like to put us all in Baltimore, Belsen. Every trash we do, every bomb we plant, is forcing the Man to repress that much more and that much more visibly. He has to buy more pigs, and more machines and the taxes go up and the people get screwed even more.

Look, we are costing the Man money, and we make him paranoid. Twenty pigs hit already – right! Every pig is looking over his shoulder, they go round in twos and threes. They can't get recruits.[30]

This strategy has now been abandoned. Underground the Weathermen appear to have reached Desolation Row. However there is little doubt that they have borne more than their own limitations, for they have introduced a new note of seriousness to all discussion in the American movement. Bombing and bomb threats jumped so high in the U.S.A. that in 1970 a National Bomb Data Centre was established in Washington. According to its report, between 1 January 1969 and 15 April 1970, 40 people were killed, 384 injured and 22 million dollars' worth of damage was done in 4,330 reported bombings. Nixon's new Crime Control Bill has sections which prescribe the death penalty for those convicted of fatal bombings.[31] Moreover thousands of extra F.B.I. agents have been hired to deal with the youth revolt. Governor Reagan has stated that if it 'takes a bloodbath to remove the student problem, let's get it over with'.

If one viewed the Weathermen phenomenon from the 'social reaction' perspective, presumably one would argue that it was the social reaction to Chicago that drove them underground; that, underground, secondary deviation occurred and that the 'life and identity' of the Weathermen are 'organized around the facts of deviance'. The problem with such a perspective is that it would do just as well for a movement that did not go underground and went meekly to jail, or again a movement which used the trials as an agitational platform (as did the earlier Chicago conspiracy trial defendants). For all the perspective states is that secondary is different from primary deviation. But in fact this is not even empirically true – some of the people who went underground were not even present at the 'Days of Rage'; they simply accepted the Weathermen's view of revolutionary action, as advanced at the Flint conference. Moreover, the implications of the social reaction approach is that increased social reaction leads to increased deviation – but, as countless revolutionary movements know, it may well have the opposite effect. Indeed most politically deviant groups are sensitively aware of the fact that their own activities can increase or decrease 'deviancy amplification' depending upon how their actions are *understood* by larger society. The Weathermen stopped bombing recently and engaged in self-criticism for precisely this kind of reason. They sent out a 'communiqué' signed (and complete with fingerprints by Bernadine Dorhn), announcing (like Dylan's recent L.P.) a 'New Morning' – 'Changing Weather'. A few extracts are enough to indicate its mood.

The deaths of three friends ended our military conception of what we are doing.... Because their collective began to define armed struggle as the only legitimate form of revolutionary action they did not believe that there was any revolutionary motion among white youth. It seemed like black and third world people were going up against American imperialism alone ... this tendency to consider only bombings or picking up the gun as revolutionary, with the glorification of the heavier the better, *we've called the military error*.* After the explosion, we called off all armed action until such time as we felt the *causes had been understood* * and acted upon. We found that the alternative direction already existed among us and had been developed within other collectives. We became aware that a group of outlaws who are isolated from the youth communities do not have a sense of what is going on, cannot develop strategies that grow to include large numbers of people; we become 'us' and 'them'.[32]

The debates around the question of the 'military error' and the suspension of bombings until the causes had been understood demonstrate a dialectically sensitive interplay between theory and practice, beliefs and reality, which is rarely allowed for in deviancy theory. Yet it is exactly this kind of interplay which is fundamental to deviant commitment, even if it is most openly recognizable only in political deviancy.

* My italics.

Conclusions

We have examined radical commitment as a means of examining deviant commitment and its treatment within the social reaction approach. We may conclude by suggesting that no fundamental advance has been made since the rejection of the viewpoint of the founding father in criminology, Cesare Lombroso, who placed radicals in the same grouping as hereditary criminals.[33] For although it is an advance upon more conservative theories of deviance, the 'social reaction' approach to deviance and commitment leaves much to be desired. Its assumptions tend to be psychological rather than sociological. It is ahistorical in its treatment of deviant meanings and in that it plays down the role of power. In refusing to see that most deviance is a quality of the act, a massive ideological edifice has been erected upon shaky foundations. This has stood in the way of more profitable directions for deviancy theory, for it has appeared in a radical guise.

The aim of this paper has been to demonstrate that some deviants exhibit purposefulness, choice and commitment in a very different manner from that allowed in the 'social reaction' interpretation. The weaknesses of the social reaction approach can be demonstrated externally but much of this critique has been immanent – from the inside of such theories. Lemert's own treatment of radicalism can be seen as a case study of the inadequacy of the 'social reaction' approach. His attempt to explain radicalism leads him to make statements like the following: 'a cross-sectional role analysis of the radicals in a given society will reveal not only a number of *symbolically disordered* persons, but also a large number – perhaps the majority – of persons who profess the extremist beliefs because of general or special situational pressures.'[34]

The 'social reaction' approach is as profoundly un-radical as its predecessors. In the meantime, the rise of contemporary political deviancy and its merger with recognizably deviant life styles has provided us with some opportunity to reassess our position and work towards new understandings. The Weathermen have been used here illustratively. I have in no sense given a full analysis of the movement. My view is that the Weatherman ideology arises from the substitution of the blacks and/or youth for class as the agency of change in contemporary America, and that it only makes rational sense in terms of such beliefs. The difficulties encountered in explaining, understanding and accounting for such a deviant phenomenon highlights the inability of contemporary social theory to move beyond social history. If this limited study has any absolute conclusion, it is that history must be brought back to social theory. If we are reflexive, we can conclude – like the Weathermen – with Bob Dylan, in saying that 'there's no success like failure and failure's no success at all'.

References

1. *San Francisco Good Times* (1970).

2. EDWIN LEMERT, *Human Deviance, Social Problems and Social Control* (Englewood Cliffs: Prentice-Hall, 1967), p. v.

3. HOWARD BECKER, *Outsiders: Studies in the Sociology of Deviance* (New York: Free Press, 1963), p. 7.

4. I. L. HOROWITZ and M. LIEBOWITZ, 'Social Deviance and Political Marginality', *Social Problems* 15(3) (winter 1968).

5. STUART HALL, 'Deviancy, Politics and the Media'; paper given to the British Sociological Association Annual Conference (Easter 1971). See P. ROCK and M. MCINTOSH, eds., *Deviance and Control* (Tavistock, 1973).

6. ALVIN GOULDNER, 'The Sociologist as Partisan: Sociology and the Welfare State', *American Sociologist* (May 1968); I. L. HOROWITZ and M. LIEBOWITZ, op. cit.; IAN TAYLOR and LAURIE TAYLOR, 'We are All Deviants Now', *International Socialism*, 34 (1968); CRESCY CANNAN, 'Deviants: Victims or Rebels?', Case-Con, 2 (1970) (the journal for revolutionary social work, London); and see STANLEY COHEN, ed., *Images of Deviance* (Penguin Books, 1971).

7. SEYMOUR L. HALLECK, in *Student Protest*, G. MCGUIGAN, ed., (Methuen, 1970).

8. E. SHORT, M.P., *The Times* (30 January 1969).

9. I. L. HOROWITZ and M. LIEBOWITZ, op. cit., p. 280.

10. IAN TAYLOR and LAURIE TAYLOR, op. cit., p. 30.

11. H. BECKER, op. cit., p. 9.

12. ALVIN GOULDNER, *The Coming Crisis of Western Sociology* (Heinemann Educational Books, 1971), pp. 296–7.

13. ALVIN GOULDNER, 'The Sociologist as Partisan: Sociology and the Welfare State', *American Sociologist* (May 1968), p. 107. Also see

IAN TAYLOR and PAUL WALTON, 'Values in Deviancy Theory and Society', *British Journal of Sociology*, Vol. XXI, No. 4 (December 1970).

14. RONALD L. AKERS, 'Problems in the Sociology of Deviance: Social Definitions and Behaviour', *Social Forces* (46), 4 (June 1968), p. 463.

15. The *Guardian* (New York, 10 January 1970), p. 14.

16. ibid.

17. See SHIN'YA ONO, 'You Do Need a Weatherman to Know Which Way the Wind Blows', in *Weatherman*, ed. H. JACOBS (Berkeley: Ramparts Press, 1970), pp. 227–74.

18. ibid.

19. ibid.

20. Quoted in 'The S.D.S's Desolation Row', *International Socialism* (February 1970). For full article see op. cit. in *Weatherman*, ed. H. JACOBS (Berkeley: Ramparts Press, 1970), pp. 184–95. This is a fairly comprehensive reader on the Weatherman.

21. The *Guardian* (New York, 10 January 1970), p. 3. See 'Stormy Weather', in H. JACOBS, ed., op. cit.

22. E. LEMERT, *Human Deviance, Social Problems and Social Control* (Prentice-Hall, 1967), p. 17.

23. ibid.

24. H. BECKER, *Outsiders* (New York: Free Press, 1963), p. 26.

25. E. LEMERT, op. cit., p. 17.

26. S. BOX, *Deviance, Reality and Society* (Holt, Rinehart & Winston, 1971), p. 218.

27. ibid., p. 219.

28. H. JACOBS, ed., op. cit., p. 311.

29. JOHN GERASSI, 'Blow Up Amerika', *Black Dwarf* (April 1970).

30. Martin Walker's second report from the American Underground, 'Strategy of Terror', the *Guardian* (27 October 1971).

31. See J. COLE, 'They Bombed in New Haven', *Workers Power* (November 1970), p. 6; and also *The Plain Truth*, Vol. XXXVI, No. 6 (1971).

32. See *The Militant* (22 January 1971) and *Peace News* (9 April 1971).

33. C. LOMBROSO, *Les Anarchistes*, 1894.

34. E. LEMERT, *Social Pathology* (New York: McGraw-Hill, 1951), p. 188.

Jock Young   **The Hippie Solution:
An Essay in the Politics
of Leisure***

Many occupational, educational, and social groups in American society are too demanding for certain individuals. The hippie movement and its many near-group pockets is an attractive organism for youths with the limited social abilities to perform adequately in the inclusive society. On the hippie scene they can do their 'own thing' (even if it is a borderline psychotic syndrome) in the sanctuary of the near-group forms that comprise the total movement.

A large number of youths, perhaps 20–25 per cent of the total movement, are clearly emotionally disturbed youths who use the malleable near-groups of the hippie movement as their syndrome. The traditional Napoleon, God, Christ, and other psychotic delusional syndromes so popular over the years may have been replaced by the hippie syndrome for many youths who have severe personal problems.[1]

(Lewis Yablonsky, Professor of Sociology at
San Fernando Valley, California State College)

No use going through Sociological crap how breakdowns of family-church-community-morals 'we lost our roots' cause fidgety kids in suburbs, build huge head-shrink industry, drives us all to dope. Let 10 grand a year people in Universities and Buck's County Mansions grind out their huge sad books on 'Grants' they call them, and let these books sit unreadable on more and more inaccessible library shelves. There is not enough time.

Instead, look at spontaneous solutions now being created by hundreds of thousands of kids who woke up early, finally, wised up to the big scram.[2]

(*Lew Welch* 'Final City')

Sociologists, depending on their political complexion, have either – with the proper modicum of scientific restraint –

* I am indebted to David Downes and Paul Walton for critical comments on earlier versions of this paper.

damned the underground, or else described it with a glowing paternalism, greeting its emergence as a confirmation of their liberal anxieties over modern democratic society. The underground, in turn, has instinctively rejected any external analysis of itself, for how can 'huge sad books' with their linear logic tell you more about the ecstasy of liberation than the briefest track on the most limited acid rock album? All of which is a pity, for the new bohemia remains a gigantic warehouse of contradictions and unexplored mystification, whilst sociology fails to gain intellectual sustenance by its refusal to enter into a critical debate with such a significant contemporary social movement.

It is my contention that the widespread occurrence of hippie cultures represents a tentative solution to emerging problems of work and leisure in the advanced industrial countries of the West. In this article I will examine the reasons for the emergence of the underground and its metamorphosis under the backlash of social reaction. Cultures may be regarded as social devices evolved to solve the problems faced by men living in particular parts of the social structure. New cultures arise when problems emerge for which there are no existing social solutions; they are collective endeavours attempting to provide for the thwarted aspirations of their members. Technological change (itself propelled by the problems of powerful groups in society) not only gives rise to such problems, which are differentially distributed throughout the social structure, but also helps create the potentialities for social change. Material change creates problems and promises or threatens solutions.

It is a recurrent fault of sociological analysis that cultures are depicted as ideal types constructed by a process of accentuation which eliminates both their internal contradictions and illogicalities. For the taken-for-granted worlds in which men exist are, as Alfred Schutz stressed, inconsistent, incoherent and incomplete. Modern sociology suffers not so much from an oversocialized conception of man as an overcoherent depiction of group norms. Thus to read descriptions of hippie culture one would be led to believe that a distant number of self-evident 'hippies' were in possession of a blueprint for social change, norm articulated against norm, with the whole plan generally agreed upon by all in the tight-knit community of the underground. Instead we find few who would call themselves hippies (although they would use this term for many others), considerable disagreement over styles of life, contradictions, illogicalities, tentative beliefs and intense internecine conflicts. In addition there are a plethora of spokesmen readily claiming to speak for all, whose statements are instantly disclaimed by others. Now the internal inconsistencies of cultures are rational in that they reflect contradictions in the values of the groups in question. They represent attempts to balance out conflicts of interests and gloss over uncertainty of solutions. Moreover, it is through conflict with other groups in society and internal conflict between members of the same culture, all of this under-pinned by clashes of material interest, that the culture develops a sense of unity and separateness over and above the rest of society. This means that our analysis must take note of the relevant conflicts, as well as the consensus of opinion, within the underground.

The Theory of Subterranean Values

In 1961 Matza and Sykes, in an examination of the value systems of modern Western societies, suggested that there existed a fundamental contradiction running through all social strata, that co-existing alongside the overt or official values of society are a series of *subterranean* values. One of these, for example, is the search for excitement: for new 'kicks'. Society, they argue, tends to provide institutionalized periods in which these subterranean values are allowed to emerge and take precedence. Thus we have the world of leisure, of holidays, festivals and sports, in which subterranean values are expressed rather than the rules of workaday existence.

The search for adventure, excitement and thrill is a subterranean value that ... often exists side by side with the values of security, routinization and the rest. It is not a deviant value, in any full sense, but must be held in abeyance until the proper moment and circumstances for its expression arrive.[3]

The Hippie Solution: An Essay in the Politics of Leisure

All members of society hold these subterranean values. Normally they are maintained in balance with the formal values and allowed expression in leisure time. Certain groups, however, accentuate these values, disdain the workaday norms of official society, and attempt to live all their life in a subterranean fashion. The juvenile delinquent and the hippie, to a varying extent, epitomize this position.

What is the precise nature of the subterranean values? Matza and Sykes are far from clear and their discussion is limited to certain working-class groups in the United States. I have therefore attempted a series of distinctions which describe in a general form the focal concerns of the two opposing value systems:

Formal work values	*Subterranean Values*
Deferred gratification	Short-term hedonism
Planning future action	Spontaneity
Conformity to bureaucratic rules	Ego-expressivity
Fatalism: high control of detail, little over direction	Autonomy: control of behaviour in detail and direction
Routine, predictability	New experience, excitement
Instrumental attitudes to work	Activities performed as an end-in-themselves
Hard productive work seen as a virtue	Disdain for work

The *formal* values are concomitant with the emergence of large-scale bureaucracies embodying a system of economic rationality, high division of labour and finely woven, formalized rules of behaviour. These values are functional for the maintenance of diligent, consistent work and the realization of long-term productive goals. They are not, however, identical with the Protestant Ethic. For whereas the latter dictated that a man realized his true nature and position in the world through hard work and painstaking application to duty, the formal values insist that work is merely instrumental. One value system provided the ideology for the *laissez faire* capitalism of the nineteenth century, the other provides the exhortation necessary for the neo-Keynsian world of contemporary consumer capitalism. You work hard in order to earn money, which is spent in pursuit of leisure; it is in his 'free' time that man really develops his sense of identity and purpose.

With the possible exception of the liberal professions, the Protestant Ethic has undergone a remarkable decline in influence. Berger and Luckmann [4] have argued that the growth of bureaucracies in almost every sphere of social life, has enmeshed the workaday world in a system of rules which preclude to a large extent the possibility of the individual expressing his identity through his job. The high division of labour and the rationalization of occupational roles has made jobs even more inadequate as vehicles of personal desires and expressivity. Work has come to be regarded instrumentally by nearly all sections of society, middle class as much as working class. Thus Bennet Berger writes:

> Whether it is the relatively simple alienation so characteristic of assembly-line work in factories or the highly sophisticated kind of alienation we find in the folk ways of higher occupations, one thing is clear: the disengagement of self from occupational role not only is more common than it once was but is also increasingly regarded as 'proper'.[5]

It is during leisure and in the expression of subterranean values that modern man seeks his identity, whether it is in 'home-centred' family or an adolescent peer group. For leisure is, at least purportedly, non-alienated activity.

It must not be thought, however, that contemporary man's work and leisure form watertight compartments. The factory-belt worker experiencing boredom and alienation does not come home in the evening to a life of undiluted hedonism and expressivity! The worlds of leisure and work are intimately related. The money earned by work is spent in one's leisure time. It is through the various life styles which are evolved that men confirm their occupational status. Leisure is concerned with consumption and work with production; a keynote of our bifurcated society is, therefore, that individuals within it must constantly consume in order to keep pace with the productive capacity of the economy. They must produce in order to consume and consume in order to produce. This places the interrelationship between formal and subterranean values in a new light; hedonism, for instance, is closely tied to what I will term the ethos of productivity. This asserts that a man is justified in expressing subterranean values, if, and only if, he has earned the right to do so by working hard and being productive. Pleasure can only be legitimately purchased by the credit card of work. For example, unlike the 'leisure classes' depicted by Veblen, modern captains of industry feel duty bound to explain how the richness of their leisure is a legitimate reward for the dedication of their labour.

The ethos of productivity thus attempts to legitimize and encompass the world of subterranean values. But there are cracks and strains in this moral code. People doubt not only the material rewards which hard work offers but the sanity of alienated work and the validity of their leisure. For they cannot compartmentalize their life in a satisfactory manner: their socialization for work inhibits their leisure and their utopias of leisure belittle their work.

Groups That Exist Beyond the Ethos of Productivity

Socialization into the work ethic is accomplished by inculcating into individuals the desirability of the various material rewards which the system offers and the efficacy of work as a means of achieving them. Work must be seen as an effective way of providing the economic substratum necessary for a satisfying leisure. The deferred gratification of labour must be commensurate with the satisfactions of consumption. Throughout the social structure such a contract is, of course, often suspect, but there are instances where a singularly blatant credibility gap occurs. Here, the problem is that the ethos of productivity is totally defunct and subcultures have arisen as tentative solutions to this predicament. The three major cases are where:

1. Work capable of realizing what is perceived as a reasonable reward is unobtainable. Thus certain groups in our society are at the edge of, or actually outside, the labour market. They have neither the skills nor the opportunities to gain entry into it at any but the most unrewarding level.

2. The material rewards are available yet scorned.

3. Material possessions are held in surplus without need for further work.

These problems occur in three different parts of the social structure and give rise to – especially amongst those groups of young people who are relatively free from adult control – bohemian solutions. It is these three strands which make up the underground and which, because of their varying coincidence and divergence of interests, give rise to the primary alliances and conflicts within hippie society. Thus we have three groups:

The Beats

The Beats are the lower underground. They come primarily from working- and lower-middle-class backgrounds, and homes which are usually either broken or disrupted. They are poor and often homeless, seeking to *avoid* the situation of *material scarcity* in which they find themselves. Conventional work, of the type available to them, could not possibly provide the income necessary to be part of the consumer spectacle. Instead they disdain conventional work and leisure and create a disparate subculture of expressivity and immediacy which exists from hand to mouth in the midst of consumer affluence. The Beats are ambivalent about material possessions, simultaneously coveting them yet disdaining *through necessity* the 'straight' world which they represent. Thus, on one hand, they take the ideology of affluence seriously – leisure is of paramount importance and possessions should be easily available – whilst, on the other hand, they are provided with singularly few opportunities for realizing this dream.[6] They do not starve, in that the physical immiseration concomitant with pre-war capitalism is no longer in force, and this meagre material base allows them the possibility of disdaining work. For as Michael Harrington noted: 'amongst the most cruelly used people in the affluent society there seems to be arising a new dignity (conservatives mistake it for laziness), which refutes the old motivations now that brutal compulsions are no longer in force.' [7] Their economic base is national assistance payments, casual unskilled work, street-level drug selling, petty crime and hustling.

The Middle Underground

This group comes largely from upper-middle-class backgrounds. They have dropped out of school or college. Richard Flacks describes them as the products of post-war affluence which:

has had the effect of liberating a considerable number of young people from anxieties about social mobility and security, and enabled them to take seriously the quest for other values and experiences. To such youth, established careers and adult roles are bound to be unsatisfying. What is the sense, after all, of binding oneself to a large organization, of submitting to the rituals, routines and disciplines of careerism, of postponing or foregoing a wide range of possible experience – when there is little chance of surpassing one's father, when the major outcome of such efforts is to acquire goods which one has already had one's fill of, when such efforts mean that one must compromise one's most cherished ideal? [8]

They would deny that *scarcity exists*:

The delusion is this: that shortage exists and is the norm. The reality is that abundance is the norm. The abundance is so great that tremendous efforts, ingenuity and loss of life are going to creating an unconvincing appearance of shortage. The abundance is so great that, even with all our present efforts at creating waste and shortage the abundance is breaking through and threatening the present set-up. We cannot cope with this problem of abundance – MORE than enough for everyone – AND retain this once-useful, but now antique and inappropriate artificiality, money.[9]

They argue that scarcity is a function of wasteful production and perverted consumer wants. The rewards from work are suspect and, furthermore, the sacrifices demanded at work are viewed with increasing dislike. For not only has there been a bureaucratization of the occupational roles which are available to them but in addition their demands for non-alienated work have increased within the context of post-war affluence and security.

The middle underground man the various community organizations; they own boutiques; they work in the record industry. Their material base is in the leisure field. Their poorer cousins subsist on parental handouts and part-time skilled work.

The Pop Aristocracy

The Pop Aristocracy are *beyond scarcity* in that they find themselves miraculously in a realm where material or sexual limitations are minimal. They come from working- or lower-middle-class backgrounds and are distinguished from previous pop singers in that they view their music as being a manifestation of bohemian art and having ideological importance in the struggle against the 'straight', non-hedonistic, anti-expressive world.

Hippie Culture

From his position of being beyond scarcity, denying scarcity or seeking to avoid scarcity, the hippie develops a bohemian way of life which is spontaneous, expressive and concerned with pleasure now rather than uncertain and ambivalent rewards in the future. The ethos of productivity is scorned. Drugs are used in order to overcome initial socialization into work values and to ease the transition into an uninhabited world of play.[10] Distinctive fashions in clothes and an international argot is evolved, the latter centring around the celebration of flamboyance and enjoyment and the denigration of the wider society as 'straight', work as a 'drag' and the businessman as 'hung up' with a life style which is a total 'bringdown'.

The culture is, however, not without inconsistencies and contradictions; in the process of constructing an alternative society based on subterranean values, certain dilemmas over strategy and conflicts over content occur. Members will often simultaneously hold two divergent positions, although empirically there is a tendency for opinions to gravitate more towards one pole of a contradiction than another. Thus a bohemian subculture emerges geared to solving the problems of a posited 'affluent' society. But its cultural answers are not flawless or consistent and any explanation of bohemian society must take note of the pertinent conflicts.

Inconsistencies and Dilemmas

I shall now deal briefly with what I consider the more important of these inconsistencies.

1. The Place of Technology

There is in the new bohemia a generalized disillusionment with many of the outward manifestations of technology. Ecological pollution, industrial alienation and mindless consumerism are all objects of criticism. But there is a dilemma as to the extent which industrialization *per se* is inimicable to human progress. Thus one writer suggests that:

the touchstone of the matter [is]; how ready are the workers to disband whole sectors of the industrial apparatus where this proves necessary to achieve ends other than efficient productivity and high consumption? How willing are they to set aside technocratic priorities in favour of a new simplicity of life, a decelerating social pace, a vital leisure? [11]

Or is technology to be the means by which liberation is to be achieved and the basis of a new electronic culture? On one side there is the argument for simplicity and scorn for the consumer society, on the other the stress upon the development of new and more sophisticated leisure goods and pastimes. It becomes difficult to argue that television sets and washing machines represent the means by which people are bribed to serve the system if you belong to a culture whose central artefacts are the electric guitar, the stereogram, and the video-tape!

191

2. The Strategy of Change

How is the millennium to be achieved? Although overall the stress is on individual rather than social revolution, there are fundamental differences of opinion about the interrelationship between the two. Is it necessary to change the system, in order for the new man of the alternative society to develop? Or is social revolution a non-event of little importance?

Thank God for the love of you Gardeners of the Soul in these times of planetary insanity and power-mania. You are the real revolutionaries for this age – the guerrillas of the inner planes – working from the grass roots of your own deep selves and not from the manufactured minds of those around you. There is nothing revolutionary about the normal run of revolutions. The rise and inevitable fall of earthly revolutions over the centuries have been products of involvement with the normal life-cycle pattern of birth-growth-decay-death to which all material things in this visible universe are subject, from microscopic mineral molecules to man. But beyond this birth-growth-decay-death syndrome lies the unchanging, undying eternal PRINCIPLE of BEING, the discovery and use of which is where the real New Age revolution is at! And those Gardeners who are delving their inner-Gardenworlds today, are the only combined force of LIGHT keeping this world in a relative state of equilibrium, by combatting the negative forces being poured into the atmosphere from the Mordor-minds of the soul-sick.[12]

Will the system be converted by love and shining self-example or is it necessary to hate parts of it and even act violently against the enemies of the alternative society? Can the individual pursue his own path to salvation or is collective action necessary? [13]

3. Possible Economic Bases

Should the underground be the leisure market of the 'straight' society or should it be independent? If independence is desired, does this involve making profit out of fellow hippies or should money be abolished and property held collectively? This contradition is most evident if we contrast the commercially-orientated boutique owner with the digger communities.

4. Cool versus Hot Hedonism

There would seem to be two fundamental modes of embodying subterranean values. Either hedonism and expressivity are articulated as a nihilistic search for kicks where emerging standards are dismantled as soon as they are erected, or, the hedonism involves a controlled seeking of identity through the pursuit of pleasure. This distinction I will call *hot* versus *cool* hedonism and in its extreme form it can be seen in the contrast between hippies and the old beat generation. For whereas the apostles of the old bohemia invoked their followers: 'to burn, burn, burn like fabulous yellow human candles', the style of the modern hippie has become more restrained. But the contradiction remains and, indeed, Davis and Munoz have suggested that the dichotomy is held in the argot distinction between 'head' and 'freak'. Thus they write:

At this level of indigenous typification, they can be seen to reflect certain ongoing value tensions in the subculture; a reflecting turning inward versus hedonism, Apollonian contentment versus Dionysian excess, a millennial vision of society versus an apocalyptic one. And that these generic extensions of the terms derive so intimately from drug experiences afford additional evidence of the symbolic centrality of drugs in the hippie subculture ... it is our further impression that 'heads' are by and large persons of middle and upper-middle class social origins whereas 'freaks' are much more likely to be of working class background. Despite, therefore, the strong legal and moral proscriptions against both LSD and Methedrine, their differential use by hippies reflects, at one level at least, the basic contrast in expressive styles extant in the American class structure; put crudely, LSD equals self exploration/self-improvement equals middle class, while Methedrine equals body stimulation/release of aggressive impulses equals working class.[14]

Although I would agree broadly with their class distinctions, ('hot' is more true of the Beats and 'cool' of the Middle Underground), I feel that this contradiction is diffused throughout the total culture. It is also true that 'cool' hedonism is associated with 'soft' drug use (marihuana and LSD) and 'hot' hedonism with multidrug use including the so-called 'hard' drugs (e.g. methedrine, heroin, injectable barbiturates).

Closely related to this hot-cool differential is the stress on aesthetic productivity compared to taking things easy. This is well expressed by Pete Townshend in an interview with Miles:

I understand life now I think, and I understand work and I think understanding work is far bigger than understanding life because work is really what keeps one living. You see it's so easy to deteriorate off into a twilight sub-culture pot-smoking world, where you sit there smoking, and work only so that you can sit in your red light and play Jimmy Reed records. Oh I did that for years! Fine, so you are in a position of great understanding but you are one of the people who watches and that's the drag. The best thing is to be so involved in something that's moving rather than saying, 'Well that's moving. Dig it! That's moving. Dig that! Look at that! Look at that plane!' It's far better to be on the plane, it's far better to have painted that picture, it's far better to have done something.[15]

These inconsistencies occur throughout hippie culture and on all levels. The Beats tend to be more political, violent, anti-commercial, millennial, social revolutionary, 'hot' and non-productive. The Middle Underground more non-political, love-orientated, individualistic, commercial and 'cool'. This reflects to some extent their different material positions and interests. But there is no one-to-one relationship between culture and structure and, as we shall see, the balance between these contradictions depends on changes in circumstances and influence of the groups in relationship to each other.

Flower Power 1967

I now want to describe the prevalent ideology of hippies in 1967 and then proceed to describe how it changed in the three years which followed.

The dominant values were the product of an alliance between the Middle Underground and the Pop Aristocracy. It was in this year that the middle-class hippie took over the bohemian tradition from the small group of Beats who had existed since the mid fifties. The Middle Underground were the first genera-tion of middle-class drop-outs who had grown up in the com-parative affluence of the late fifties and early sixties. They en-visaged a world where leisure was the problem and work on the point of being automated out of existence. The ethos of pro-ductivity seemed inapplicable to the age of leisure. Poverty was a residual phenomenon which a benevolent Welfare State would finally eradicate. What was necessary was that people must be 'turned on' to the possibilities of the alternative society. How was this to be achieved? Two powerful catalysts of change were invoked: drugs and music. The psychedelic drug LSD and, to a lesser extent, marihuana, were seen as powerful ex-panders of consciousness which would unfailingly reveal to the initiate the transcendental possibilities of a new world. As Allen Ginsberg put it:

I propose, then, that everybody including the President and his and our vast horde of generals, executives, judges and legislators of these states go to nature, find a kindly teacher or Indian peyote chief or guru guide, and assay their consciousness with LSD.

Then, I prophesy, we will all have some ray of glory or vast-ness beyond our conditioned social selves, beyond our government. beyond America even, that will unite us into a peaceable com-munity.[16]

Secondly there was the Rock Revolution. Rock'n'roll music was envisaged not only as embodying a subterranean aesthetic (it was the music that got the white man back 'inside his body') but as having ideological undertones. 'When the mode of the music changes, the walls of the city shake!' became the slogan. Music together with drugs would 'turn on' the 'straight' society and precipitate change. On the personal level what remained was to show the rest of society how to act. The initiated, those 'out front', must display the benefits of their insight. This would be accomplished by love both for fellow hippies and even seem-ing enemies. Thus after a demonstration protesting against *International Times* being 'bust' by the police, Tom McGrath, its editor, wrote:

Mike Lesser, part-owner of the Badge Boutique, took part in the ceremonies and was ecstatic about them. 'It is really happening here in London, with no leaders or nonsense like that.' But he felt that when we make future Street Happenings we must be more gentle, loving and understanding with the police. During the funeral, the strategy was to give the police flowers. This was done, but Mike saw some of the mourners THROWING the flowers hard at the police. We have to remember that even policemen are human; perhaps because of their singularly unpopular position in society, they need more love than most of us.[17]

A parallel set of alternative institutions would be set up, shops, work, families, communities and even banks:

Thus loans of credit could be made by the scene through the 'bank'. If all credit-worthy account customers on the books of the various u/g retail outlets: i.e. Middle Earth, Musicland, Indica, Flying Dragon, Cornucopia, Macrobiotic Restaurant, Granny's, Hung on you, Arts Lab, etc., etc., were issued with credit cards valid at all member organizations then anyone 'shopping on the underground' could get one bill at the end of the month from the central accounting office and would need no bread.[18]

But most important of all what is necessary is an alternative communication system. For given:

the rapid onslaught of the Marxian 'surplus' the laws are becoming redundant, many already are, even in terms of maintaining the status quo. In the not too distant future ownership of material goods will have little meaning, power will lie in the hands of the owners of the communications systems.[19]

Moreover, underground propaganda must be directed primarily at young people, for these are seen as the new class, who are most open to new ideas, and share a common interest in progress.

The alliance between the Pop Aristocracy and the Middle Underground was a product of symbiosis between the two. The Pop Aristocracy was composed of upwardly mobile youth, who had tapped the leisure market, by providing music that was unambiguously hedonistic and expressive. It was music tailor-made for the youth culture which grew up, on the edge of the ethos of productivity and squarely in the subterranean tradition. Their problem was to create and confirm their identity as the agents of a new expressive artistic culture, and to explain their extraordinary position in the world. To do this they turned to the Middle Underground, which viewed itself as the true repository of bohemian knowledge, and which was in the process of evolving theories to describe and explain the affluent society of the sixties and beyond. A series of alliances were forged, the paradigm case of which was the marriage between John Lennon and Yoko Ono. The Middle Underground, in turn, praised the Pop Aristocracy as the apostles of the Rock Revolution and looked up to the artists as living incarnations of subterranean ideals existing in a world without scarcity. Thus they come either from the cushioned limbo of the middle-class young or from part of a supremely successful meritocracy who had propelled themselves by their own efforts into a position of almost unparalleled material and sexual surplus. Either way they saw little structural opposition to the age of leisure; the problem was not so much to change the *status quo* of power and interest, as to change the way men thought. They lacked any experience of being surrounded by coercive institutions which impinged upon them. They knew little of exploitation: their theories focused on the isolated individual. Little wonder that the main obstacle to change was portrayed as being inside man's head. What was necessary, therefore, was to defuse inhibitions with rock and drugs and to shame and lure people by the example of Love. All this directed at a youth culture whose economic divisions were perceived as negligible, and at a society where opposition was viewed solely in terms of individuals being 'uptight', 'evil' or emanating 'bad vibrations'.

The Forces of Change

A subculture can be viewed as having three major components: a *material base* which is the economic technical and organizational substructure of the group; *ideals* which are the desired goals, the thwarting of which created the subculture as a possible solution to their achievement; and finally, it has a series

197

of *hypotheses* which relate to the world view of the subculture. That is, its interpretation of its position in the world and, closely related, the means which it suggests might achieve its ideals.

There are four distinct yet interacting areas of conflict which transform the subcultural project:

1. Contradiction between Ideals and Material Base

When the material base of a culture is insufficient to achieve its ideals, either those ideals must be changed or the hypotheses linking base to ideas must be substantially revised.

2. Contradictions between Ideals

When incompatibilities exist between ideals in terms of possible future action then these will either be eliminated in the course of the subcultural project or result in the break up of the group into factions closely related to differences in material interests within the subculture.

3. Contradictions of Material Interests

Where conflicts of material interest within the subculture become manifest in the attempted resolution of the project, then the subcultural consensus will divide and factions emerge with conflicting ideals.

4. Contradictions between Subculture and the Wider Society

Social reaction can fundamentally alter the material base of a subculture; it can create or intensify problems and it can prove or invalidate hypotheses.

The Base of Social Reaction Against the Hippie

The reaction of powerful forces against bohemian subcultures occurs not because wider material interests are threatened but because the bohemian threatens the reality of the 'straight' world. By invoking a world of pleasure unrelated to productivity, of expressivity divorced from work roles, he is a caustic to the moral legitimacy of the system. What price hard work and conformity, if the shiftless youth across the road enjoys all the rewards and openly refuses to work a stroke?

The bohemian was blissfully unaware of the hornet's nest of reaction which he was to stir up. Only half knowingly, he had aimed a severe blow at the moral plexus of the system. Thus at the same time as threatening the affluent citizen's world of discipline and consumption he mocked the poverty of the working-class poor. Both the strata of society which relentlessly created its own scarcity and that which desperately attempted to rise beyond scarcity, were at odds with the long-haired youths who demanded: 'the storming of the reality studio and the retaking of the universe'.

The effect of social reaction on the degree of deviancy of a particular group can take three courses: it can intensify the original problem so as to result in increased deviancy which in turn elicits increased social reaction further increasing the problem, the deviancy and the reaction and so on, to form what is termed a *deviancy amplification spiral*.[20] It can ameliorate the problem experienced by the subculture, opening up possibilities of re-entry into normality and form a *deviancy elimination* sequence. Lastly, it can take steps to ensure that the group deviates no further, but at the same time prevent re-entry. The deviant is petrified in the role circumscribed by his transgression. *Ossification* of deviancy has occurred. All three of these processes have affected different segments of the underground.

The Politics of Leisure

I want now to discuss the changes which occurred within the hippie movement between 1967 and 1971. To begin with, as we have seen, there was an alliance of flower power; a consensus uniting the Beats, Middle Underground and Pop Aristocracy. Rock'n'roll, drugs and love were envisaged as about to transform a world over-ripe for change. I want to examine the significant factors, both internal and external to the subculture, which brought about a re-examination of ideals, an alteration of hypotheses and an awareness of the limitations of its material base:

1. The Media Backlash

The newspaper industry has discovered that people read avidly stories which play on their own normative worries. The hippies' commitment to subterranean values fascinates the reader, although his disdain of work repels. The newspaper provides a myth which luridly describes the deviant, dwells on his hedonistic transgressions, teases out moral outrage, and then plumps for the system by pointing to the disgrace, pain and suffering in which such behaviour *must necessarily* be seen to culminate. In a segregated society much of our knowledge of groups with norms unlike our own stems from the mass media. The latter can suddenly focus on a particular group and over a short space of time a relatively unknown subculture can become a social problem. Precisely such a moral panic, utilizing stereotypical information, occurred over hippies in 1967. The result was a forceful backlash of social reaction and at the same time a widespread dissemination of bohemian ideals amongst the young.[21]

2. Love Fails

The Middle Underground was, to echo Raoul Veneigem, like 'those Walt Disney characters who rush madly over the edge of a cliff without seeing it, so that the power of their imagination keeps them suspended in mid-air; but as soon as they look down and see where they are, they fall.'[22] They predicted a world of affluence with their role as innovatory precursors, but found themselves either with no economic base or one in which they had no idea of its future implications. They envisaged a world transformed by Love, then found themselves objects of hate and derision. Worst of all they woke up to find themselves bedfellows with a lumpenbohemia that was to their minds parasitic on their limited resources. For the Lower Underground had a tendency to over-stay their welcome at the flats of the Middle Underground, an irritating habit of taking the ideals of shared money and property literally.[23] They were 'uncool' about drugs and tended to get involved in political action such as the Piccadilly squat which, to quote a prominent member of the Middle Underground 'gave youth a bad image'. In the flourishing 'Arts Lab' movement the conflict centred around those who wished to evolve progressive arts centres which might be eligible for Arts and Local Council grants (the Middle Underground) and those who wished to establish the Laboratories as communal experiments (the Lower Underground).[24] On the part of the Lower Underground rapid disillusionment set in, as this letter to *International Times* illustrates:

If youth has now become a 'class' would you mind telling me why some members of this 'class' are very much better off than others? I'm at a loss to understand what the rest of us are supposed to have in common with the underground journalists on their expense-paid flights to witness this 'new' supergroup or that 'youth revolution' with the Hoppy's of this world mapping out their careers with the Sony Corporation; or with the Chelsea groover in his pretty suede trousers pondering the decor of his new boutique (he's probably flicking thru the latest issue of 'Communes' in between pulls on £15-an-ounce Afghani joints, but boy he's careful not to drop any ash on those trousers!). Are our interests really the same as those of the 101 promotion men and hustlers who seduce us with their goodies thru your columns? [25]

3. Drugs Fail

The notion that LSD and marihuana were elixirs which produce instant altruism took a severe beating. Although it is true that the hallucinogens by disorganizing the incoming stimuli to the brain can bring the drug-user to question the 'taken for granted' reality that surrounds him, the interpretation of this effect is tightly structured by the social norms of the individual taking the drug.[26] There is no reason to believe, for instance, that if marihuana were legalized it would not be easily contained within the existing culture. The effects experienced by the early 'heads' were related to their own perspectives on the world. The diffusion of marihuana to a wider public did not create the love generation prophesied.

4. The Alternative Market Place

'The revolutionaries are on CBS' is the slogan of the famous international record company. Commercial interests soon realized that because of the hippies' development of subterranean modes of expression they were not only a new market for leisure goods, but excellent innovators in the fields of music, design, clothes and fashion. Business opportunities opened up for a limited number of the Middle Underground. The new bohemia found its 'leaders' selling out rapidly:

> This rapid-turnover, status-ridden, fashion-infested shit heap is the perfect playground for straight society. Through the culture-market, the POWER (overground) and the GLORY (underground) are re-united in the person of the hip financier; the boutique-owning deb; the Hippie Jet Set; Cosmic Comics Incorporated; the frilly-shirted, Vidal-scissored, teenage-toy tycoon. Having no style of their own, they culture-slummed and bought yours. Freak Revolution becomes straight rave. You kicked them in the balls: they calmly took a polaroid shot of it, framed it and hung it in the middle of the lounge wall, along with the Picasso print and the Oxfam subscription card, and all their other claims to a tolerant liberal conscience. No, I'm not sufficiently purist or naive to claim that everything that's a commercial success is automatically a hype or a sell-out. But it generally is, or at least paves the way for one. Pats on the head, or cheques in the bank, can be rather more lethal than machine-guns.[27]

The New Shape of the Underground

The successful part of the Middle Underground became more involved in the commercial individualistic, reformist and non-political side of the bohemian contradiction. They were ossified in their jester roles as accepted deviants of whom there has been a long history in music, design and painting. Society provided them with the secure expressive economic base that they had been seeking. On the other, the Beats became more harassed, persecuted and subject to a process of deviancy amplification which led in a minority of cases to the tragedy of 'hard' drug use and in others to the odd spurt of almost millennarian political action. In between, a growing body of middle-class drop-outs became disenchanted with the Middle Underground. Some grew sick of an alternative society where as Roy Harper puts it: 'the festive consumer was consumed by the feast'; where it cost more to dress like a hippie than a business executive whilst the clothes lasted half as long. They re-entered the 'straight' society relatively easily, for unlike the Beats they had skills which were readily marketable. Others remain committed to bohemian ideals and were faced with the problem of realizing the individual revolution in a world where an economic base was necessary to survive and social hostility a commonplace. Three solutions were evolved:

(i) A minority argued that the subterranean doctrines of hedonism and expressivity were not the route to individual revolution. What was necessary was renunciation of material and sexual desires. This disciplined puritanism finds evidence in the Hare Krishna Temple and the Jesus Freak.

(ii) A further minority saw in the reaction they had suffered the message that capitalism could buy up anything and would contend with no opposition. They retreated to the country or to the bohemian colonies of Tangier and Nepal. Here a little money would go a long way and in the meantime they could wait for the inevitable collapse of the system. Not willing to enter into activism against a corrupt society, they made resort to ecological or transcendental forces which would bring about, without their efforts, its eventual disintegration. The initiated, with their Tarot cards, and knowledge of UFO dragon lines, eating their macrobiotic foods and practising their Yoga, would survive. The meek would inherit the earth and the wicked destroy themselves with their own devices.

(iii) The largest group scorned both puritanism and quietism. They discovered that the road to individual revolution must necessarily involve politics.[28] It is this group which is undoubtedly forming the central ethos of the new underground.

Politics and Deviance

This involves a radical political stance distinct from the New Left in that it is more hedonistic and expressive:

Getting stoned, drunk or laid is maybe the aim of revolution, but it is not the sole means to achieve it. If it was, Ladbroke Grove would be a free state ... Basically we are being ruled by a bunch of fat rich honkies who are going to do nothing that will benefit us unless we really force them to, and forcing honkies to do what they don't want to do is commonly called revolution.[29]

Or as Abbie Hoffman put it:

In the past few years our numbers have grown from hundreds to millions of young people. Our conspiracy has grown more militant. Flower children have lost their innocence and grown their thorns. We have recognized that our culture in order to survive must be defended. Furthermore we have realized that the revolution is more than digging rock and turning on. The revolution is about coming together in a struggle for change. It is about the destruction of a system based on people and co-operation. The old system is dying all around us and we joyously come out in the streets to dance on its grave. With our free stores, liberated buildings, communes, people's parks, dope, free bodies and our music, we'll build our society on the vacant lots of the old and we'll do it by any means necessary. Right on![30]

Conclusion

We have seen how the bohemian consensus which grew up in 1967 was transformed in the following years as the hypotheses of the culture palpably failed and the unshaky configuration of groups were re-aligned under the influence of differential social reaction and underlying conflicts of material interest. I hesitate, however, to suggest with many theoreticians on the Left, that the changes within the new bohemia are merely indicative of the absurdity of their ideals. I do not wish to argue that the hippie movement is an example of false consciousness, ill conceived in totality and historically insignificant. For as Martin Nicolaus put it:

Radical social ideas are radical not because they express the demand for some imagined desirable society, not because they

The Hippie Solution: An Essay in the Politics of Leisure

protest against some inequality in the present social order. Their radicalness derives from their ability to express the *repressed potential* of the *present* social order, from their accuracy in pointing to the possibilities which the status quo *negates*.[31]

The hippies were ill advised in that they sought change through individual revolution alone, and inaccurate in that they generalized from their upper-middle-class world of affluence to the rest of society. They were not unrealistic, however, in their sensing the imminent potential of advanced industrial societies for providing material abundance and the concomitant changes in social relationships and industrial consciousness which such a change would facilitate.[32] Thus Nicolaus comments:

I do not intend to suggest that the hippie subculture is or will become a revolutionary force, in the sense that it will develop the power to alter the basic political and economic structure of capitalist society. It is possible, however, that it will have the effect of seriously undermining the fundamental value system which is essential to the smooth functioning of capitalist society. As Antonio Gramsci wrote, the ultimate subjugation of the oppressed occurs in the ideological or cultural realm; a social system can maintain its repressive effectiveness only so long as the oppressed share the fundamental ethos of the oppressors. This, I take it, is what Gramsci implied in the notion of hegemony. In the history of the two great revolutions of the modern world, the French and the Russian, we may observe a long preliminary process during which the culture and the ethos of the dominant class were challenged and undermined by an antagonistic worldview. It may well be that the hippies are to be *philosophes*, that Allen Ginsberg and Abbie Hoffman and Paul Krassner are the Rousseau and the Diderot and the Voltaire, of a new American revolution. The present style and appeal of the hippie subculture may well fade away, but the vision of a practical culture in which man is free from labour, free to begin at last the historic task of constructing truly human relationships, probably has been permanently launched and will continue to haunt capitalist society as the spectre of its own repressed potentialities. The official attempt to suppress and crush the hippie subculture must be viewed as an effort to commit social infanticide.[33]

The new bohemia questions not only the present social order, but a certain orthodoxy of the Left. It points to the radicalizing potential of affluence rather than its role in 'repressive desublimation'.[34] It calls for the need for changes in consciousness and relationships *now*, rather than envisaging such transformations as mere camp followers of material change. The emerging political underground stresses the necessity for the individual and social revolution to be dialectically related and, in this way, forms a critique of vulgar materialism.[35] For the revolution in consciousness is futile without the social revolution and the revolution called for in the social structure is abortive without a revolution in consciousness and intimate relationships. They would sympathize with Raoul Vaneigen when he wrote: 'People who talk about revolution and class struggle without referring explicitly to everyday life, without understanding what is subversive about love and what it positive in the refusal of constraints, such people have a corpse in their mouth.'[36]

References

1. L. YABLONSKY, *The Hippie Trip* (New York: Pegasus, 1968), pp. 294–5.

2. L. WELCH, 'Final City', *International Times*, 34 (1968), p. 5.

3. D. MATZA and G. SYKES, 'Juvenile Delinquency and Subterranean Values', *American Sociological Review*, 26 (1961), p. 716.

4. P. BERGER and T. LUCKMANN, 'Social Mobility and Personal Identity', *European Journal of Sociology*, 5 (1964), p. 331.

5. B. BERGER, 'Sociology of Leisure', *Work and Leisure*, ed. E. SMIGEL (New Haven: Cambridge University Press, 1963), p. 34.

6. For a description of a parallel culture amongst Chicago Negroes *vide* H. FINESTONE, 'Cats, Kicks and Color', *The Other Side*, ed. H. S. BECKER (New York: Free Press, 1964).

7. M. HARRINGTON, 'Why We Need Socialism in America', *Dissent* (May–June 1970), p. 267.

8. R. FLACKS, 'Social and Cultural Meaning in Student Revolt', *Social Problems*, 17 (1970), p. 350.

9. H. LOMAS, 'Money: A Once-Useful Device', *International Times*, 45 (1968), p. 11.

10. *Vide* J. YOUNG, *The Drugtakers* (MacGibbon & Kee, and Paladin, 1971).

11. T. ROSZACK, *The Making of a Counter Culture* (Faber & Faber,

1970), p. 68. For a critique of Roszack's position, see my review of his book in *International Socialism*, 45, pp. 30–31.

12. 'Mind Revolution', *Gandalf's Garden*, 5, p. 4.

13. A related problem to this is the problem of order within the underground itself. The notion that love alone would hold the community together contrasted with the need for some degree of organization, especially in large gatherings. It led in the case of pop festivals to the employment of Hell's Angels as 'outlaw policemen' and to the disastrous events at Altamont. *Vide: Altamont*, ed. J. EISEN (New York: Avon Books, 1970).

14. F. DAVIS and L. MUNOZ, 'Heads and Freaks', *Journal of Health and Social Behaviour* (1968), p. 161.

15. 'Miles Interviews Pete Townshend', *Some of IT*, ed. D. MAIROWITZ (Knullar, 1969).

16. A. GINSBERG, 'Public Solitude', *Some of IT*, pp. 62–3.

17. T. McGRATH, 'UFO Dies', *Some of IT*, p. 58.

18. Miles, 'The Phragmented Philosophy', *International Times*, 38 (1968), p. 12.

19, Miles, 'Design for Positive Effectiveness', *International Times*, 27 (1968), p. 3.

20. *Vide* J. YOUNG, 'The Police as Amplifiers of Deviancy, Negotiators of Reality and Translators of Fantasy', *Images of Deviance*, ed. S. COHEN (Penguin Books, 1971).

21. I dicuss this in detail in 'The Consensual Image: the Portrayal of the Drugtaker in the Mass Media' in *Explorations in Sociology*, ed. M. McINTOSH and P. ROCK (Tavistock Publications, forthcoming).

22. R. VANEIGEM, *Traité du Savoir Vivre* (London: Agiprop Publications, 1970).

23. The decline of Haight-Ashbury, usually portrayed as due to the influx of lower-class predators, might be better seen as a community torn apart by its own theoretical inadequacy.

24. *Vide* the discussion in *International Times* (1969), 45, p. 19; 53, p. 2; 54, p. 10.

25. *International Times*, 81 (1970), p. 11.

26. *Vide* the discussion of this point in *The Drugtakers*.

27. F. COOK, 'The Reality Makers', *International Times*, 76 (1970), p. 9.

28. An interesting parallel to these three positions is the development of the consciousness of the American Negro from the subterranean world of the hustler, to the puritanism of the Black Muslims, to the political activism of the Black Panthers. *Vide: The Autobiography of Malcolm X* (Penguin Books, 1968); and B. SEARLE, *Seize The Time* (Arrow Books, 1970).

29. M. FARREN, 'A Record Review of Sorts', *International Times*, 75 (1970), pp. 11 and 14.

30. A. HOFFMAN, *Woodstock Nation* (New York: Vintage Books, 1969), p. 77.

31. M. NICOLAUS, 'The Contradiction of Advanced Capitalist Society and its Resolution' (mimographed paper delivered in Seminar Department of Politics, Sociology and Anthropology, Simon Fraser University, 2 October 1967), p. 15.

32. *Vide* discussion by M. NICOLAUS, ibid., pp. 12–13, of PAUL A. BARAN and PAUL M. SWEEZY, *Monopoly Capital* (Penguin Books, 1968), who calculated that at least 56 per cent of the American gross national product in 1963 was expended in maintaining the social order of capitalism, and represented productive forces of which the population at large was deprived. Relative abundance was thus imminently possible but contrary to the interests of the capitalist system.

33. ibid., pp. 17–18.

34. For a critique of Marcuse on this point see M. HARRINGTON, op. cit., p. 274; and A. McINTYRE, *Marcuse* (Fontana, 1970).

35. STUART HALL in 'The Hippies: An American Moment' in *Student Power*, ed. J. NAGEL (Merlin Press, 1969), presents an interesting discussion of the hippies as representing the expressive pole of an expressive-activist dialectic in the underground.

36. R. VANEIGEM, *The Revolution of Everyday Life* (London: Agit-prop Publications, 1970).

A Note on the National Deviancy Conference

Membership Secretary:
Laurie Taylor
Department of Sociology
University of York
Heslington, York

The National Deviancy Conference was formed late in 1968 by a small group of sociologists and criminologists, with a view to widening the nature of debate and the focus of concern in British academic criminology, and with a view, also, to forging links with people active in radical social work, in psychiatry, in community organizing, and so on.

Since 1968, the N.D.C. has held fourteen symposia (all of them, except one, at York University), attended by some 1,300 people. A list of the papers given at these symposia is attached (short abstracts of these papers being available on application). We have also published two books of papers given at the symposia (*Images of Deviance*, edited by Stanley Cohen, Penguin Books 1971, and this collection itself).

In line with the concern to act also as some kind of umbrella organization for radicals involved directly in action, N.D.C. members have built links, on an individual basis and via the organization itself, with groups like Radical Alternatives to Prison, Preservation of the Rights of Prisoners, the Squatters, the London Street Commune, *Case-Con* (the journal for revolutionary social work), Red Rat (the journal for alternative psychiatrists), and others. Individual members have been and are involved in various campaigns in the country at the moment, notably the Prescott-Purdie Defence Committee and the movement to reopen the Stafford-Luvaglio case.

Politics and Deviance

The N.D.C. is now one of the largest alternative quasi-academic bodies in Britain, with over 400 members. It is a radical but non-sectarian body, and the range of the membership's interests is well displayed in the attached list of papers given at the symposia, and in the Register of Research (available on application to Roy Bailey, Department of Applied Social Studies, Sheffield Polytechnic).

Membership of the symposium is open to all, and costs £1 a year. Members receive regular details of N.D.C. activities, the Research Register and a set of abstracts of the papers given at each symposium. Symposium funds (which are not great) are also used to subsidize the attendance at the symposium of individuals with little or no income. Membership fees should be sent to the Membership Secretary.

The committee of the symposium is well spread throughout the country, and any committee member will be happy to inform you of further activities in progress. The committee is:

Gail Armstrong, Department of Social and Economic Research, University of Glasgow.

Roy Bailey, Department of Applied Social Studies, Sheffield Polytechnic.

Stan Cohen, Department of Sociology, University of Essex.

David Downes, Department of Social Administration, London School of Economics.

Mike Hepworth, Department of Sociology, University of Aberdeen.

Mary McIntosh, Nuffield College, Oxford.

Paul Rock, Department of Sociology, London School of Economics.

Mike Smith, Department of Sociology, Bath University.

Ian Taylor, Faculty of Law, Sheffield University.

Laurie Taylor, Department of Sociology, University of York.

Paul Walton, School of Social Sciences, University of Bradford.

Jock Young, Department of Sociology, Enfield College of Technology.

Papers Given at the National Deviancy Symposium

First Symposium (1–3 November 1968)

Paul Rock, 'The Police as Agents of Social Control'
Maureen Cain, 'On the Beat: Interactions and Relations in Rural and Urban Police Forces'
Jock Young, 'The Role of the Police as Amplifiers of Deviancy, Police as Negotiators of Reality and Translators of Phantasy'
Ian Taylor, ' "Football Mad" – A Speculative Sociology of Football Hooliganism'
Stan Cohen, 'Middle-Class Violence'

Second Symposium (11–12 January 1969)

Laurie Taylor and Paul Walton, 'Industrial Sabotage: Motives and Meanings'
Mary McIntosh, 'Changes in the Organization of Thieving'
David Downes, 'Studying Gambling'
Kit Carson, 'White-Collar Crime and the Enforcement of Factory Legislation'

Third Symposium (12–13 July 1969)

John Lambert, 'Cops and Colour'
Dermont Walsh, 'Deviant Appearance and Deviant Action: Some Hypotheses'
Mike Hepworth, 'Deviants in Disguise: Blackmail and Social Acceptance'
Phil Strong, 'Notes on the Management of Sexual Interaction'
Eric Colvin, 'Con-Men'

Politics and Deviance

Fourth Symposium (3–4 January 1970)

Maxwell Atkinson, 'Explaining Suicide'

Mike Smith, 'The Sociology of Mental Illness: Ideology and Research'

Mike Brake and Ken Plummer, 'Bent Boys and Rent Boys: Preliminary Theoretical and Conceptual Comments on the Social Intercourse of the Male Homosexual Prostitute'

Jock Young and Mary McIntosh, 'Wide, Camp and Cool: A Study of Argot in Three Deviant Groups'

Laurie Taylor and Stan Cohen, 'Long-Term Imprisonment in a Maximum Security Wing'

Fifth Symposium (11–12 April 1970)

Gail Armstrong and Mary Wilson, 'City Politics and Deviancy Amplification'

Margaret Voysey, 'Parents of the Disabled'

Peter Lassman, 'Aspects of the Phenomenological Approach to Sociological Theory'

Paul Wiles, 'Private Security Companies in the United Kingdom'

Frank Pearce, 'Cicourel's Contribution to Deviancy Theory'

Stuart Hall, 'The Hippies – An American Moment'

Sixth Symposium (2–3 October 1970) Theme: *The Politics of Social Work*

Mike Phillipson, 'Juvenile Delinquency and the School'

Ron Bailey, 'Social Workers as Social Policemen'

John McKinlay, 'The Other Side of the Typificatory Coin' (clients' perception of social work and other agencies)

Phil Cohen, 'Youth Subcultures in Britain'

Paul Corrigan, 'Interactionist Theory and Social Work'

Ian Taylor, 'Soccer in Mexico: Who Gets the Kickback?

Seventh Symposium (8–9 January 1971) Theme: *The Politics of Psychiatry*

Simon Maddison, 'Mindless Militants? Psychiatry and the University'

Papers Given at the National Deviancy Symposium

Jeff Coulter, 'A Critique of Bio-Genetic Theories in Explaining Cognitive Disorders'

Ken Nuttall, 'The Ideology of Psychiatry'

Roy Bailey, 'The Family and the Social Management of Intolerable Dilemmas'

Colin Campbell, 'Religious Deviancy and Deviant Religion: An Exploration of some Neglected Areas'

Eighth Symposium (10–11 July 1971)

Graham Murdock, 'Pop Fans and Pupils'

Jerry Palmer, 'Thrillers: The Deviant Behind the Consensus'

Bob Roshier, 'Crime Reporting and the Press'

Paul Walton, 'The Case of the Weathermen: Social Reaction and Radical Commitment'

At this symposium, the guest speakers were Peter Hughman and David Lewis, authors of the Penguin Book *Most Unnatural: An Enquiry into the Case of Dennis Stafford and Michael Luvaglio,* and Robert Traini, head of the Crime Writers Association.

Ninth Symposium (7–8 January 1972) Held at the University of Sheffield

Mary McIntosh, 'Gay Liberation and Gay Ghetto'

Iain Manson, 'Sociological Aspects of Pornography'

Paul Willis, 'A Motor-Bike Subculture'

Gerry Stimson, 'Patterns of Heroin Addiction'

Steve Alwyn, 'The Politics of Eysenck'

David Widgery, 'The Politics of the Underground'

Tenth Symposium (14–15 April 1972)

Frank Pearce, 'Crime Corporations and the American Social Order'

Paul Rock, 'Phenomenonalism and Essentialism in the Sociology of Deviance'

Ian Taylor, 'Two New Conflict Theorists of Deviancy'

Richard Daventry, 'Problems of Participant Observation in a Gambling Setting'

Peter Archard, 'The Alcoholic Dosser: Some Problems of Research for the Participant Observer'

Peter Sedgwick, 'Mental Illness *is* Illness'

Politics and Deviance

Carol Riddell, 'Transvestism and the Tyranny of Gender'
A session on Prison Movements was also held with contributions from Stan Cohen, Troy Duster, Tove Stang Dahl; and representatives of the National Association for the Care and Resettlement of Families, Radical Alternatives to Prison, and Preservation of the Rights of Prisoners.

Eleventh Symposium (18–19 September 1972)

Bernie Simons and Jeremy Smith, 'Prospects for a Radical Legal Profession'
Thomas Mathiesen, 'Strategies of Resistance within a Total Institution'
Mike Hepworth, 'The Deviance of Privacy'
Geoff Mungham and Geoff Pearson, 'Radical Scholarship and Radical Action'
David Woodhill, 'Ideology and Responsibility in the Juvenile Court'
Andy Tudor, 'Popular Culture: Light Fantasy – Heavy Baroque'
Jock Young, 'Romantics, Keynesians and Beyond'
Charles Smith, 'Mass Education and Deviance'
Paul Corrigan and Bob Fryer, 'The Industrial Relations Act: A Suitable Case for Deviance?'
Geoff Pearson, 'Misfit Sociology: A Study of Scholarship and Action'

Twelfth Symposium (12–13 January 1973)

Discussion session on 'The Policy and Ideological Implications of the New Deviancy Theory' introduced by Albert Cohen, with contributions from Herman Bianche and Bernard Cassen

John Gagnon, 'Every Exit is an Entrance Somewhere: Some Notes on Ewing Goffman'
John Auld, 'Explanation or Mystification? Some Comments on the Social Functions of Drug Use'
'Comrade X', 'The British Campaign to Stop Immigration'
Peter Manning, 'A Dramaturgical Perspective on Social Control'
Stuart Hall, 'The Uses of Structuralism'
Peter Leonard, 'Community Action'
David Lewis and Peter Hughman 'The Prosecution Process'

Notes on Contributors

Gail Armstrong graduated in Sociology from Strathclyde University in 1966. She then went into social work. From 1969–70, she worked as a research assistant in the Department of Sociology at Strathclyde, where the present study was started. She has taught part-time in the Mackintosh School of Architecture in Glasgow. She is now a research fellow in the Department of Social and Economic Research in the University of Glasgow, and with Mary Wilson, she is writing up the Easterhouse research for publication in book-form (George Allen and Unwin, 1973).

Ron Bailey is a graduate of the London School of Economics, where he gained a B.Sc.(Econ), and Southampton University, where he obtained a certificate of Education. For three years he was a teacher, until July 1968, when he became involved full time in direct action on housing. He joined CND in 1959 and supported all its major marches and Committee of 100 demonstrations. On several occasions he has been arrested on minor charges of obstruction. When he tried to prevent Stan Orme, M.P. from addressing the Easter Rally because, in the period of a slender Labour majority in the Commons, Orme had voted in favour of the defence estimates, Bailey was again arrested, under the Public Order Act. He has been involved in campaigns to expose the government's Civil Defence plans and was found guilty in 1964 of breaking into official headquarters and stealing documents. In October 1967 he was fined £30 for taking part in the occupation of the Greek Embassy. On this occasion he conducted his own defence; and he has since been studying law with a view to discovering ways in which ordinary people can use it in campaigns 'as an additional tool'. Ron Bailey has also contributed to direct action in picketing Social Security Offices, schools and hostels for unmarried mothers.

Martin Loney graduated in Politics and Economics from Durham

University in 1966. From 1966 to 1969 he was a graduate student in the Department of Political Science, Sociology and Anthropology at Simon Fraser University in Vancouver; and in 1968 he went to Cuba to carry out field-work for his M.A. thesis. In 1970 he became President of the Canadian Union of Students, and subsequently returned to Britain to work as a Research Assistant in Sociology at the University of Bradford. After a period as Director of the Research/Action Unit of the World University Service in Geneva, he was appointed Director of the National Council for Civil Liberties in 1973.

Simon Maddison graduated in Sociology from York University in 1968. After a year abroad, he returned as a research student at Durham University. He is now a tutor-organizer for the Workers' Educational Association, and is doing research on the identification and definition of mental illness amongst students.

Jerry Palmer graduated in French and German at Southampton University in 1961, and followed this with an M.A. thesis on Jean-Paul Sartre. His Ph.D., also from Southampton, is concerned with the application of structuralist methods to classical theatre. He is also writing a book on pornography, and a book on thrillers as the incarnation of the bourgeois social order. The article in this volume is a part of the latter work.

Frank Pearce graduated in Sociology from Leeds University in 1967. He was a research student at the University of Kent for a year. He is now Senior Lecturer in Sociology at North London Polytechnic, and has lectured at California State College in Los Angeles. He is interested in sociological theory, particularly the relationship between Marxism and phenomenonology, and is currently engaged on a research project into the social meanings of homosexuality.

Paul Walton graduated in Sociology from the University of York in 1968; did postgraduate research at Durham University, and is at present lecturer in Sociology at the University of Bradford. He is interested in sociological theory and the sociology of deviance. His published works include a book on Marxism entitled *From Alienation to Surplus Value* (Sheed and Ward, 1972), which was awarded the Isaac Deutsche Memorial Award for 1972, and with Ian Taylor and Jock Young he has written *The New Criminology* (Routledge and Kegan Paul, 1972).

Mary Wilson graduated in Sociology from Strathclyde University in 1968, following this with two years' work as research student in the Strathclyde department. She teaches part-time in the Mackintosh School of Architecture and is currently writing up the Easterhouse research with Gail Armstrong for publication.

Jock Young completed his first degree and M.Sc. in Sociology at the London School of Economics. He is Senior Lecturer in Sociology at the Middlesex Polytechnic and has completed a Ph.D. on the relationship between drug use and bohemianism. He has recently published *The Drugtakers* (Paladin, 1971), a study in the social meaning of drug use. He is working on three books: *Media as Myth* (an investigation of the mythical portrayal of deviancy in the mass media), a reader on the relationship between the hippies and the Romantic movement, and has completed, together with Paul Walton and Ian Taylor, *The New Criminology*, a textbook on deviancy theory.

Crime in a Changing Society

Howard Jones

Throughout the Western world crime is on the increase: in America four serious crimes are committed every minute and in Britain the number of people involved in crime has more than doubled since the 1930s. The causes and treatment of criminal behaviour are now of urgent interest to the man in the street, and it was for him that Professor Jones wrote *Crime in a Changing Society*. It is the first general survey of the history, methods, and aims of criminology and penology to have been aimed specifically at the general reader.

The discussion ranges from 'criminal areas', the psychology of abnormal offenders and the influences of heredity and intelligence to the 'punishment versus treatment' debate, the structure of penal reform, and the meaning of teenage violence.

Here is both a simple, concise account of the crime problem and a social critique of the relation of criminal behaviour to patterns of social change in contemporary Britain.

The Young Offender

D. J. West

Criminal statistics are often quoted to prove that crime is increasing, above all among young people. Actually the picture is more complicated and less dismal.

In this balanced study Dr Donald West, of the Cambridge Institute of Criminology, fully examines the extent, nature, causes, and prevention of offences committed by those under twenty-one in England. Most convicted persons, he admits, are young males: but that is nothing new. It remains true that the incidence of conviction declines dramatically after the age of fourteen (which is the peak) and begins to peter out among those in their twenties. Delinquency, in short – and that means, to a large extent, theft in one form or another or very petty crime – is a passing phase of youth.

Donald West devotes his central chapters to the social, hereditary and psychological factors in delinquency and his final chapters to the penal and remedial measures at present being applied. A special chapter covers the more sensational topics of girls, sex, drugs and violence, which rate the bold type in the press but feature quite small in the statistics of crime.

Psychological Survival

The Experience of Long Term Imprisonment

Stanley Cohen and Laurie Taylor

What good do you think you do?
Do you think that I'll be different when I'm through?
sang Johnny Cash in the 'Ballad of San Quentin'.

What is it like to live under the eye of a TV camera; to
sleep with the light on all night; to be unable to close a
lavatory door; or to spend ten years sewing mailbags?

Stanley Cohen and Laurie Taylor are two young
sociologists who taught and talked to the inmates of
Durham Prison's maximum security block, where they
gained an insight into the problems peculiar to long-term
imprisonment. In this book, which grew out of their
experience there, they show how such prisoners fear
psychological deterioration, how they react to disrupted
emotional relationships, and how they manage to adapt
to prison conditions without losing their sense of personal
identity.

Images of Deviance

Edited by Stanley Cohen

During the present century we have been taught to regard the sexual offender, the drug taker or the vandal not as degenerate but as sick: he has a 'kink', a 'warped mentality' or a 'twisted mind'. The attitude of society towards those who deviate from its rules has turned from the *punitive* to the *therapeutic*. But too often the psychiatric remedies proposed (such as electric shock, brain surgery and compulsory hospitalization) smack of the same authoritarianism under a liberal guise.

The seven papers in this volume were given at the York Deviancy symposium and adopt a sceptical position to crime, deviance and social problems. The subjects studied range from marijuana smoking to football hooliganism, from industrial sabotage to the functions of coroners. In all these the parts played by the press, television and the police are inextricable. These writers are not unanimous in every detail, but each is concerned with the criteria by which behaviour is considered deviant and the standing of the deviant in society.